KU-300-042

Stefan,

I hope you find this interesting, & look
forward to your comments. Is there, for
example, an O.R. dimension to leadership?

Andrew   27·03 99

THE SIX DIMENSIONS
OF LEADERSHIP

One of the most original and enlightening books on leadership I've read in recent years. I think Andrew Brown's approach is especially appealing to (and badly needed by) global leaders.

Warren Bennis

Without leadership, management loses meaning. Andrew Brown's masterly exploration of what leadership itself means thus goes to the heart of managing. So managers of all kinds badly need to understand his six dimensions of leadership – and, above all, to apply the lessons in practice.

Robert Heller

The Six Dimensions of Leadership is a stimulating and wide-ranging exploration of the mystery of leadership. I commend Andrew Brown's book to all who aspire to excellence in this difficult, demanding, and yet essential art.

John Adair

Andrew Brown brings a refreshingly new angle to a time-honoured subject. You will be entertained by the book's biographical anecdotes which bring leadership successes and failings vividly to life. Whatever your entrenched views on leaders and leadership, *The Six Dimensions of Leadership* will give cause for thought.

Sir Adrian Cadbury

Leadership, like all buzz words in management, risks losing its meaning as its popularity grows. Andrew Brown's book is therefore especially timely by bringing back real meaning into the subject. The many faces of leadership are introduced in a way that promises to be a source of stimulus and challenge to all managers aspiring to greater heights.

Meredith Belbin

A refreshingly original look at leadership-in-the-round, with all its richness and variety. In this pantheon of colourful characters, each reader will find his favourite profile.

Charles Hampden-Turner

THE SIX DIMENSIONS OF LEADERSHIP

Andrew D. Brown

RANDOM HOUSE

BUSINESS BOOKS

© Andrew D. Brown 1999
All rights reserved

Andrew D. Brown has asserted his rights under the Copyright, Designs and
Patents Act, 1988, to be identified as the author of this work

First published in 1999 by Random House Business Books,
Random House, 20 Vauxhall Bridge Road, London SW1V 2SA

Random House Australia (Pty) Limited
20 Alfred Street, Milsons Point
Sydney, New South Wales 2061, Australia

Random House New Zealand Limited
18 Poland Road, Glenfield
Auckland 10, New Zealand

Random House South Africa (Pty) Limited
Endulini, 5a Jubilee Road, Parktown 2193, South Africa

Random House UK Limited Reg. No. 954009

Papers used by Random House UK Limited are natural, recyclable products
made from wood grown in sustainable forests. The manufacturing processes
conform to the environmental regulations of the country of origin.

ISBN 0 7126 8470 0

Companies, institutions and other organizations wishing to make bulk
purchases of books published by Random House should contact their local
bookstore or Random House direct:
Special Sales Director
Random House, 20 Vauxhall Bridge Road, London SW1V 2SA

Tel 0171 840 8470 Fax 0171 828 6681

www.randomhouse.co.uk
businessbooks@randomhouse.co.uk

Typeset by SX Composing DTP, Rayleigh, Essex
Printed by Biddles

For my wife BiYu and son Tristan

ACKNOWLEDGEMENTS

A great many people have helped in the preparation of this book. My editor, Simon Wilson, has been extremely helpful, and I am grateful for the advice and encouragement he has provided. Without his perceptive comments this book would be far less interesting and readable. Mike Humphreys also deserves special mention for the time and effort he has expended assisting me in writing this book. Not only did he have insightful comments to make on the text, but many of the photographs that appear here do so due to his research work. My thanks also are due to Sandra Dawson for her assistance. A number of people have read earlier versions of part, or all, of this manuscript, and to them I owe a debt of thanks for their incisive commentary. They are: Jonathan Allen, Owen Atkin, Susan Bartholomew, BiYu Brown, Charles Hampden-Turner, Rachel Jones, Beryl Patten, and Jessica and Charles Wells. I would also like to record my thanks to the support staff at the Judge Institute of Management Studies, University of Cambridge, who helped me in various ways, notably our technician John Martin, and the staff of the Institute's library.

Contents

One

INTRODUCTION

It is the paradox of our times that precisely when the trust and credibility of leaders are at their lowest, when the beleaguered survivors in leadership positions feel unable to summon up the vestiges of power left to them, we most need people who can lead. (Warren Bennis)[1]

NELSON MANDELA IS arguably the most gifted, and certainly the most widely admired leader of our age. From being denigrated as a terrorist he has become a world figure courted by politicians, business leaders and royalty. He is the man who took on the racist apartheid system in South Africa using passive resistance and non-violent opposition. He is the man who was imprisoned in 1962 and not released until 11 February 1990, aged 71. He is the man who was jointly awarded the Nobel Peace Prize, and won the 1994 elections to assume the presidency of South Africa. And he is the man who has done more than anyone else to unify disparate races and factions, and to hold South Africa together. Nelson Mandela, then, is a natural starting point for an analysis of what makes a leader effective.

The biography of Mandela is that of an epic *hero*, whose experiences impress and amaze all who are familiar with them. A man of tremendous courage and determination, he has for decades been a symbol of justice for oppressed people. His skills as an *actor*, and especially his impassioned and uplifting oratory, are legendary. They were first brought to the attention of a world audience in 1963 when, in opening the case for his and his co-accuseds' defence, he delivered a speech that gripped and electrified the court which sentenced him to life imprisonment. Moreover, Mandela has always been more than a wide-eyed idealist. He is a man of profound vision, an *immortalist*, whose benign persona has been written into the cultural fabric of South Africa and the world. And what is more, when hard pressed, he has been found to possess the *power-broking* talents required to unite not just a political party and a mass movement, but a whole nation. A persuasive and sensitive *ambassador*, he has moved seamlessly from travelling his country fermenting revolution, to the role of one of the world's elder statesmen. Perhaps most impressively of all, he was for years a *victim* of a morally bankrupt regime, yet refused to renounce the cause in which he believed at the expense of his freedom. And, finally, a man whose release brought catharsis and political change to his country.[2,3]

As the example of Nelson Mandela shows, to be truly great, leaders must be convincing heroes, consummate actors, self-confident immortalists, shrewd power-brokers, effective ambassadors, and, when necessary, willing victims. These are the six dimensions of leadership. While relatively few people can excel in all, or even most of these dimensions, those that can have often proved themselves exemplary. They are iconic business leaders such as Walt Disney, Henry Ford and the Siemens brothers; great military and naval strategists like General Patton and Admiral Horatio Nelson; and political giants ranging from Napoleon, Chairman Mao and Indira Gandhi to President Kennedy and Margaret Thatcher. Such individuals are, despite weaknesses, multi-dimensional leaders. What is more, as I illustrate, they are people from whom contemporary and aspiring future leaders can learn.

New leadership ideas are certainly required. Ours is, after all, a world in which between 35% and 50% of all corporate CEOs are replaced within five years of being appointed.[4] What is more, the technical possibilities opened up by new information technologies, the internet, the rise to prominence of global media corporates, and the growth of a worldwide market in which every item of news has a monetary value, place a heavy burden on our leaders. Further, a better educated populace knows more, expects more, and is more insightfully critical than any previous generation. In short, leadership has become more difficult to sustain in our personality-centred, performance-oriented, information-rich age. To compensate, to survive and prosper, business leaders must be multi-talented, multi-dimensional men and women.

Who should read this book – and why

This book is for anyone with an interest in what leadership is and what leaders do. I first became fascinated with leaders, and especially political leadership, while a student at Oxford University. My focus was later broadened to include business leaders worldwide while a fellow at the Manchester Business School. Having now lectured on leadership as a faculty member of three different universities, I thought it was time to commit my ideas to a wider audience. The result is this book, which attempts to look afresh at leaders, and the roles they play. It is composed largely of stories drawn from biographies, autobiographies and corporate histories that offer a commentary on the nature of leading and leadership. Most importantly, this book is designed to be read and enjoyed.

The Six Dimensions of Leadership

James E. Burke, former chairman of Johnson & Johnson, has written that: 'Early in my career, I felt that the concepts of leadership that I inherited were worn out in terms of the way in which the world was working . . . This was true 20 years ago, certainly 10 years ago, and now more than ever.'[5]

I agree. The voluminous literature on leadership in organizations is filled with ageing labels which act as straitjackets on our imagination. An increasingly ancient vocabulary, time-honoured but also time-wearied, has ossified our thinking if not our curiosity. A few favoured words and the images they evoke – democratic/autocratic, charismatic/non-charismatic, participative/non-participative – constrain our thoughts. The once fresh insights they seemed to offer have now, inevitably perhaps with the passage of time, become jaded.

To retain our vitality and sharpen our analytical skills, we need constantly to make new discoveries regarding what it means to be a leader. New ideas and novel images make for new ways of seeing, and are a liberating and energizing force. Familiar images breed mundane understandings, while extraordinary images challenge us to explore and to learn. Here, then, is my attempt to provoke you with the six dimensions of leadership. My argument is that effective leaders are:

- *Heroes.* Great leaders are liberating heroes and role models who devote themselves to the collective good.
- *Actors.* The best leaders are skilled actors, able to deliver authentic and convincing performances.
- *Immortalists.* Admirable leaders are visionaries with high self-esteem, whose organizations take on their personalities.
- *Power-brokers.* Excellent leaders are shrewd dealers in power, who accomplish goals by mobilizing others to act on their behalf.
- *Ambassadors.* High performing leaders are diplomats, who use their interpersonal skills to develop valuable networks of external supporters.
- *Willing Victims.* Effective leaders are, when necessary, content to make a personal sacrifice for the sake of a cause in which they believe.

To be fully effective leaders need to be adept in all these dimensions of leadership. Perhaps the biggest single danger for any aspiring leader is that of *role capture*, i.e. being captured by a single role, or narrow set of related roles. Rather than being able to switch with ease between different dimensions of leadership, some individuals' lives are dominated by their attachment to a single role. They are people such as the narcissistic French fashion designer, Pierre Cardin, and power-broking despots like Ed Artzt, ex-CEO of Procter & Gamble. Such people lack the self-insight and intuitive skills to modify their behaviours to fit changing circumstances. They are the prisoners of their own psychic limitations. And while such people may be successful in the short term, they will never be able to exploit to the maximum the opportunities available to them. What is more, over time, the chances are that eventually their inability to adapt themselves to multiple settings will prove their undoing.

The key to avoiding role capture is broad-minded self-examination. Indeed, in many ways the heart of my argument and this book is this: a plea for self-awareness, and self-critique. And these accomplishments, as I argue in the conclusion, are intimately bound up with the attainment of wisdom and maturity, a recognition of the importance of integrity, and courage.

My promise to you, the reader, is that the next six chapters contain a wealth of informative and entertaining examples of leaders engaged in the business of leading. My belief is that, except for the already perfect leader who is reading this book for entertainment only, this material opens up the possibility for you to rethink the job of leading and the function of leadership. My hope is that you take up this challenge.

Nelson Mandela

TWO

LEADER AS HERO

The great demigods of the management culture who are honoured everywhere, the equivalents of Theseus, Hercules, Perseus and Jason, are such men as Andrew Carnegie, John D. Rockefeller, Henry Ford, Lord Northcliffe, Lord Nuffield, Alfred Nobel . . . (Cleverley)[1]

GREAT LEADERS NATURALLY assume the status of heroes. From George Washington to Chairman Mao and Nelson Mandela, leaders have been attributed with superhuman qualities. The idea that effective business leaders have heroic qualities too, also has a lengthy pedigree. Henry Ford and J. Paul Getty have been cultural icons for decades, and have helped to define the *corporate hero* genre for later aspirants such as Lee Iacocca, John DeLorean, Richard Branson and Bill Gates. The heroic CEO, say Terrence Deal and Allan Kennedy,[2] is 'The magician, the person everyone will count on when things get tough . . .' And what is more, they argue, 'America's boardrooms need heroes more than Hollywood's box offices need them.' Corporate heroes are liberating forces: they are incorruptible, no-nonsense people who counteract the forces of anarchy and disorder, and restore peace and tranquillity to their organizations.

It is hardly surprising, then, that demand for heroes is invariably high, nor that they are generally in short supply. The value of heroes to corporations, most of whose members are more concerned with satisfying their own personal needs, is twofold. Firstly, the devotion of heroes to their organizations is of great practical importance, especially on those occasions when the organization is under threat. What price then a charismatic Sir John Harvey-Jones (ex-head of ICI), a ruggedly determined Ted

Turner (founder of CNN), or a shrewdly calculating Bill Gates? Equally important, however, is the symbolic value of company heroes, who represent an extreme conformity with the ideal of putting collective above purely personal interests. Heroic acts dramatically assert that the ideal of devotion to the collective organizational good is not mere fantasy, but instead lies within human capacities.[3]

Heroes are characters with whom we naturally identify, and these processes of identification diminish our own anxieties, fears and loneliness.[4] Such people make success seem attainable for ordinary employees, symbolize the culture of the organization and what is unique about it, and foster loyalty in others. Most importantly of all, heroes are role models for other employees, personifying organizational strengths and setting standards for performance. People learn a lot from modelling themselves on others, and the privileged position of leaders as the most obviously available models in organizations, makes it imperative that they play their heroic roles with flair and guile. The commentators on business leadership, James Kouzes and Barry Posner, recognize this when they write that 'Leaders go first. They set an example and build commitment through simple, daily acts that create progress and momentum. *Leaders model the way through personal example and dedicated execution.*' [italics in original][5]

The importance of leadership modelling has been noted many times and in many contexts. As Albert Schweitzer has said, 'Example is not the main thing in influencing others – it is the only thing.'[6] Leaders as diverse as the Russian revolutionary Lenin, the English Victorian engineer Isambard Kingdom Brunel, Alexander the Great, and Lawrence of Arabia, all exercised leadership by their own example. Of Lenin, a friend once wrote, 'There is no one else who for the whole twenty-four hours of every day is busy with revolution, who thinks, even dreams of the revolution.'[7] When progress on an engineering work fell behind schedule, Brunel 'inspired willing work by occasionally rolling up his sleeves and working alongside' his men.[8] Alexander the Great was particularly noted for sharing in his men's dangers, eating the same food while on campaign, and taking considerable physical risks, as they did, in combat. Similarly, Lawrence of Arabia lived as an equal with the Bedouin tribespeople he sought to lead.

Being an exemplar hero is not an optional extra role that leaders can choose to ignore or play down. Failure in this respect can mean total failure as an organizational leader. By the same token, by role modelling behaviours that impress others, otherwise ordinary individuals can exercise a leadership influence. Consider, for example, the vivid story related in *USA Today* concerning a stewardess in a plane crash, in which most (twenty-four out of twenty-nine) people survived. The article reads in part:

> Passengers credit [Robin] Fech, 37, with keeping them from panicking when the plane faltered after it lost a left engine.
>
> They say her demeanor was that of a drill sergeant as she tested passengers one by one to make sure they knew how to brace themselves and calmly pointed out the exits as the crippled plane lurched toward a hayfield.
>
> 'I think because of her, everyone in the cabin was calm,' said Air Force Maj. Chuck LeMay, a passenger. 'There was no screaming, no yelling.'
>
> In the nine minutes between a loud bang and the crash itself, Fech never raised her voice and made all the passengers demonstrate the doubled-over crash position, correcting them when they did it wrong, he said.
>
> As the turboprop grazed treetops and sharply descended, she pointed out exits. She told some passengers to switch seats so the most able-bodied were near the emergency exits.
>
> After the crash, Fech, her face bloodied, pulled passengers from the wreckage, and she didn't sit down until the emergency workers arrived, LeMay said.
>
> 'She just did an absolutely fantastic job.'[9]

Fech was effective because she was a model of calm and controlled efficiency. But while she had only to keep up the act for nine minutes, business leaders have the more difficult task of acting as role models every hour of every working day. What is more, while organizational leaders can and must serve as heroic exemplars, there are dangers here. Leaders who pretend that the success of a large company is uniquely a function of their own abilities often fail to impress. For example, while corporate transformations such as those undertaken by Iacocca at Chrysler owe much to one individual, their success also depends on the empowerment and involvement of others. There can be little doubt that some would-be heroic leaders expend their energies in a fantasy world of powerful and pervasive images of what 'real heroes' are like. Seduced by inappropriate archetypes, such people tend to be over-controlling and uninventive. The leadership writers Daniel Bradford and Allan Cohen, for instance, have identified a category of American managers who 'secretly view themselves as direct descendants of the frontiersman, that quiet but tough adventurer who was constantly setting out for new territory'. They maintain that 'Even many women who have made it into middle management tend to think in these heroic terms, although their specific imaginings may resemble Wonder Woman: beautiful, strong, surrounded by admirers but still the cleverest, toughest, miracle worker around.'[10]

The term hero may seem to have become an over-used descriptive label. This has led some commentators to write off the idea that there is anything positive to say about leaders as heroes. It has led others to claim that there are more dangers than advantages in acknowledging heroes, who can be intimidating, demotivating and disruptive to normal organizational life.[11] The bizarre attempts undertaken by some organizations to artificially create corporate heroes out of very ordinary people have done nothing to quell these anxieties. I acknowledge these difficulties and dangers, but maintain that this is, nevertheless, a vitally important dimension of leadership. At General Electric, for instance, it is obvious that heroes such as Thomas Edison, the inventor, and Gerald Swope and Jack Welch, the CEO entrepreneurs, are important figures. Perhaps what we need to do then is to rediscover not the word *hero* but its important meaning.[12]

In this chapter I identify four heroic leader roles. My argument is that effective leaders are, when required, able to cast themselves:

- as *epic* heroes who claim a right to lead by virtue of the difficulties they have overcome;

- as *symbolic* heroes whose authority derives from their association with some idea, movement or achievement;
- as *playful* heroes whose leadership style makes use of humour, and who blend the worlds of work and play; and
- as *warrior* heroes who understand their role as being akin to that of a general leading their organizations into battle.

Each is a role which all actual and aspiring leaders can learn to deploy to their advantage in appropriate circumstances.

Leader as Epic Hero

Hired by his elder brother John to help run a sanitorium, William Kellogg spent two decades working twenty hours a day at humiliating chores. Stories are told of how John would attend meetings insisting that his brother wait outside the door until he was finished, and then drive him home late at night with orders to return by 5 a.m. the next day. During this time the brothers experimented with different kinds of health foods in an effort to improve the care provided to the sanitorium patients. The wheat and corn flake breakfast cereals were developed during this period. While William recognized the potential commercial worth of the products, John vetoed the idea of setting up a company to exploit them. Years of bickering with his brother went by before William eventually established the Battle Creek Toasted Corn Flake Company. Just six months into production William's factory burned down. The facility was rebuilt and production recommenced. Twelve months later John's sanitorium burned down, and William returned to assist him. The Battle Creek Corn Flake Company became his night-time endeavour. Despite this inauspicious start, William continued with his cornflakes, and today Kellogg's is one of the world's largest businesses.[13] William Kellogg's is the story of an epic hero.

The epic hero is someone who has undertaken (or often who is undertaking), a perilous journey involving a crucial struggle. The journey itself tends to be a melodramatic one, and is most usually characterized by three phases. First, there is an initial stage in which the individual either appears indistinguishable from the crowd, or if marked out in some way, still has it *all to prove*. Second, the individual then undergoes a dangerous ordeal involving many hardships. Typically this struggle involves a battle against factors such as harsh and unfair competition, restrictive government legislation, incompetent staff, or a world recession. In general, the more problems the hero faces, and the more hurdles that are overcome, the more venerated the hero will eventually be. Finally, there is the redemptive phase, in which the questor achieves his or her goal: the world-beating organization is born, a dominant market share is achieved, a breakthrough technology is devised and harnessed . . . Whatever the form of the redemption, the number of radical transformations and/or restructurings that have occurred, the outcome is always the birth, rebirth or burgeoning of the organization.

As a result of their endeavours, the epic hero is not infrequently able to invest him or herself with mystical qualities. Some corporations have deliberately traded on their founder's epic rise to prominence and sought to reinvent their mission as being moral as well as commercial. For example, at the UK-based confectionery manufacturer Cadbury the founder, John Cadbury, who established the company in 1824, and his two sons Richard and George who revived the firm's fortunes in the nineteenth century, are now venerated in various in-company publications as having been motivated not merely by profits, but by the moral principles of Quakerism.[14]

A similar phenomenon is evident at Procter & Gamble, which was founded in 1837 in Cincinatti by two brothers-in-law, William Procter, an English candle maker, and James Gamble, an Irish soap maker. Both men, says the official company biography, were devout Protestants to the point where 'The law of the Lord superseded all else . . . It was as if Procter & Gamble had a demanding third partner named God.'[15] The *special* qualities and motivations of the founders were so influential, readers are told, that Procter & Gamble was the first company to offer comprehensive benefits to employees, and by 1887 had a profit-sharing plan, the oldest in the United States. The message of the official publications of Cadbury and Procter & Gamble is clear and appealing: our founders were not just commercial but moral crusaders, and we will continue their work.

A Japanese leader with a classic epic hero biography, and who also redefined his company's goals as not just economic but moral, is Konosuke Matsushita, founder of Matsushita Electric Industrial (MEI), one of the largest Japanese corporates. In 1932, when MEI was already a big concern, Matsushita himself gave a watershed speech in which he argued that the aim of MEI should be to manufacture products in ways which would help eliminate poverty: 'Beginning today, this far reaching dream, this sacred calling, will be our ideal and our mission, and its fulfilment the responsibility of each one of us.'[16] The idea of benefiting mankind by producing more, and more necessary goods, proved appealing to stakeholders. Over time the message was refined to include the creation of high-paying and secure jobs for the good of society. Matsushita the man as much as the company became imbued with a new moral authority that gilded his epic hero status and reaffirmed him as an icon of good business practice.

Another renowned epic hero figure is Ted Turner, the founder of Cable News Network (CNN). Variously described by his critics as an obnoxious bully, a rascal and a gambler, he is above all a combative survivor. Twice expelled from Brown University in Providence, Rhode Island, in 1960 he went to work for his father, Ed, who had built up a small billboard business in Atlanta. On his father's death he fought to retain control of the company and used the profits it generated to purchase three radio and one obscure UHF (Ultra High Frequency) TV station. In 1972 he outbid rivals for the rights to televise Atlanta Braves games to the hometown fans the following year. This proved a turning point in Ted's fortunes. Now for the first time Atlantans had to tune their sets to channel 17 on the UHF dial and advertisers began to notice him. A series of deals with thirty-two other TV stations and the booking of space on the satellite Satcom-1 signalled his intent to challenge the three big national networks of the time (ABC, NBC and CBS). Key to making this jump was CNN, a twenty-four-hours news service. It was not until 1980 that he managed to sign a reasonable deal with the cable TV operators, pull together the high quality news team required to give CNN respectability, book the space he needed on Satcom-1, and gather sufficient advertising revenue and customers to fund the venture. Post-launch further triumphs (such as the purchase of MGM) and disasters (notably when the value of his company's stock slipped to $11) lay ahead. Interestingly, while the epic nature of Ted Turner's leadership journey is hard to dispute, it seems certain that some industry observers will always regard him as nothing more than 'a crackpot Southern entrepreneur with delusions of grandeur'.[17]

Asia, too, has its fair share of epic heroes, as the case of Chung Ju Yung, the man who developed Hyundai into a vast conglomerate, illustrates. Chung grew up in a poor rural area of Korea where, as he says, 'Survival itself was very difficult.'[18] As a young man he moved to Inchon where he became a stevedore unloading ships, eventually becoming a rice delivery boy. Unable to ride a bike, he nevertheless attempted to pedal around the city streets with 175 pounds of rice and beans. He fell off so many times the handlebars were bent out of shape. Yet nothing – including inexperience and inability – could deter him. Through dint of hard work he won the trust of the rice shop owner, eventually taking it over aged twenty-one. When the Japanese occupied Korea and closed the shop down Chung borrowed money and set up a car repair shop. When the shop burnt down he borrowed more money and rebuilt it. By the time the Americans took over Korea he was an experienced and ambitious businessman. He then borrowed money on generous terms from the Korean government to purchase the Hyundai Construction Company, which prospered. By the time he bowed out as chairman at the end of 1991 his forty Hyundai companies accounted for 16% of Korea's GNP, with sales of $53.2 billion, making it the eleventh or twelfth largest company in the world.

Guglielmo Marconi was an Italian, whose epic story continues to inspire would-be inventor entrepreneurs to this day. Born in 1874, Marconi demonstrated an original mind from an early age. His first efforts to develop a wireless apparatus were offered to the Italian government, which rejected his overtures. His family then sent him to London where he was granted the world's first patent for wireless telegraphy. On 20 July 1897 he initiated the Wireless Telegraph and Signal Company Limited, and the omens looked good. General interest in his work, however, did not translate into orders. Worse still, competitors started to enter the field. Eventually he managed to set up stations on both sides of the Atlantic and sent messages more than 2,000 miles, something that was previously unheard of – and that many said was impossible. One notable highlight occurred on 18 January 1902 when the President of the USA used the service to communicate with the King of England:

> HIS MAJESTY KING EDWARD THE SEVENTH BY MARCONI'S TRANS-ATLANTIC WIRELESS TELE-GRAPH IN TAKING ADVANTAGE OF THE WONDER-FUL TRIUMPH OF SCIENTIFIC RESEARCH AND INGENUITY WHICH HAS BEEN ACHIEVED IN PERFECTING A SYSTEM OF WIRELESS TELEGRAPHY I SEND ON BEHALF OF THE AMERICAN PEOPLE MOST CORDIAL GREETINGS AND GOOD WISHES TO YOU AND ALL THE PEOPLE OF THE BRITISH EMPIRE.
> THEODORE ROOSEVELT. WHITE HOUSE WASHINGTON.

It was, however, a brief triumph, and technical problems soon caused the service to be shelved. Only the fanatical energy of Marconi and his small band of associates kept the hopes of the company alive. Slowly, the commercial possibilities of wireless technology became evident to a broad audience, and orders began to come in. Continued technical breakthroughs, such as the diode valve and the directional antenna, made the wireless an ever more reliable and popular means of communication. The use of the wireless in the First World War consolidated its position, and from then on there was a ready market for Marconi's high quality products. By 1936 the Marconi Company (as it was now styled) and its subsidiaries and associates had been granted 800 patents, and Marconi broadcasting transmitters were in service at 180 stations in 32 countries. Yet this is only part of the story. In cash terms the company had been in poor shape from the 1920s, and in

1929 had been forced into an unequal merger with Cable and Wireless. Marconi's epic adventure was, sadly, from then on limited to research, invention and manufacture.[19]

What conclusions can we draw from these colourful characters? Most importantly, it is that successful leaders are able to cast themselves as epic heroes. They tell stories about themselves and encourage others to tell stories about them that illustrate the positive qualities they wish to inspire in others – tenacity, determination, single-mindedness, clarity of vision, and so forth. Commenting on the need for leaders to cast themselves as epic heroes, Melvin R. Goodes, chairman and CEO of the giant diversified pharmaceuticals company Warner-Lambert, has sagely noted that:

> Those who step into the top jobs of the world's largest companies soon learn that their lives have become much like the heroes in myths. In fact, their task bears a strong resemblance to the labors of Hercules. They're only given a few years – never enough – to make their mark and to triumph. Then the Fates whisk them off the glittering stage.[20]

Such leaders often emphasize their own uniqueness in an effort, which is not always fully conscious, to create an organizational mythology centred on them. This was in part how Dwight D. Eisenhower, American general and president, came to be described as 'perhaps the greatest American hero of the twentieth century'.[21] Indeed where these stories are oft repeated, elaborated and refined in a culture, newly cast epic leaders can, through the symbolic messages they give out, influence activities at all levels of even the largest institutions.

Leader as Symbolic Hero
In 1947 Dr Takeshi Mitarai took charge of the Japanese organization Canon. He remained chairman until his death in 1984. Mitarai reformed Canon after the Second World War, taking advantage of the US Occupation Forces to make the company a success. During his tenure, he instilled a code of ethics which

emphasized the corporation's obligations to improve society, especially by providing jobs. He was the man most responsible for Canon's stress on the importance of R&D, with the result that Canon under Mitarai was usually at or near the top of the list of companies winning US patents. It is Mitarai who is credited with ensuring that Canon's workers are promoted on their merits rather than seniority, or contacts, to a greater extent than other Japanese companies. According to one corporate biographer, 'Almost everything that Canon makes . . . is a result of the pioneering of Dr Mitarai, and in line with his philosophy, almost everything made by Canon today has a value to society other than simply economic.'[22] Mitarai and his philosophy of Three J's – *ji-hatsu, ji-kaku, ji-chi* (self-motivation, self-awareness, self-management) – is now a potent in-company symbol of modernization, rationalization and humanitarian values.

A symbolic hero, like Dr Takeshi Mitarai, is someone who has come to represent something significant to others. This is most usually achieved through their association with a big idea or movement, a particular way of organizing, or as a result of some special achievement. Some heroic leaders are symbolic on only a local scale, within a given organization or industry. At the other extreme are leaders who become cultural icons on the world stage. Historical figures such as George Washington and Ho Chi Minh, and contemporary leaders ranging from Fidel Castro to Boris Yeltsin have images which are known and discussed around the world. While relatively few leaders of organizations are likely ever to figure in a list of world cultural icons, the idea that leaders take on symbolic significance is an important one. It suggests that leaders should be sensitive to how their key constituencies see them, and especially to the ideas their audiences associate with them, because these images will have implications for subordinate commitment and performance.

Many symbolic heroes operate in something of a sociological and psychological vacuum: they are 'types' that have an emotional resonance for mass audiences without the assistance of any organizational or institutional infrastructure. A symbolic leader moves people through the images associated with him or her, the kind of person he or she seems to be, and the lifestyle and attitudes he or she projects. Princess Diana is a prime example of recent times. Symbolic heroes provide their audiences with a vicarious experience of another, and usually more appealing – richer, more beautiful, more virtuous, more powerful – life. The relationship between symbolic hero and audience works through the principle of identification. Those people who identify with a particular hero's role often 'experience a thrilling sense of uplift, triumph or achievement'.[23] In those instances where the hero plays a role that serves an organization, the members of that institution are also likely to derive a sense of security and well-being. Symbolic heroes can boost morale, provide positive self-images for groups, dramatize causes, crystallize and mobilize movements, and even develop cult followings. Most importantly of all they can act as role models of diverse sorts -champion, defender, crusader, martyr, moral leader, splendid performer and self-made man or woman.

John DeLorean in the 1970s was considered 'an authentic American folk hero'.[24] Andy Grove is a symbol of Intel and of contemporary corporate America, celebrated on the covers of business magazines and by Intel shareholders to whom he delivered 40% annual returns during his first decade at the helm. Jack Welch, who made General Electric the world's most profitable and most valuable company, seems set to be judged the 'quintessential CEO of the late twentieth century, symptomatic of our times'.[25] In Korea, the mystique of Hyundai's founder, Chung Ju Yung, pervades not just his own company but the entire business community. The importance of such corporate symbolic heroes should not be underestimated, and is symptomized by comments of employees. For example, of Jim Treybig at Tandem, one employee has been quoted as saying: 'Jimmy is really a symbol here. He's a sign that every person here is a human being. He tries to make you feel part of the organization from the first day you are here. That's something people talk about.'[26]

In-company symbolic heroes, with limited reach, but of great significance to individual organizations, are plentiful. At the German company Siemens plc the three brothers (Werner, Karl and William) who founded and grew the organization in the latter part of the nineteenth century, are powerful symbols of the importance of combining both technical ability and business competence. As in many organizations their formative exploits are celebrated in a variety of commemorative books published by Siemens today, ensuring that the important messages they symbolize are not forgotten by succeeding generations of employees. At the Transport and Trading Company that forms part of Royal Dutch Shell, the founding influence of Marcus Samuel (1853–1927) is remembered in a glossy video which traces the history of the 'Shell' Transport & Trading Company through its first century. As the man most responsible for transforming a small family business trading in sea shells and other curios in London's East End into an international oil giant, with operations worldwide, Marcus Samuel is another powerful in-company symbol of business acumen and determination.[27]

Some corporate leaders have managed to establish themselves not just on an organizational, but on a world stage. Alfred P. Sloan, John D. Rockefeller, Henry Ford, Walt Disney, and latterly Bill Gates, have all achieved the status of cultural icons with symbolic resonance for millions of people. Alfred Sloan has been described as a paragon of American industry who was looked to for guidance by the American nation during critical times such as the Second World War. Indeed, at least one commentator has suggested that Sloan occupies a possibly unique position as the first industrialist to define a nation (America) in terms of business.[28] Equally synonymous with American capitalism is John D. Rockefeller, the man who entered the oil business in its infancy, formed the Standard Oil Company in 1870, and eventually came to own most of America's oil industry. A great part of his contribution to later generations was not just his vision, but the systems of professional management he developed, which has led the business historian Alfred Chandler to assert that 'An understanding of the history of the Standard Oil Company is essential to the understanding of the rise of the large corporation in the American economy.'[29]

Henry Ford achieved iconic status by deploying assembly line technology for the manufacture of Model T automobiles. His vision of corporate life metamorphosed the car from a luxury item into a virtual necessity for ordinary people. Born in 1901, Walt Disney achieved iconic status by making a commodity out of childhood fantasies. He developed popular cartoon characters, used them in full length cartoon films, re-engaged them in cross-marketing and merchandising ventures, and finally featured them in theme parks with incredible success the world over. Perhaps the most obvious contemporary industrialist with a claim to have achieved iconic status is Bill Gates of Microsoft. Co-founder of the organization that has made him a fortune measured in billions, he has stamped his personality (as well as his products) on the currently buoyant computer industry.

What all these people have in common is not only huge public recognition, but acknowledgement on the part of the public that they have in some way been influenced by them. These icons of the corporate world are not merely well known, but have become emblems of success and advancement which spur on and inspire others.

Powerful and charismatic political leaders such as Winston Churchill in the UK, Kemal Ataturk in Turkey, and Nelson Mandela in South Africa have also achieved world iconic status. A particularly interesting example is George Washington, who was fashioned into the symbolic centre of the American nation in his own lifetime, coming to define 'Americanism' both internally and externally. Views of him as the Father of the country, Sunday School figure, General, and fearless revolutionary continue to live in the collective memory of Americans in numerous stories and myths. That Washington remains such an important symbol of American cultural identity is a tribute to the efforts of influential individuals who have continually reconstructed him as a cultural icon. Witness, for example, Senator Daniel Webster's words during the centennial of Washington's birth in 1832:

> Washington stands at the commencement of a new era, as well as at the head of the New World. A century from the birth of Washington has changed the world. The country of Washington has been the theatre on which a great part of the change has been wrought; and Washington himself a principal agent by which it

has been accomplished. His age and his country are equally full of wonders; and of both he is the chief.[30]

The same social processes that created the symbolic-iconic Washington are, of course, operative today. Gandhi is known not just in India but around the world as a symbol of freedom and humanitarianism, as the man who broke the moral hold of the British over India, and as the embodiment of personal courage and resistor of injustice. Similarly, Martin Luther King capitalized on his personal appeal and media attention to become a symbol of the African American people's struggle for equality in the USA. Somewhat more conventional politicians have also struck a global public chord by force of their personality and achievements. Dwight Eisenhower, one of the most endearing post-war US presidents, quickly became a symbol of traditional individualist values and of America's global power. His image was that of the Christian crusader, and in the 1940s and 1950s he inspired immense public confidence and pride. The fact that Eisenhower's public face of courage, cooperation and congeniality was a simple stereotype far removed from the complex and less pristine private man, has not proved important: his immense symbolic value to the West has meant that those acquainted with his faults have found it useful to protect his public reputation.[31]

Perhaps most potent of all of the newly created iconic leaders is Nelson Mandela, symbol of the new South Africa. After spending years as a political revolutionary and then political prisoner in a South African jail, he was sworn in as President of South Africa on 10 May 1994. On his inauguration Mandela said:

> We have triumphed in the effort to implant hope in the breasts of the millions of our people. We enter into a covenant that we shall build the society in which all South Africans, both black and white, will be able to walk tall, without any fear in their hearts, assured of their inalienable right to human dignity – a rainbow nation at peace with itself and the world . . .[32]

His eloquence as much as his life story suggest that Nelson

Mandela may well turn out to be one of the more enduring symbolic leaders of our century.

While I have focused attention on a few particularly well-known individuals, it is important not to lose sight of the main message here. The same principle of empathic identification which creates world icons also operates within relatively small organizations. Individuals the world over are naturally drawn to role models with whom they can identify and images of whom they can use in the development of their own self-concepts. Employees in organizations base many of their work behaviour patterns on close-at-hand individuals who seem to personify that which is admirable. Leaders at all levels in organizations need to remind themselves that they are, though possibly only with a small reach, symbols. They will do well to reflect that their words and deeds will be carefully scrutinized by their subordinates, and that the messages they consciously and unconsciously project will have an influence on the thoughts and behaviours of their constituents. Little wonder then that shrewd leaders cultivate appealing personas, tailor the symbolic meanings their audiences read into their actions, and employ their corporate propaganda machines to refine and bolster their public faces.

Leader as Playful Hero

Sitting for hours in State House, Entebbe, Uganda, Tiny Rowland, chief executive of Lonrho, was waiting to see President Muraseveni. A colleague who was waiting with him turned and asked whether he thought they would get lunch. Said Tiny, 'Well, we should get at least a sandwich – we gave them £6 million for uniforms.'[33]

Like Tiny, the playful hero is someone who agrees with Rosa Luxemburg that 'Happiness is salubrious and elevating to the soul',[34] and who uses humour in the exercise of their leadership role. Of course, playful heroes vary along a wide spectrum. At one end of this spectrum are those who, like Fred Smith of FedEx and the US General, Pagonis, use a gentle and restrained style of witticism in their daily interactions with their colleagues. At the other end of the spectrum there are leaders such as Richard Branson of Virgin and Wayne Huizenga of Blockbuster Video, some of whose exploits would not be out of character in the repertoire of professional comedians. The difference here is between those who believe that work should be enjoyable, and those who believe that it should be fun. In addition, there are those leaders, such as the Dutchman Paul Fentener van Vlissingen, for whom humour is best employed occasionally, as a cathartic release from the pressures of work. What all these types of playful hero have in common is a recognition of the importance of humour in sustaining effective and meaningful organizational life. Such leaders tend to found and develop cultures where playful activity is not just tolerated, but encouraged with good grace.

In extreme cases, the inclination to find a humorous angle even on difficult problems may be so strong that the search for jokes precedes the search for solutions. This is not quite as bizarre as it might at first sight appear. Commentators on corporate leaders have long recognized that not only do many highly effective CEOs have a profound sense of adventure and play, but that they capitalize on these inclinations to maximize their organizations' creative capacities. Warren Bennis and Burt Nanus,[35] for example, have suggested that leaders tend to manifest 'a felicitous fusion between work and play'. Another perceptive analyst of organizational leaders, Peter Vaill,[36] has argued that in organizations 'Where members have learned how to operate at high levels of quality, they take pleasure in the sheer conduct of the process and attach great importance to proper execution . . . play and enjoyment are integral to getting the job done.' The leader who can adopt the role of the playful hero is one from whom we can all learn, a sort of reduced-threat role model.

A multitude of talented leaders have explicitly recognized and commented on the importance of humour in business. Matt Weinstein, founder of Playfair, argues that the intentional use of fun at work can be a positive force in team building, customer service and boosting employee morale and company loyalty.[37] When asked what he did better or differently from other CEOs, Fred Smith of FedEx replied, 'I have more of a sense of humor than a lot of them, I'll tell you that much.'[38] Harold Geneen, ex-head of ITT, claims that 'I often told colleagues that business was as much fun as golf, tennis, sailing, dancing, or almost anything else you might want to name.' Says Geneen, his role as CEO was to create an organization in which people achieved for the company, their careers, 'but also for the fun of it. I wanted them to enjoy the process of tackling a difficult piece of business.'[39] Marjorie Scardino, the first female chief executive of a FTSE 100 company (Pearson), says that she regards humour as a vital tool of management, and describes her management style as firm but fun.[40] In a similar vein, John Pepper, chairman and chief executive of Procter & Gamble, says he switched the company over to casual attire because 'I want to see people enjoy themselves.'[41]

A nice example of someone whose style involved a restrained form of humour was Lieutenant General William G. Pagonis, who ran the theatre logistics for Desert Shield and Desert Storm. Reflecting on his own behaviour he claimed that 'I use a gentle kind of humor quite a bit. Humor helps me make contact with other people.'[42] Another style of playful hero is illustrated by the Dutchman Paul Fentener van Vlissingen, the ex-head of SHV holdings which employs 65,000 people in more than twenty countries. Van Vlissingen became CEO back in 1984 with the philosophy that people must enjoy their work to do good work. One story he liked to tell was how he invited 120 managers and their spouses on an all-expenses-paid trip on the Orient Express across Europe. In telling the story his main point was that 'We had a lot of fun, a lot of laughter on that trip . . . and afterwards they put together a little cabaret making fun of me. Wonderful! Very funny.'[43] The point? Van Vlissingen is able to play his leadership role without being too self-conscious. He casts himself as a member of the team, not separate from it.

Some noted political figures, such as Tony Blair, also know how to use humour to good effect. At the age of thirteen Tony Blair, the future Prime Minister of Britain, attended Fettes College in Edinburgh. The school was strong on tradition, and the younger boys like Blair were expected to 'fag' (act as a sort of servant) for the older boys. Blair was made a dedicated fag to a boy named Mike Gascoigne, for whom he had to clean shoes, run errands and make toast. Furthermore, if Blair committed any misdemeanour the older boy was empowered to thrash him as he saw fit, which occurred on a number of occasions. Blair soon became disillusioned with this system, and now jokes that his opposition to fagging was his first act as a modernizing politician. On one occasion, twenty-five years after Blair and Gascoigne had last met, Blair was invited to be the guest of honour at a function organized by an Edinburgh lawyers' dining club. Spotting Gascoigne – who was now a senior partner in an eminent Edinburgh law firm – in the audience, Blair seized his opportunity for some good-natured 'revenge'. Departing from his prepared speech he 'pointed to Gascoigne and, to general amusement, expounded humorously on the rigours he had endured as Gascoigne's fag'.[44]

By contrast, Scott McNealy, the CEO of the highly successful computer company Sun Microsystems, tends to deploy a more robust sense of humour. It has been said of him that 'He has a mouth that won't quit, constantly spewing one-liners – usually very funny ones and usually jabs at Microsoft or its founder, Bill Gates . . .'[45] Scott himself readily admits that this same mentality is deliberately projected internally within Sun on the grounds that 'If we work hard and have fun doing it, we'll win.'[46] Similarly, Herb Kelleher, CEO of Southwest Airlines which earns $2.6 billion in revenues, is often described as having an offbeat sense of humour which infects the whole organization. For example, it has been reported that at Southwest Airlines '. . . people looking for jobs, from pilots to mechanics, are routinely asked, "Tell us how you used humor to get out of an embarrassing scrape", and "What is the funniest thing that ever happened to you?" And at least on one occasion, applicants were tested to see how well they responded to a practical joke.'[47]

Wayne Huizenga's partner at the $10 billion corporation Waste Management once said of him that 'He creates an aura of excitement. He has a tremendous sense of humor and he's fun to be with.'[48] When Huizenga left Waste Management to develop Blockbuster Video he did not let the intensity of putting together another hugely successful business destroy his penchant for fun. At themed parties he is reported to have dressed up as a tacky tourist, a motorcycle gang member and a beaded hippie. His sensitivity to comedy also paid direct business dividends. Says one biographer, 'Huizenga has a strong sense of one-liners and timing, and used them often to break the tension, in negotiating or other situations.'[49]

The importance of humour in fostering good interpersonal relations is also well illustrated by Ross Perot. On one occasion, when taking EDS public with the blue-chip firm R.W. Pressprich & Company, he took the lawyers out to lunch at a less than salubrious barbecue pit. Reporting the event at a later date, the senior liaison man from R.W. Pressprich remembers:

> 'And we go down there, and obviously Perot has prearranged this, the guy who owns the place has a filthy rag and he wipes the top of the counter. We ask what is available and the guy behind the counter says "You oughta try that barbecued armadillo, it's real good." Now these lawyers are figuring they can't afford to offend Perot – this is his place – and they take the "armadillo", which was probably pork, to the table, and Perot's sitting there, and he's watching. There are five of us pushing the food around the plate and trying not to eat it, and Ross is having a great time.' Needless to say, the deal went through.[50]

Perhaps the best known of the more extreme playful heroes is the young Richard Branson, founder and leader of Virgin. According to one biographer, Branson uses practical jokes to create intimacy with both friends and strangers. Jumping into swimming pools while pulling others in with him, and bread-roll and meatball throwing contests over dinner characterize his lifestyle. On one occasion Branson is reported as having invited friends round for dinner only to retreat to the kitchen, smear himself with a mixture of ketchup and iodine, and lurch theatrically into the dining-room crying 'call an ambulance'. Watching his friends' faces frozen in horrified disbelief, Branson then slowly transformed his expression of pain into one of hilarity to a chorus of groans, oaths, and a barrage of bread rolls and insults.[51] On another occasion when his trusted confidant Al Clark let it be known that he was considering moving on, the playful side of Branson was evident once again, and the results, as usual, were positive:

Branson's response was to pull a water pistol from his desk and start firing at him, grinning broadly all the while. Later that afternoon, Branson telephoned Clark's wife, pretending to be the managing director of the company to which Clark was going, and talked gibberish down the telephone. Clark capitulated and stayed with Virgin, on the grounds that idiosyncrasy and fun was worth more than conventional careerism.[52]

The playful hero can, of course, always tinge humour with menace when required. Tiny Rowland's subordinate, Hynett, once arranged a meeting between his boss and the leader of Nigeria to discuss an oil deal. Just two months later the president was removed from office in a coup. The same night, Rowland dictated a telex for Hynett: 'Why on earth do you waste my time and introduce me to a load of has-beens?'[53] There is also sometimes a fine line between practical joking and outright sabotage. For example, when the media tycoon Robert Maxwell checked into a US hotel which did not live up to his expectations, he paid a visit to the National Institute of Health where a strain of large fleas was being bred. He acquired a small box full of them – several thousand in all – arranged to check out of the hotel, and then released the fleas into the lift shaft. In the early hours of the morning, it is reported, the other guests in the hotel had to be evacuated.[54]

Playful heroes recognize the importance of humour in breaking down barriers between individuals and bolstering group cohesion. The comic act and the amusing aside melt the cold ice of hierarchy, allowing us to interact as people rather than impersonal job titles with powers and responsibilities, if only for an instant. Through humour, leaders can encourage others to confront problems and vices which might otherwise be ignored or downplayed, with renewed vigour and insight. Through humour the playful hero is able to reveal a little more about him or herself, and thus to make empathic contact with others in their work group. Even Oliver Cromwell, a man noted by historians as dour and puritanical, had a sense of fun. For example, at the wedding of his daughter Frances to Robert Lord Rich in November 1657 he is reported to have thrown wine over the dresses of the women guests and 'dawbed all the stools where they were to sit with wet sweet meates'.[55] And this from the man who was at that time Lord Protector of England, and who was soon to turn down the opportunity to become king. As one academic has written: 'Comedy is sanctioned doubt, a permitted and honoured way of expressing doubt over the majesty and wisdom of our superiors, the loyalty and devotion of our inferiors, and the trust of our friends.'[56] It is a wise leader indeed who recognizes the value of playfulness, and who is willing and able to incorporate it into his or her portfolio of available roles.

Leader as Warrior Hero

The Aztecs waged war and practised human sacrifice to feed the gods and maintain cosmic order. Modern business leaders also tend to cast themselves as warrior heroes. They wage war against other companies and sacrifice the careers and livelihoods of those both inside and outside their organizations through the closure of subsidiaries, redundancies and by forcing competitors out of the market. And they do so not just to maintain their own self-esteem and reinforce their own sense of self, but to please shareholders and preserve free market capitalism. Shareholders and markets have taken the place of gods and the cosmic order, but the warrior ethos is the same. Just as with the Aztecs, business wars not only destroy but create. The warrior hero weeds out unproductive individuals and units from his or her own organization and unfit competitors from the battlefield of the market. By destroying others the warrior hero fulfils his or her martial mission of protection and salvation. Expressed in warrior rhetoric: strategies are often daring and risky, requiring bravery and courage. Victories result in leaner, more efficient and effective organizations, better able to exploit commercial opportunities, fitter to survive in a cut-throat, unpredictable and unforgiving world.

The parallels between military and business leaders have occasionally been recognized by corporate heroes themselves, and their subordinates. Robert Lutz, ex-president of Chrysler, once asserted that 'If by now you've gotten the idea that I view life as a battle – or at least as a heated conversation – you're right.' In describing what he believes makes for effective leadership, Lutz quotes General

Patton's view that 'Success in war lurks invisible in that vitalizing spark, intangible, yet as evident as lightning – the warrior's soul.'[57] One former GE employee has likened Jack Welch to a warrior hero, claiming that 'The basic problem is this – we have Patton, he thinks he's Eisenhower, we need Bradley. Welch needs to win the way other people need to breathe.'[58] It is ex-military leaders who have moved into politics, however, who provide the best examples of this genre. Fidel Castro overcame the Batista regime in Cuba by seizing 'the imagination of many Cubans starved of heroic models among the politicians of the day'.[59] Ho Chi Minh, the North Vietnamese leader who led a long and brutal war against France and the USA, is seen in his country as a warrior-hero and father-figure personification of the nation.

The warrior hero is, above all things, an exemplary figure for those he or she attempts to lead. The German tank commander Erwin Rommel once said: 'Be an example to your men, both in your duty and in private life. Never spare yourself, and let the troops see that you do not, in your endurance of fatigue and privation.'[60] General Schwarzkopf, US military commander in the Gulf War, sought to make the same point by describing the failings of a colonel who was once his commanding officer. Says Schwarzkopf:

> His personal habits . . . alienated the men: the first time we went out on manoeuvres, he declared that there was no reason a man – meaning himself – should not be comfortable in the field. 'We all deserve a good night's sleep,' he said. He had a little tent set up next to the operations tent, and each night he'd put on pyjamas, a maroon satin dressing gown, and fuzzy slippers made of lamb's wool. He'd sit on his cot where troops walking by in their dirty fatigues could see him. 'Look at that candy ass,' they said.[61]

Those executives safely ensconced in their fiftieth floor luxury offices surrounded by choirs of adoring personal assistants and a phalanx of oh-so-very-reassuring yes men; whose lunches are taken in the civilized environs of the corporate dining room reserved only for the most senior managers; and whose journey to work in the company Rolls is made still more pleasurable by the knowledge that the reserved parking space awaits them, may care to reflect on Schwarzkopf's homily.

There are other interesting parallels between military and corporate leaders. Just as military heroes may experience 'battle ecstasy' – the blind enjoyment of the battle – so too may executives. J. Glenn Gray, writing of men in the Second World War, characterized battle ecstasy with great acumen when he wrote that:

> Men who have lived in the zone of combat long enough to be veterans are sometimes possessed by a blind fury that makes them capable of anything. Blinded by the rage to destroy and supremely careless of consequences, they storm against the enemy until they are either victorious, dead or utterly exhausted. It is as if they are seized by a demon and are no longer in control of themselves.[62]

No wonder, then, that warriors not only symbolize bravery, honour and social responsibility, but are prone to excess, and to violating social rules. No wonder, also, that business leaders like the late media mogul Robert Maxwell, and the failed Australian entrepreneur Alan Bond, for whom the corporate equivalent of battle ecstasy was a way of life, excite as much antipathy as admiration.

At their best, however, warrior heroes are incredible achievers. Take, for example, Ray Albert Kroc, born on 5 October 1902 into a respectable lower-middle-class neighbourhood in Chicago. Following stints as an ambulance driver and pianist he signed on as a paper cup salesman. It was at this early stage that he found the motto (borrowed from President Coolidge) that both summed up his attitude to life and later bedecked his empire:

NOTHING IN THE WORLD CAN TAKE THE PLACE OF PERSISTENCE.
TALENT WILL NOT: NOTHING IS MORE COM-MON THAN UNSUCCESSFUL MEN WITH TALENT.
GENIUS WILL NOT: UNREWARDED GENIUS IS ALMOST A PROVERB.

EDUCATION WILL NOT: THE WORLD IS FULL OF EDUCATED DERELICTS.
PERSISTENCE AND DETERMINATION ALONE ARE OMNIPOTENT.'

It was this warrior fervour that ultimately made him his fortune. He resigned from the paper cup business to become the world's exclusive sales agent for a gadget that could make six milk shakes at a time. He travelled to various eating establishments, and learned first-hand about different sectors of the restaurant market. Then in 1954 he met the McDonald brothers. Says one biography of this moment: 'Kroc had arrived at the once-in-a-lifetime juncture of the right man, the right time, and the right product.'[63] Persuading the brothers to sign a deal with him was not easy, and was later fought out in traditional American style through lawyers, threats and legal clauses. Kroc eventually took control of his own destiny by buying out the McDonald brothers for $2.7 million in the early 1960s. Despite being enormously in debt, by 1972 Kroc had opened 1,500 McDonald's outlets. Explaining why he had been so successful, he told one reporter: 'Look, it is ridiculous to call this an industry. This is not. This is rat eat rat, dog eat dog. I'll kill 'em, and I'm going to kill 'em before they kill me. You're talking about the American way of survival of the fittest.'[64]

The qualities of the warrior hero are not restricted to men, as the example of Indira Gandhi, Prime Minister of India for sixteen years, makes clear. Helped to power by a 'Syndicate' of powerful individuals who thought they could control her, she soon exerted her independence. Despite the opposition of her cabinet and army chiefs, she first declared war on Pakistan and then unilaterally declared a ceasefire, and then recognized Bangladesh as a new sovereign country. Pursuing a socialist agenda, she nationalized private banks, commercial banks and general insurance agencies, and inclined in foreign policy toward the USSR rather than the USA. These decisions took remarkable qualities of courage and statesmanship.[65, 66]

While Indira's attributes as a warrior hero were plain to all, there were 'costs' as well as benefits associated with them. On the one hand, she strengthened India's place in the world. She led her country to become the fifth military power, the sixth member of the elite nuclear club, the seventh to the space race and the tenth industrial power. On the other hand, she was intolerant of those who questioned her dominance, and she encouraged sycophancy to the extent that some in the Indian Congress began to compare her with the Goddess Durga (Goddess of Power). Further, democracy in India declined and the institutions of party, parliament and judiciary were twisted. The Indian political culture became amoral and the style authoritarian. Such are the dangers of political leaders captured by the warrior hero role.

While business and political leaders may occasionally identify themselves as a new breed of warrior hero, leaders of armies are frequently fully captured by the images evoked by this single category. The American Second World War general, George S. Patton, is an extreme example. A tank commander in an age where tanks had taken on the romantic symbolism of the cavalry, his old-fashioned, classic style, flamboyance and gallantry, all contributed to his self-definition as the personification of warrior virtues. Reckless regarding his own safety, he once said that the 'inspiration of an heroic act will carry men to victory . . . the blood of heroes like the dragon's teeth will sprout new leaders to replace his loss.'[67] On another occasion on 20 December 1941 he regaled a division with the thought that: 'Battle is not a terrifying ordeal to be endured. It is a magnificent experience wherein all the elements that have made men superior to the beasts are present: courage, self-sacrifice, loyalty, help to others, devotion to duty.'[68] His view of war as a sacred event echoed the ancient mythology of the Aztecs, but also eventually rendered him seemingly obsolete in a new world of peace. His sense of personal mission, has, however, led at least one commentator to describe him as 'the most recent and possibly the last total warrior in America'.[69]

The warrior hero provides another label by which corporate leaders can and frequently do identify themselves. Naturally there are many sub-types here. There is the Chevalier, a warrior who leads by his daring and gallantry; the rifleman, who mixes geniality and brutality, who is both callous and sentimental, being martial but not disciplined in the military; then there is the executioner, who is a killing machine detached from the bigger picture or rationale. These different types – and there are surely many more than listed here – evoke distinct images that will appeal to different personalities, and no one needs or indeed is able to play all the roles suggested by them. But many subordinates expect their leaders to adopt a warrior stance in certain situations, perhaps especially when times are hard, competition intense, the future uncertain. In such instances corporate leaders need to be able to adopt the role of the warrior, to exhibit courage and determination, to provide a role model of sacrifice and loyalty, and to promise to bring future order out of current chaos.

Learning Points for Leaders
The great corporate leaders naturally assume the status of heroes. When things get tough, they are the people everyone counts on. Equally importantly, they are the role models that subordinates look to for guidance and inspiration. Convincing heroes cast themselves in one or more heroic genres: epic, symbolic, playful and warrior. To succeed, leaders must avoid retreating into their own fantasy world where followers are relegated in importance. Instead, they must realize that their status and power as heroes depends on the perceptions of others, which must be astutely managed. At their best, corporate heroes are awe-inspiring exemplars of what others ought to aspire to become. Like J.D. Rockefeller and Andrew Carnegie, they stand the test of time to become regarded as outstanding symbols of their industry and their age.

The most effective leaders of organizations are able to play the role of the hero with aplomb. Like Chung Ju Yung and Ted Turner, they gain moral authority by casting themselves as epic heroes. Like President Reagan and Prime Minister Thatcher, who for a time came to personify the positive qualities of America and Britain, the best organization leaders strive for symbolic status. As with Herb Kelleher and Richard Branson, admirable leaders are able to deploy humour to spark creativity and enrich the lives of their followers. And, like Ray Kroc and Indira Gandhi, excellent leaders have the courage and inspirational qualities of warrior heroes.

While I have chosen to describe individual leaders under one specific category, it is important to recall that many have successfully cast themselves in multiple hero roles. Henry Ford, for example, gained considerable moral authority from the epic nature of his rise to prominence and the vicissitudes he faced. His stature as a symbol of American industrial frontiersmanship who also wrested secrets from nature and used them to transform society, is undisputed. His strength of will, courage and simple-minded determination to stamp his vision of good business practice on the world are traits of the warrior hero. In the words of one biographer: 'Henry Ford was an original. No matter what avatar he assumed, he was never consistently identified with another figure, but stood alone as a new kind of American hero.'[70]

Yet, while heroes may be their organizations' greatest assets, not everyone is able to play the role of the hero with consummate ease, and even fewer are able to give great performances. As with the other dimensions of leadership, to be fully captured by the roles implied by 'the hero' category is always likely to be self-defeating. The most impressive leaders are more than just heroes. Indeed, role capture in this dimension can have particularly telling consequences in the form of 'hero's neurosis'. This is the pathological condition wherein people who have participated in their own casting as heroes are then racked by doubts, being uncomfortably aware of a discrepancy between what they are and what people think they are. Consider, for instance, Lawrence of Arabia's account of his feelings when supposedly at the height of his powers:

> My craving for good repute among men . . . made me profoundly suspect my truthfulness to myself. Only too good an actor could so impress his favourable opinion. Here were the Arabs believing me, Allenby and Clayton trusting me, my bodyguard dying for me: and I began to wonder if all established reputations were founded, like mine, on fraud.[71]

The French national hero De Gaulle also seems both to have

recognized and sometimes suffered from this condition, writing that:

> The price they [men of character] have to pay for leadership is unceasing self-discipline, the constant taking of risks, and a perpetual inner struggle. The degree of suffering involved varies according to the temperament of the individual; but it is bound to be no less tormenting than the hair shirt of the penitent. This helps to explain those cases of withdrawal which, otherwise, are so hard to understand. It constantly happens that men with an unbroken record of success and public applause suddenly lay the burden down.[72]

Even for those untroubled by such anxieties, it is a rare individual who can, in miniature, stir the same sorts of feelings that Cubans have for Castro or many Americans felt toward President John F. Kennedy in 1960. As a basic condition for so doing one must be fit for one's times. We should remember that JFK's impact in part reflects that: 'It was a hero that America needed, a hero to his time, a man whose personality might suggest contradictions and miseries which could reach into the alienated circuits of the underground, because only a hero can capture the secret imagination of people, and be so good for the vitality of his nation.'[73] JFK's genius was to capitalize on the advantages with which he was presented, advantages that President Carter, for instance, was signally unable to exploit. The same point holds true for iconic heroes of business such as Walt Disney, who, with Hollywood plagued by accusations of immorality, was thrust to prominence by the success of the first commercially viable sound cartoon, *Steamboat Willie*. Said one biographer, 'if ever an industry needed a new hero, the movies did now' – and there was Walt Disney, 'just in the nick of time' and 'about to become the least likely savior of an industry'.[74]

We should recall, too, that not everyone is sufficiently astute and manipulating to be able to modify their behaviour as required by what are often fickle and hypocritical audiences. Of few individuals could it be written, as it has been regarding Dwight Eisenhower, that he:

adapted himself to the managerial techniques of the modern state. He managed his own personality and temperament, restraining his more intemperate impulses. He managed men and resources effectively as a military commander and politician. Most skilfully of all, he managed his image and standing with the American public.[75]

Finally, casting oneself as a hero, we should recall, comes at a price. And many great men – Lincoln, Washington, Jefferson and Nelson among them – have suffered from the caprices of a public that adored them as heroes one moment only to redefine them as villains the next.[76]

To conclude, then, effective leaders are often exemplary heroes. Some leaders unselfconsciously realize that they need to cast themselves in a heroic mould. Most learn the value of assuming the hero role as they ascend the corporate hierarchy by observing how other high performers conduct themselves. If you are in doubt regarding your own heroic status then you probably need to start by following the advice of Melvin Goodes of Warner-Lambert, and re-examine what can be learned from traditional cultural heroes such as Hercules and King Arthur. Some specific questions to consider when evaluating how well you perform in this dimension of leadership are:

- *As an Epic Hero.* Have you succeeded against the odds and in the face of many daunting hurdles? Are your followers aware of the 'epic' nature of your rise to a leadership position? Do others attribute 'special' (moral, spiritual, etc.) qualities to you that reinforce your personal authority?

- *As a Symbolic Hero.* Are you clear in your own mind what values and 'big ideas' you stand for? Do you frequently and consistently voice and role model these values and ideas? If asked, would the majority of your subordinates be able to identify the values and ideas you believe you symbolize?

- *As a Playful Hero.* Do you tend to use humour in the exercise of your leadership function? Are you a believer in the value of humour in sparking creativity, relieving social tensions, and maximizing motivation? Do your subordinates recognize and respond to your sense of humour?

- *As a Warrior Hero.* Do you have the courage of your convictions? Do your followers have confidence in your ability to successfully complete difficult and risky tasks? Do you tend to think of business as a war in which there are winners and losers?

William J. Kellogg

Ray Krock

Alfred P. Sloan

Bill Gates

Three

LEADER AS ACTOR

All one needs to realize . . . performances and to regard them as worth while is a powerful leader, a willing cast and an empathetic audience. A triadic collusion, the stuff of the theatre and of organization. (Mangham & Overington)[1]

WITH THE FUTURE of Apple crucially dependent on the Mac, Steve Jobs launched the new product to a mix of shareholders, the media and Apple employees. Jobs, with his shoulder-length dark hair and rock star good looks, opened the meeting by quoting lyrics from Bob Dylan's 'The Times They are A-Changin'':

> Come writers and critics who prophesy with your pens
> And keep your eyes wide the chance won't come again.
> And don't speak too soon for the wheel's still in spin
> And there's no telling who that it's naming
> For the loser now will be later to win
> For the times they are a-changin'.

In 1958, continued Jobs, IBM failed to spot the potential of xerography technology, and lost out to Xerox. Ten years later IBM dismissed the mini-computer as insignificant, leaving the way open for DEC to become a multi-hundred-million-dollar corporation. Another decade passed, and in 1977 the fledgling company Apple invented the Apple II, the first personal computer as we know it today. IBM again dismissed the PC as too small to perform serious computing. Yet by the early 1980s the Apple II had become the world's most popular computer, and the Apple corporation the fastest growing company in American business history. IBM at last recognized that Apple was its major competitor, and set out to retain its dominance. 'Will Big Blue really dominate the entire information age?' asked Jobs, rhetorically. The crowd, by this stage whipped up into a frenzied hysteria, shouted back a chorus of 'No's' as a fantastically slick and expensive 'Orwellian-1984' themed commercial lit up a huge screen behind him. As the ad finished, Steve walked over to a bag and took out the Mac. He turned it on with the theme music from the movie *Chariots of Fire* blasting from the auditorium's speakers. Writing about the event years later, John Sculley, one-time head of Apple, commented that 'It was a brilliant bit of theatrics', and 'The audience roared its approval.'[2,3]

Steve Jobs' performance, beautifully described by his old friend Sculley, is a marvellous example of poetic, rhetorical, storytelling and showmanship skills being effectively deployed. Jobs provides his audience with a history of computing that both emphasizes Apple's leading role and takes every opportunity to knock IBM, their biggest and most dangerous competitor. Apple is the fastest growing company in American business history, while IBM is so blinkered that it passed up the opportunity to buy Xerox, and then entered the mini, and later the personal computer markets, late in the game. IBM is George Orwell's Big Brother out to dominate computing. Apple are the heroes of the information world, who with the Mac, will wrest victory from the stultifying and menacing Big Blue. The setting, the action, the visual impact of the commercial, the music, and Steve Jobs' charismatic performance are all in synergy. The result was surely what every leader would hope for: a mesmerized audience roared its approval.

As the example of Steve Jobs aptly demonstrates, effective leaders need often to be consummate actors. It has long been recognized that managing and leading are both forms of performance. Back in 1978 the management guru Tom Peters argued that executives do not synthesize chemicals or operate lift trucks; they deal in symbols.[4] And what is more, their overt verbal communications are only part of the story. Consciously or unconsciously, leaders are constantly acting out the vision and goals they are trying to realize in an organization that is typically far too vast and complex for one person to control directly. As the legendary J. Paul Getty has said, businessmen, like theatrical personalities, can be catapulted into stardom by one good performance, and see their popularity wane after a flop. Like intelligent theatrical stars they turn down roles that do not suit them, refuse to appear in productions that fall below their standards, and once having accepted a role do the best they can. Not every performance can win an Academy Award, 'But the top names are those whose average of hits is highest and who consistently do their utmost to do their best.'[5]

Rather than exercise control through formal systems and procedures, leaders exert much of their influence through their roles as poets, rhetoricians, storytellers and show-men and -women. Many modern corporations are so huge, and their operations so sophisticated, that no single individual can hope to master all their intricacies. No one person can accumulate all the specialist knowledge required to undertake every task, let alone the chief executive, most of whose time tends to be spent contemplating broad strategic issues. What is more, the normal levers of power available to those who direct enterprises – the rule book, the HR policies governing aspects of organizational life from appraisal to compensation to promotion – are rather blunt instruments. Given these limitations – of leader time, energy, knowledge and ability – and the often ineffectual nature of formal powers, leaders have no choice, and no less is expected of them by their subordinates, but to control and direct through their words and deeds.

The importance of this dimension of leadership is signalled by analysts' suggestions that those who would lead must 'tap into a deeper sense of meaning for their followers'[6] in order to achieve what Peter Vaill[7] has described as a form of 'managerial artistry'. Parallels between the work of corporate leaders and that of artists, poets and actors, litter the business literature. The management scholar Paul Bate has likened leaders of cultural change to 'artists who create a work of art'.[8] Harold Geneen of ITT was once described as 'the Michelangelo of management'.[9] And, according to Robert K. Lifton, 'If artists give up the world's pleasures to pursue their calling, people understand it. What they don't understand is that many businessmen have the same creative drives and derive the same satisfactions as artists – but what they are doing is translated into dollars and cents.'[10]

The striking agreement among commentators on the need for leaders to be actors has led to considerable attention being focused on *how* leaders perform. A key question here, is what differentiates a 'good' from a 'poor' performance. The good performance is one which is authentic, believable and convincing. By contrast, the poor performance is one that appears contrived and self-conscious. In striving to describe how organizational leaders can deliver credible performances, the business school academics Iain Mangham and Michael Overington draw on the problems faced by theatre actors. They argue that:

> . . . the way in which actors present themselves on-stage, not as themselves but as their characters, nothing but their characters, is the key to maintain the audience's attention to the staging of theatrical reality. Any hint in the playing of their parts, any suggestion that there is an actor present in a character . . . will erode the taken-for-granted nature of this special form of consciousness. If an actor forgets a line, audibly breaks wind, has problems with his costume or his props or loses his wig in the middle of the action, the reality so delicately maintained until that point is rendered more precarious.[11]

From the audience's viewpoint, then, a competent performance is one which holds its attention, is plausible and coherent, and which strikes it as in some sense 'real'. In an organizational context this translates as a performance, like Steve Jobs' at the launch of the Mac, that captivates subordinates, and that does not seem contradictory or hypocritical. More than this, if the leader is an actor then it is an actor of a particular sort: someone who makes the organization and its activity seem logical and sensible. The leader as actor gives his or her employees an attractive role in the world to which they can relate and which is deeply meaningful. The leader is the star who allows all others in the organization to perform their roles without the stress and distress of uncertain goals, vague objectives, or an underdeveloped sense of what the future may hold. Leaders act to integrate their organizations, and are the linchpins on which all other acts depend. What is it like to be a leader giving a great performance in a successful organization? The actor Simon Callow's description of what it feels like to give a superb theatrical performance provides some insight. It involves, he says:

> A feeling of power, but not power *over* anyone or anything; simply energy flowing uninterrupted and unforced through your body and your mind. You are the agent. You are above the performance – *it* is performing, not you. You sense the audience's collective identity and you speak directly to it . . . You are always forward moving: the thread unbroken . . .
>
> You are the master of time and rhythm, and you play with them like a jazz musician. You create a pleasurable tension and then you relieve it pleasurably . . . The performance is not so much new as newly revealed, the varnish stripped off, the paint bright again, detail discernible . . .[12]

How is such a performance, that satisfies both the leader and his or her audience, to be achieved? There are those who argue that if the actor/leader believes in the reality of his or her own performance, then this will carry an individual through to success. The idea that authentic performance is more about immersion than technique has proved beguiling, and has many adherents. Others have suggested that a range of different skills, attributes and abilities is required. According to the critic Kenneth Tynan, the essential attributes of great acting are: complete physical relaxation; powerful physical magnetism; commanding eyes; commanding voice; superb timing; and finally *chutzpah* – the Jewish word for that combination of cool nerve and outrageous effrontery. To these the theatre critic Michael Billington[13] adds acute interpretative intelligence, required not least because the modern actor – and we might add the modern leader – has to be a kind of histrionic chameleon able to adapt a performance quickly to suit changing conditions and audience expectations.

Arguments over the precise combination of factors and talents most likely to result in a convincing leadership performance have, of course, run for decades. None of the magic formulae so far suggested has attracted a widespread following, and the reason is not hard to discern. It is illustrated by a story about the actor Laurence Olivier: Olivier once gave a performance of Othello so brilliant that even the cast applauded him at the curtain call. When it was over, he tore back to his dressing room in a towering rage and slammed the door behind him. One of the actors timidly knocked on the door and said: 'What's the matter, Larry – don't you know you were brilliant?' To which Olivier is reported to have replied, 'Of course I fuckin' know – but I don't know *why*.'[14] By the same token, and for the same reasons, we cannot formulate simple lists of success factors that hold good for all people in all situations for all times. Reality is too complex – there are just too many variables to be taken into account. Moreover, an individual giving a great performance will likely be so wrapped up in the role he or she is playing that acute self-insight is just not possible, while those attracted by the performance will have their critical faculties dimmed by admiration: great performances, it seems, are more easily enjoyed than analysed.

This chapter is an exploration of what the critic James Agate meant when he claimed that 'Whoever has seen a great actor knows that he is not an animal to be stalked in its lair but a tiger leaping out on the spectator from the bush of mediocrity and the brake of competence.'[15] The same can surely be said of great business leaders too. The importance of this insight has, as we shall see, been recognized by commercial leaders as diverse as Mary Kay Ash, J. Paul Getty and Richard Branson; political leaders of the stature of Winston Churchill, John F. Kennedy and Fidel Castro; and military leaders of the calibre of Nelson and Napoleon. In this chapter I examine leaders:

- as *poets*, who frame convincing images for their sub- ordinates;
- as *rhetoricians*, who energize their audience through their language;
- as *storytellers*, who focus and amplify others' beliefs; and
- as *show-men* and *-women*, who dramatize, and who explain through action.

Leader as Poet

Faced with the considerable challenge of turning around the performance of the Scandinavian airline SAS, Jan Carlzon sought to induce culture change by promoting notions of customer service. The headline image he identified as key, was the abstract but appealing notion of *'moments of truth'*. Said Carlzon:

> Last year, each of our 10 million customers came in contact with approximately five SAS employees, and this contact lasted an average of 15 seconds each time. Thus, SAS is 'created' in the minds of our customers 50 million times a year, 15 seconds at a time. These 50 million 'moments of truth' are the moments that ultimately determine whether SAS will succeed or fail as a company. They are the moments when we must prove to our customers that SAS is their best alternative.[16]

Just as great poets are able to frame images that guide the sensitivities of their readers, so great leaders develop images that mould the behaviours of their subordinates. Like poets searching for a theme or aspect of existence that no one else sees in quite the same way, the corporate leader must wrest a coherent image of the way ahead from the chaos of conflicting trends and data items with which he or she is continually bombarded. According to business academics like Linda Smircich and Gareth Morgan,[17] leadership is essentially about framing and defining reality for others. Successful corporate leaders give direction to the organization in a strategic sense, and they do so by providing an image or pattern of thinking in a way that has meaning for those directly involved. Very frequently, for organizational leaders the framing of an image involves describing some visionary end state, thus providing a snapshot of the organization's purpose. To be successful the image framed must evoke a strong emotional impact among subordinates, build confidence and excitement, and be appropriate to the history and culture of the organization as experienced by employees: only then will it have the power to inspire.

One of the most important functions of the leader is to present an appealing organizational mission and identity. Mary Kay Ash, founder of the Dallas-based Mary Kay Cosmetics Company, defines her image for the corporation in terms of equal rights for women and an explicitly Christian outlook. At various times she is reported as saying 'My objective was just to help women' and 'Our company motto is: God first, family second, and business third. In that order, everything works, and out of that order, nothing works.'[18] Through these statements, and others like them, the principal identity components of the Mary Kay corporation have been established, reinforced and transmuted into fundamental tenets for ordinary employees. Anita Roddick, founder and co-chairperson of the UK-based retailer The Body Shop, frames her organization's key images in terms of assisting the development of disadvantaged trading communities. For example, she has written that 'We absolutely believe in the power of community economic initiatives to affect and change lives. Our trade with these communities is our way of participating in and encouraging these initiatives.'[19]

When in 1980 Asea Brown Boveri (ABB) was formed by the merger of two European manufacturers of electrical power systems and equipment, the president and CEO, Percy Barnevik, faced the difficult task of framing an image that would help generate a coherent identity for the new entity. His response was to try and make a virtue of the transnational nature of the organization:

> ABB is a company with no geographic center, no national axe to grind. We are a federation of national companies with a global coordination center. Are we a Swiss company? Our headquarters is in Zurich, but only 100 professionals work at headquarters and we will not increase that number. Are we a Swedish company? I'm the CEO, and I was born and educated in Sweden. But our headquarters is not in Sweden, and only two of the eight members of our board of directors are Swedes. Perhaps we are an American company. We report our financial results in U.S. dollars, and English is ABB's official language. We conduct all high-level meetings in English.
>
> My point is that ABB is none of those things – and all of those things. We are not homeless. We are a company with many homes.[20]

Political leaders, especially those who survive for extended periods of time, learn to deploy salient images which capture the public mood. In Canada, René Levesque created the Parti Québecois, led it to victory in creating the government of Quebec, and then directed that government in a referendum that sought a mandate to negotiate 'sovereignty-association' with the rest of Canada. Key to this vision was the image of an association, which married well with the concept of sovereignty, and which had none of the absolutist and rigid connotations of 'independence'. While the image of sovereignty-association took Levesque a long way, the Canadian public ultimately turned against him, and he saw his vision of an independent Quebec collapse when defeated in the referendum.[21] In the UK, Prime Minister Margaret Thatcher created a series of images linked to notions of privatization, free market economics and British nationalism, all of which were subsumed under the general label of 'Thatcherism'. This served her well for more than a decade, by which time these images and their associated ideology had begun to pall, and the British public (not to mention her own Conservative Party) were ready for change. Images, then, may well need to be updated in the light of changing circumstances: audiences, whether they are national electorates, organizational participants or shareholders, are nothing if not fickle in their affections.

The felicitous consonance of imagery with context is something that the young Masayoshi Son, the founder of the Japanese software distributing company Softbank, had to learn the hard way. Masayoshi Son relates how, when he first started the organization in 1981, he had just two part-time workers and a small office. Thinking big from the beginning, however:

> I got two apple boxes, and I stood up on them in the morning as if I was giving a speech. In a loud voice, I said to my two workers, 'You guys have to listen to me because I am the president of this company.' I said, 'In five years I'm going to have $75 million in sales. In five years, I will be supplying 1,000 dealer outlets, and we'll be number one in PC software distribution.' And I said it very loudly.

> Those two guys opened their mouths. They stood up and opened wide their eyes and mouths, and they thought, this guy must be crazy. And they both quit.[22]

This did not stop the company becoming successful, and by 1992 Masayoshi Son had 570 employees and sales of $350 million. What this example does do, though, is to illustrate the dangers associated with framing palpably unrealistic images with which employees cannot easily identify. If leaders have to be poets, then they should be sensitive and careful in their choice of imagery. To think too far ahead, and to predict too long into the future, is to risk formulating images so detached from the everyday experiences of ordinary folk that they are unable to accept them. The leader as poet must be as much a populist as an idealist, and his or her poetry must be for a mass not an elite audience.

To summarize, then, effective leaders are able to capture the essence of their organization and its mission in instantly appealing images. As Jack Welch of GE has said, as a chief executive, 'You need an overarching message, something big but simple and understandable. Whatever it is – *we're going to be No. 1 or No. 2, or fix/close/sell, or boundarylessness* – every idea you present must be something you could get across easily at a cocktail party with strangers. If only aficionados of your industry can understand what you're saying, you've blown it.'[23] One final, and particularly compelling example of a leader playing the role of the poet with some sophistication concerns George Merck. In the 1930s Merck sought to alter his corporation from a chemical manufacturer into a preeminent drug-making company on the basis of its research capability. Describing this envisioned future at the opening of Merck's research facility in 1933, he said:

> We believe that research work carried on with patience and persistence will bring to industry and commerce new life; and we have faith that in this new laboratory, with the tools we have supplied, science will be advanced, knowledge increased, and human life win ever a greater freedom from suffering and disease . . . We pledge our every aid that this enterprise shall merit the

faith we have in it. Let your light so shine – that those who seek the Truth, that those who toil that this world may be a better place to live in, that those who hold aloft that torch of science and knowledge through these social and economic dark ages, shall take new courage and feel their hands supported.[24]

Leader as Rhetorician

Born the son of an influential baptist minister in Atlanta in 1929, Dr Martin Luther King delivered speeches that helped to foster a sense of common identity, and destiny, among African Americans. Perhaps his most bravura, and certainly his best known use of rhetoric to move others, is his 'I have a dream' speech. A brief excerpt of which will serve us well:

> . . . When the architects of our republic wrote the magnificent words of the Constitution and the Declaration of Independence, they were signing a promissory note to which every American was to fall heir. This note was a promise that all men, yes, black men as well as white men, would be granted the unalienable rights of life, liberty, and the pursuit of happiness.
>
> It is obvious today that America has defaulted on this promissory note in so far as her citizens of color are concerned. Instead of honoring this sacred obligation, America has given the Negro people a bad check, which has come back marked 'insufficient funds'. But we refuse to believe that the bank of justice is bankrupt. We refuse to believe that there are insufficient funds . . .
>
> So I say to you, my friends, that even though we must face the difficulties of today and tomorrow, I still have a dream. It is a dream deeply rooted in the American dream that one day this nation will rise up and live out the true meaning of its creed – we hold these truths to be self-evident, that all men are created equal. This will be the day when all of God's children will be able to sing with new meaning – 'my country 'tis of thee; sweet land of liberty; of thee I sing, land where my fathers died, land of the pilgrim's pride; from every mountain side, let freedom ring' – and if America is to be a great nation, this must become true.[25]

Here King cleverly introduces his theme centred on the American ideals of life, liberty and the pursuit of happiness through an avowedly Christian lens. He then refracts it through American historical and contemporary events, evoking a powerful emotional response in his audience as he does so. To understand why this speech was (and still is) so compelling, we must consider both the context in which it was delivered and the origin of the imagery it references. The speech was given with Congress considering President Kennedy's Civil Rights Act of 1963 – a highly charged time in American politics. The speech itself was designed to appeal to white as well as to African Americans, and to do this King drew on lines from the song 'America' and quotes from both Lincoln's Gettysburg Address and the Declaration of Independence. It was by means of this subtle framing of his movement's values in terms of the nation's values (which he therefore seemed to cherish and protect), that King heightened the significance of the African American people's struggle for every American. By so doing he maximized his and his movement's appeal and potential acceptance by Americans generally.[26]

Rhetoric is the art of writing and speaking both impressively and persuasively. Leaders, if they are to be effective communicators, must not only be lay-poets, but, like King, adept in the crafts of the rhetorician. If the management of organizations is, in part, a performing art, then this centrally involves the shaping of direction and the marshalling of support through appropriate rhetoric. The most important aspect of the leader as rhetorician is the ability to use language in ways which are emotionally expressive, and which energize, motivate and inspire others to action. A focus on the role of the leader as rhetorician is useful because the many textbook reminders that leaders need to be effective communicators are still ignored or at best only partially understood. In short, there are still many executives who, like second-rate actors, are careless of speech, inattentive to words, pronounce them in a thoughtless and slipshod manner, and thus end up with completely mutilated, incomprehensible phrases.

A particularly noteworthy Asian rhetorician, again from the world of politics, is the ex-leader of Pakistan, Benazir Bhutto. In a country blighted by mass illiteracy, oratory is an especially important political tool. An excellent example of her abilities is the speech she gave in 1986 in Peshawar. Desperate to convince the conservative and male-dominated Pakistani society that a woman could lead them, she rose before a large crowd, 99% of which consisted of men, and addressed them with a mixture of fire and poetry:

> People think I am weak because I am a woman. Do they not know that I am a Muslim woman, and that Muslim women have a heritage to be proud of? I have the patience of Bibi Khadija, the wife of the Prophet, Peace Be Upon Him, I have the perseverance of Bibi Zeinab, the sister of Imam Hussain. And I have the courage of Bibi Aisha, the Prophet's favourite wife, who rode her own camel into the battle at the heads of the Muslims. I am the daughter of martyr Zulfiakr Ali Bhutto, the sister of martyr Shah Nawaz Khan Bhutto and I am your sister as well. I challenge my opponents to come and meet me on the field of democratic elections.[27]

While the Muslim and historical references will be unfamiliar to many, the power of Benazir Bhutto's rhetoric is evident to all. The parallels with the rousing speeches of other world class rhetoricians like Martin Luther King need no further comment. In part at least because of her rhetorical finesse, Ms Bhutto duly won national elections in 1988, and assumed power.

Few corporate leaders have been so candid as John Sculley of first Pepsi and then Apple, regarding the pains he took to ensure that he was rhetorically competent. In his autobiography, Sculley relates how he had to work for many hours to improve his oratorical skills, overcoming a severe stammer and a lack of confidence in addressing large groups. So determined was he to build a strength out of what had originally been a weakness that he went to the theatre just to watch how actors performed on stage, practised his own performances for hours on end, and even hired a speech coach to perfect his technique. On one occasion, having been named as marketing vice president for Pepsi, he began preparing for a forty-minute speech a full three months before it was due to be delivered. By sheer dint of hard work Sculley, like his mentor Don Kendall, the man who built PepsiCo into a formidable multinational enterprise, was able to deliver fine performances to vital constituencies.[28]

An impressive example of a naturally proficient business leader–rhetorician is Lee Iacocca of Chrysler. His particular skill was to employ vivid metaphors and analogies to justify his strategic choices and to mobilize the energies of his workers. In the depths of a major crisis, Iacocca likened Chrysler's position to America in the midst of world war and economic depression. The necessity for closing plants he described in terms of triage: 'I felt like any army surgeon. The toughest assignment in the world is for the doctor who's at the front during a battle . . . it's a question of priorities . . . They would pick the ones who had the best chance of survival.' The unmistakable suggestion is that, while painful, the plant closures are in the best interests of long-term healing for an organization at war with an enemy. In 1979 and 1980 Chrysler laid off 15,000 blue- and white-collar workers. The mass firings are described by Iacocca as a family tragedy: 'To cut expenses, we had to fire a lot of people. It's like a war – we won, but my son didn't come back.' These images of war and family were deliberately used to conceal the culpability of Chrysler in its own bankruptcy, as well as the divergence of interests between its managers and workers, while simultaneously underlining the need for loyalty and joint action. Iacocca may or may not have *believed* his own rhetoric, but it worked powerfully for those around him, and he commanded much respect in troubled times because of it.[29]

The leader as rhetorician galvanizes the energy of his or her subordinates, and anyone else who happens to be in their orbit. During the Second World War, with Britain facing the threat of invasion from Germany, Prime Minister Winston Churchill used his powers of rhetoric to unite the British nation. Consider, for example:

> Hitler knows he will have to break us on this island or lose the war. If we can stand up to him, all Europe may be free, and the life of the world may move forward into broad, sunlit uplands. But if we fail, the whole world, including the United States, including all we have known and cared for, will sink into the

abyss of a new Dark Age, made more sinister and perhaps more protracted by the lights of perverted science. Let us therefore brace ourselves to our duties and so bear ourselves that if the British Empire and its Commonwealth last for a thousand years, men will still say, 'This was their finest hour'.[30]

A generation later President John F. Kennedy gave speeches which captured and exploited the mood of the times. There can be few people in the Western world of that generation who cannot remember or continue to be inspired by the words from JFK's inaugural address: 'Let every nation know, whether it wishes us well or ill, that we shall pay any price, bear any burden, meet any hardship, support any friend, oppose any foe, in order to assure the survival and the success of liberty.'[31] The force of the words is a tribute to the power of rhetoric. And while not everyone can hope to be as skilled as a Churchill or a Kennedy, or even an Iacocca, most can, like Sculley, improve with dedication and practice. Like Franklin D. Roosevelt, who learned to use colloquial phrases and folk imagery in his fireside chats, leaders can tailor their language to different audiences. And, as with Martin Luther King, all can try and employ repetition, rhythm and metaphor to create a special bond with an audience.

In summary, effective leaders are those who are excellent orators, able to deliver speeches impressively and persuasively. The best litmus test of one's abilities is the reaction of followers and subordinates. Positive reviews such as 'Hal Geneen taught us to aspire higher',[32] and Ross Perot's 'ability to communicate was the best I'd ever seen'[33] are accolades to which we can all work towards. For those who lack confidence in their abilities, the marketing guru David Ogilvy recommends the use of ghostwriters and speech coaches. Ghostwriters were employed to good effect by notable rhetoricians like Presidents Franklin, Roosevelt and Kennedy, while John D. Rockefeller employed talented publicity agents to put an 'appropriate' spin on his words and deeds.[34] The bottom line here is that the benefits of being a skilled rhetorician are so great for corporate leaders, that some considerable time and resource investment is surely merited.

Leader as Storyteller

The nineteenth century British statesman Benjamin Disraeli once said that 'With words we govern men.' Later commentators on leadership have added that words are most effective when they tell a story. Stories are not just messages or themes; they are explanatory accounts. As the business scholars Noel Tichy and Eli Cohen have noted, effective leaders embody their teachable points of view in living stories which explain their learning experiences and their beliefs.[35] What is more, they create stories about the future of their organizations that engage their followers, both emotionally and intellectually, to attain the winning future that they describe. The stories great leaders tell are highly selective, focusing their subordinates' attention on salient, non-trivial issues. Through their familiarity with and understanding of stories, people are able to reduce complexity to manageable levels. Leaders ensure that their followers discard the chaff – the marginal and irrelevant information – rather than the grain. Stories are easily remembered guides to action that people enjoy telling and retelling. They not only extend a leader's reach into the furthest corners of his or her organization, but enrich its cultural fabric.

All leaders tell stories, and most become the central characters in stories told about them by their followers. The most distinguished leaders revel in their role as storytellers, and fully exploit stories as vehicles for exercising power and control. Through stories leaders connect with their followers, allowing them a glimpse into their minds and their lives. Complete with their human protagonists and fascinating dramas, stories engage listeners on an intuitive level not touched by purely rational arguments. Given the importance of stories as tools of leadership, there is no point in narrating ordinary stories that merely incorporate the latest faddish thinking of a favourite management guru. Such organizations are led by the Gerald Fords and the George Bushes of the business world: people who tell traditional, unexciting and unadventurous stories. They may be effective, but they are rarely inspirational. The modern corporate world requires innovative and visionary story-tellers – such leaders are the corporate equivalents of Confucius or Moses. They are leaders who can voice novel plotlines, bring attention to latent but vital aspects and relationships of their organization, and incite radical new thinking.

One way in which stories can be employed is to build and destroy culture. For example, while heading up a division at General Motors, John DeLorean told stories that undermined the company's established culture. One particular story that DeLorean liked to tell concerned a trip by a senior sales officer to the Chevrolet sales zone. The sales zone staff learned from Detroit that the boss was keen on his hotel room having a refrigerator full of cold beer, sandwiches and fruit for him to snack on at night. They booked a suite in one of the city's best hotels, rented a refrigerator and ordered food and beer. Only then was it discovered that the fridge was so big that they could not get it through the hotel room door. What was more, the hotel refused them permission to rip out the door and part of the adjoining window. Unperturbed, the quick-thinking zone staff hired a crane operator to put them on the roof of the hotel, knocked out a set of windows in the suite, and manoeuvred the fridge into the room through this gaping hole. Enjoying his beer and sandwiches that night, the Chevrolet executive no doubt thought, 'What a great bunch of people we have in this zone.' The next day the executive left for another city, and another refrigerator. Meanwhile, says DeLorean, the zone people were once again dismantling hotel windows and employing the services of a crane.[36]

It is not hard to see DeLorean's point. GM's culture was one that venerated respect for authority, conformity with established norms, and loyalty to superiors. This was an organization where subordinates were expected to meet their visiting superiors at the airport, carry their bags, pay their hotel bills and drive them around. In fact, the higher the status of the superior, the larger was the retinue required to meet him at the airport: a chief engineer necessitated at least one assistant engineer, while the chairman of the board would be met by literally dozens of senior personnel. DeLorean's story ridicules this mentality by providing a graphic illustration of the sorts of bizarre behaviour that it generates. His message is that there are limits to the deference that one should pay to bosses, and that just because everyone else is hiring cranes and ripping out windows, this does not mean that it is appropriate let alone acceptable behaviour. Stories such as this one caused waves within GM that threatened the dominant ethos. No wonder, then, that DeLorean was ultimately forced out.[37]

Leaders who, like DeLorean, are skilled storytellers, often use stories to increase their own personal standing. One notable historical example of this is the English naval hero Horatio Nelson, who told and wrote stories about his own exploits that contributed to his own mythology. In describing his famous indiscipline at the Battle of Cape St Vincent, Nelson is at his myth-making best. He relates how, in 1797 in the war against Spain, he divined what the Spanish admiral had in mind and following his instincts disobeyed orders. Departing from the *Fighting Instructions* was normally seen as an act of cowardice and invariably entailed a court martial. Flouting convention, Nelson took it upon himself to sail directly into the Spanish fleet, and with three other British ships engaged the enemy. In a clever manoeuvre Nelson captured the *San Nicolas* (at the cost of only seven English men dead and some others wounded), and then used it to board the largest Spanish ship (the *San Josef*) which lay alongside her. In his account of the battle, Nelson wrote:

> When I got into her main-chains, a Spanish Officer came upon the quarter-deck rail, without arms, and said the Ship had surrendered. From this welcome information, it was not long before I was on the quarter-deck, when the Spanish Captain, with a bended knee, presented me with his Sword, and told me the Admiral was dying with his wounds below. I gave him my hand, and desired him to call to his Officers and Ship's Company that the Ship had surrendered, which he did; and on the quarter-deck of a Spanish First-rate, extravagant as the story may seem, did I receive the Swords of the vanquished Spaniards, which as I received I gave to William Fearney, one of my bargemen, who placed them, with the greatest sang-froid, under his arm.[38]

Nelson continues to describe how the crew of the *Victory*, surging past after the fleeing enemy, lined her rails and gave three cheers as the men looked with wonder at the astonishing sight. The style is epic, his tone triumphant, the description unapologetically self-congratulatory. The storyline is simple, clear and appealing. His intelligence, courage and determination are so woven into the fabric of the narrative that they do not have to be mentioned explicitly. Of course, Nelson informs us, his tactics were forgiven and he was commended by his commanding officer for his part in the proceedings. Through stories such as these Nelson managed to write himself into history as a world-historical figure. Napoleon did much the same through his publication of a reflective and grandiloquent account of his achievements, the *Mémorial de Sainte-Hélène*, published in 1823. And if not all corporate leaders can perform on a world stage, they can at least inscribe themselves into the history of their own organizations.

Less flamboyant but no less effective in creating memorable and impactful storylines was the American chief of staff during the US involvement in the Second World War, George C. Marshall. In the years leading up to the war Americans were disinterested in conflicts abroad, and Congress adopted an overtly isolationist stance. Recognizing the dangers inherent in such an approach to world affairs, Marshall worked both behind the scenes and in public to persuade Americans of the need to strengthen the US army. The story of the necessity for strong defensive forces was not new, but it was one that had to be learned by a new generation. As the public mood turned in his favour he provided more specific storylines: that conscription should apply to all, that officers had to be well educated and direct operations using the best military thinking, that technology had to be state-of-the-art, that older and outmoded officers needed to be replaced, and that unnecessary rules and regulations had to be dispensed with.

Marshall's combination of mastery of the facts, articulate testimony and deep belief in the necessity of mobilization proved highly effective. According to one commentator, it was 'Only because he told his stories with exquisite persuasiveness, and because he embodied these messages so transparently in his own life', that Marshall succeeded 'so remarkably in influencing American public opinion'.[39] Indeed, such was his pervasive influence that he managed to redefine military service in the US as a form of disinterested service to one's country, promoting an attitude that prevails to this day.

Smaller-scale examples, but no less important to specific organizations, can be found in a business context. Jan Carlzon of SAS, for instance, used to skilfully relate the details of the search and find procedures that on one occasion had led to the return of an American businessman's misplaced air ticket in order to demonstrate what it meant to be a customer-driven company.[40] Similarly, J.W. Marriott Jr of the Marriott hotels group, narrates stories telling how his staff have assisted a range of clients to meet their personal and business goals. The most compelling of these concerns a woman who phoned up to change her reservation for a honeymoon at a Marriott hotel because her future husband had just been diagnosed with terminal brain cancer, and her wedding plans needed to be brought forward. Says J.W. Marriott Jr, his staff not only made the hotel available, but offered her an upgrade, waived all fees, and found an airline that would take her and her husband on a first-class and complimentary basis.[41] Mary Kay Ash likes to tell a simple parable to the effect that engineers have discovered that bees should not be able to fly because their bodies are too heavy for their wings. Not knowing this, however, bees fly very well. In the same way, says Ash, American housewives do not know what they are capable of until they come to Mary Kay, where they find they can pursue a career and achieve financial independence.[42]

As these examples illustrate, the leader as storyteller focuses and amplifies selected beliefs amongst his or her followers. Leaders with a sophisticated understanding of this role tailor stories to communicate quite precise messages. Further, they always remember that, to work well, there must be a snug fit between the message on the one hand, and the context and culture of the organization on the other. Our final example here concerns Fred Smith of FedEx, who has recognized these features of effective stories, and built them into a vignette he uses to illustrate what Rosabeth Moss Kanter has referred to as *kaleidoscope thinking* – looking at complex problems from different angles. Smith tells how Dr Hans Selye, as a young research assistant at the University of Rochester, found his experimental cultures were infested with green mould. His reaction was one of mortification, thinking that a year of his life was now down the drain. A little later a doctor in Britain, called Alexander Fleming, looked at similar-type moulds, saw their life-enhancing properties, and discovered penicillin.[43]

Leader as Show-person

In addition to being a poet, rhetorician and storyteller, a leader must also be a show-person, sensitive to the theatrical potential of his or her position. A good show-person is someone who strains to give a quality performance that harmonizes with audience expectations. Leaders as show-people are expressive and spontaneous, and able to project their individuality through action in creative and imaginative ways. The successful show-person gives performances in which are blended the most appropriate combinations of settings, costumes, messages, rhythms, colour, pitch, emphasis and pace. This is what Jan Carlzon of SAS had in mind when he claimed that leadership: '. . . involves more than a little show-manship. If you want to be an effective leader, you cannot be shy or reticent. Knowing how to appear before large audiences and persuade them to "buy" your message is a crucial attribute of leadership.'[44]

Carlzon's own showmanship had a broad range. He abolished the dining room at corporate HQ, forcing executives to lunch with other employees to signal that 'we were all . . . to work together'. On one occasion, noticing that his airport staff were not permitting passengers to board a plane until he was seated, he deliberately waited behind and boarded last. On other occasions his staff were prone to ask him to select a newspaper or magazine before offering them to other passengers. Carlzon always declined to be first, telling his staff, 'Out of the question . . . I cannot take any myself until I know that all the passengers have gotten what they want.' He recognized that leaders are watched very carefully, and that their behaviours are highly likely to be mimicked by subordinates. More than this, he saw that the behaviours he most valued in others had to be modelled in dramatic, theatrical ways which people would remember and relive in the company of others. As Carlzon himself has said, 'Showmanship demands that you sometimes turn yourself inside out a little to communicate the message. The entertainer who fails to give something of himself will never reach the audience no matter how polished the performance.'[45]

Leaders with a flair for showmanship, like Steve Jobs, Lee Iacocca and John DeLorean, are, as we have already seen, capable of extremely memorable theatrics. But just about every leader plays the role of the show-person at some stage in their career. In 1991, for example, Bill Gates rode into the annual employee meeting at Microsoft on a Harley Davidson motorcycle, leading a 'gang' of bikers – somewhat predictably, more than 7,000 of the faithful 'went wild'.[46] When the Australian entrepreneur Alan Bond's natural ability to divine land that would attract investors deserted him, he had the sand hills painted green to make the brochures look better.[47] The flamboyant Englishman Richard Branson has dressed up as a cossack to launch Virgin Vodka, worn a bridal dress to advertise his wedding business, and paraded in an air hostess uniform to serve passengers on his airline. Still more outrageously, the self-made billionaire recently posed nude in a national UK paper, his modesty preserved only by a copy of the newspaper, bearing the title of his autobiography, *Losing My Virginity*.[48]

While our modern, publicity-oriented, sound-bite fixated world encourages CEOs to engage in ever more eye-catching acts, successful leaders have always used theatre to get their point across. Henry Ford, surprised by his workers with an updated version of the Model T they had built while he was away, responded by kicking in the windshield and stomping on the roof. Said one employee, 'We got the message . . . the Model T was god and we were to put away false images.'[49] When Robert Johnson, president and CEO of Johnson & Johnson, saw his company's damaged goods in a store, he sent his staff out to purchase every damaged product they could find. He then put them all on a large table, called in his marketing director and said, 'Correct this problem.'[50] More extreme still, it is rumoured that Forrest Mars brought packaging problems to the attention of his executives by throwing poorly wrapped Mars Bars across his boardroom. Such events tend to live on in the collective memory of organizations, enriching as well as guiding the working lives of ordinary employees.

An individual with a particular talent for ballyhoo was Richard Warren Sears, co-founder of the mail order company. His startling promotions were something of an extension of his naturally dynamic personality. As one commentator has noted, 'When Richard Warren Sears bestrode the stage, the remainder of the cast had perforce to bask in his reflected glory.' A few examples give a flavour of the man. When a customer complained that his son had broken his leg riding a Sears bicycle, and that his leg had been improperly set by a local doctor, Sears employed the services of a well-known surgeon to reset the bone of the boy's leg at the company's expense. On another occasion, finding an employee searching for a five-dollar bill he had lost in the Sears Roebuck plant, Sears handed the man five dollars from his own pocket, saying that he did not want his friends losing money on his premises. At another time, Sears was riding a streetcar when the conductor dropped and broke his Sears Roebuck watch. Sears had him given a new watch free of charge, claiming, 'We guarantee our watches not to fall out of people's pockets and break.' The goodwill that reports of such acts generated for the Sears Roebuck company underscores the importance of this facet of leadership.[51]

H.J. Heinz, founder of the giant Heinz food corporation, has been described by one biographer as having 'carried his company's products and his own industrial philosophy to four continents with a promotional flair and showmanship that probably have never been surpassed'. His efforts to attract visitors to his stall at a food manufacturers' exhibition in 1893, illustrate his talents as a showman. Exhibiting from a magnificent pavilion of hand-carved antique oak, which was attended by four beautiful girls charged with dispensing a variety of free Heinz products, the venture nevertheless failed to attract many people. Seizing the initiative, Heinz produced and distributed cards promising that anyone who presented one at the Heinz Company exhibit would receive a free souvenir (a plaster pickle). According to one biographer, 'By the thousands the people headed for the Agricultural Building, swept by the foreign food exhibits, and climbed the stairs to the Heinz display.' So big were the crowds he attracted that policemen had to be summoned to regulate their attendance, and the *New York Times* reported that 'the gallery floor of the Agricultural Building has sagged where the pickle display of H.J. Heinz Company stood, owing to the vast crowd which constantly thronged . . .'. Arthur Baum, editor of the *Saturday Evening Post*, referred to the Heinz pickle as 'one of the most famous giveaways in merchandising history' while historians of advertising still speak of it with admiration.[52]

Unsurprisingly, the world of advertising has produced some of the most remarkable show-leaders, and of these Charles and Maurice Saatchi are particularly notable examples. Extravagant expenses, luxurious offices and large salaries were all symptomatic of the brothers' natural flair for self-publicity. Their quirky show-manship skills had many admirers. On one occasion in the company's start-up phase the brothers thought they needed more staff to impress a potential client. Their solution was typically off-the-wall: they asked their staff to invite their friends and relatives into their offices, and then when this still did not yield sufficient bodies, they sent subordinates out on the streets to offer passers-by £5 just to come in and look as if they were working.[53] It was creativity such as this which led to the famous advertising cam-paigns that helped to sustain Margaret Thatcher in power through-out the 1980s, and which assisted in making her privatization programme successful.

The showmanship engaged in by leaders of more moderate disposition may be no less memorable or effective. For instance, Michael Edwardes, the head of the old UK automotive company British Leyland, heralded his decentralization initiative by closing down the vast corporate HQ and closeting himself in rather modest accommodation surrounded only by key staff. Leo Bontempo, president of Ciba-Geigy's US Agricultural Group, sought to demonstrate the importance of trust in his organization by revealing the results of a survey which showed what his sub-ordinates thought of him.[54] Chung Ju Yung, founder of the Korean conglomerate Hyundai, was noted for his tendency to roll up his sleeves and work on assembly lines and, shovel in hand, on building sites: by so doing, he handsomely demonstrated the importance of menial tasks in the fabrication of large, prestige buildings and products.[55] Tom Murrin, the ex-president of Westinghouse's Public Systems Sector, used videotapes of competitors' factories to bring quality and productivity issues to the attention of his senior team, declaring:

> Frankly, gentlemen, my perspective of our competitive strength is tempered with caution and concern after gazing about the boardrooms, offices, laboratories and factories of our competition . . . From Fairfield to Dallas, to Munich, to Tokyo and around much of the rest of the world, what I see is both exciting and alarming. In particular, findings in Japan scare the hell out of me . . .[56]

The perils of giving a poor performance are, perhaps, best illustrated by the now legendary fiasco of the launching of New Coke. On Tuesday, 23 April 1985 Roberto Goizueta, CEO of Coca-Cola, launched a press conference to tell the world about New Coke. All seemed set to go well as he stepped onto the podium of the Vivian Beaumont Theater at Lincoln Center. With the stage awash with red, a video montage interspersed shots of Americana, Coke imagery and a retrospective of Coke commercials, to the beat of a patriotic ballad. But, as the lights came up, instead of storming across the stage with an air of purpose and promise, Goizueta wrung his hands and appeared visibly nervous as he delivered the script. Then, with the script played out, the press corps seized control of the agenda, and a barrage of difficult and sceptical questions ensued. Goizueta's responses did not impress. Worse still, when the reporters tasted the New Coke it is said that 'many visibly grimaced', and some even spat it out. The press and media generally mounted a negative campaign, and complaints to Coke's hot line reached 1,000 a day. In the end, even though New Coke outperformed Old Coke in repeated taste tests, consumers, led by the media, rejected the New Coke concept.[57]

Great acting is something you recognize the moment you see it. Poor showmanship is equally apparent. One of the best 'compare and contrasts' we have to reflect on here is that between US Presidents Reagan and Carter. Reagan had been a professional actor before assuming the mantle of the Presidency, and carried off his public performances with ease and authority. For example, according to an ABC poll, support for the US invasion of Grenada *doubled* immediately after Reagan's explanatory speech. In contrast, Carter, despite being one of the best informed presidents this century, was, for the American people, an implausible showman. Indeed, one of his own cabinet officers remarked that working for him was like looking at the wrong side of a tapestry, where life was blurry and indistinct.[58] History favours Reagan over Carter, the showman over the administrator. A good leader is a skilled social architect who understands the craft of stage management, the need to be an actor and a show-person.

Learning Points for Leaders

In many ways organizations are like theatres and their leaders star actors. Great leaders tend often to recognize the theatrical potential of their position, and to exploit it with consummate skill. To be truly effective in this dimension of leadership means being a poet, rhetorician, storyteller and show-person. To succeed, leaders must give authentic and convincing performances that generate confidence in their followers. As a minimum requirement this means performing sufficiently well to build trust. At their best, leaders are captivating artists whose sheer physical presence inspires others. The most admirable leaders are those who, like Steve Jobs, are capable of giving spectacular theatrical displays that ignite the enthusiasm and creativity of their followers.

Many notable historical and political figures have been adept actors. It was De Gaulle's rhetorically incisive wartime radio broadcasts that transformed him into the personification of *free France*.[59] The basis of Fidel Castro's popularity in Cuba is the unique rapport he is able to strike with the masses, whether on the television screen or in public meetings. Even when she finally resigned on 22 November 1990, Mrs Thatcher still managed to astound parliament and the public with a dazzling and dramatic performance in the House of Commons. Nelson and Napoleon both managed to write themselves into our history books through elaborating their own personal mythology. To act well is, of course, to be exercised in a very demanding way: it is a form of callisthenics of the psyche.[60] And it is much harder for leaders than it is for professional actors, having no pre-set script, no director or stage manager to serve as guides, and with the responsibility for many people's careers on their shoulders.

Yet we must also acknowledge that some otherwise outstanding corporate leaders have failed to come to terms with this dimension of leadership. Konosuke Matsushita, founder of the vast Japanese corporation Matsushita Electrical Industrial, was a notoriously poor public speaker.[61] Pierre du Pont, the man most responsible for the success of the Du Pont Powder Company and General Motors, always too shy to be a good actor, was never comfortable with public speaking and for a long time dreaded public appearances.[62] Alfred Nobel, who initiated the famous series of prizes for outstanding achievements, was never a social success, was noted for his melancholic personality and experienced near-horror at the thought of all kinds of pretence and show.[63] Such leaders have relied on their prowess in other dimensions of leadership: Matsushita was a determined visionary, du Pont had a calculating razor-sharp rational intellect, and Nobel was a virtuoso inventor who greatly improved on existing formulas for dynamite.

Despite such exceptions, it is nevertheless true that most business leaders find it a necessity to hone their skills as actors. They have to communicate sometimes simple, sometimes complex, messages across what are often vast and fragmented organizations. They have to promulgate their ideas with disciplined frequency and consistency, always remembering to reward with positive feedback when their messages are heard and enacted by others. And they would do well to recall Richard Nixon's famous saying: 'About the time you are writing a line you have written so often that you want to throw up, that is the time the American people will hear it.'[64] Furthermore, leaders should note, as an ex-president of the electronics giant Philips reminds us, that 'In a way, each CEO is a new light in the firm's sky who must set the stage for the next decades.'[65] The play does not come to an end when the CEO departs, and succession planning to find the next corporate star must always be a high priority concern.

It is the example of those who have not coped well with this dimension of leadership who throw its importance into the sharpest relief. John M. Stafford, who ran Pillsbury for three years in the 1980s, always struck people as weak and dithering. His emphasis on numbers rather than people and his inflexible approach to business issues led to his being ridiculed as 'the wooden soldier'.[66] Stafford, and numerous others like him, could have learned much from the example of Michael Dell, founder and head of the Dell Computer Corporation. As a young man Dell was a poor public speaker and uncertain actor – but he was willing to learn. Under the tutelage of Lee Walker, who was president and Chief Operations Officer of Dell between 1986 and 1990, Dell developed his abilities to cope with this dimension of leadership. Says one of Dell's subordinates, he is now 'a very charismatic leader, a great speaker. He can go into any department and know what hot button to push' to motivate his staff.[67]

Just being a proficient actor is, of course, not in itself sufficient to make an individual a good leader. It takes more than sparkling communication skills and showmanship to build and evolve successful organizations or lead a nation. To be fully captured by the narrow set of roles associated with the leader as actor constitutes a pathological condition. Such people will always seem to lack substance. In my terminology they are uni-dimensional. To be a wise, mature and consistently successful leader means being able to play the multiple roles associated with many (and ideally all) the dimensions of leadership.

What is more, prowess in this dimension does not come easily and naturally to everyone. If your artistry is suspect then, like John Sculley and Michael Dell, you can proactively take steps to improve your performances. Close observation of professional actors, combined with the specialist advice of speech coaches and constant practice, can have impressive results. Even without professional assistance you can do a lot to refine your acting skills by identifying high-performing role models and modifying your behaviour in line with theirs. Some specific questions to bear in mind when evaluating your competence in this dimension of leadership are:

- *As a Poet.* Do you employ instantly comprehensible and appealing images? Are you able to frame and define what is important about your organization in ways which motivate and inspire? Do you have the ability to reduce uncertainty and confusion in the minds of your followers?
- *As a Rhetorician.* Are you able to evoke a positive emotional as well as an intellectual response from others when you speak? Do you use language in ways which energize and motivate your staff? Are you sensitive to the appropriate use of linguistic techniques such as metaphor, repetition, and rhythm?
- *As a Storyteller.* Have you developed a repertoire of easily-remembered stories that embody your beliefs? Are you able to tell these stories so convincingly that they influence the behaviours of your subordinates? Do your followers narrate stories about you that reflect well on you and your organization?
- *As a Show-person.* Are you sufficiently at ease with yourself and others to give consistently good leadership performances? Are you able to project your individuality in creative and imaginative ways that others find admirable? Are you an effective social architect able to draw others into giving their best possible performances?

George Merck

H. J. Heinz

Anita Roddick

Percy Barnevik

Four

LEADER AS IMMORTALIST

An institution is the lengthened shadow of one man. (Ralph Waldo Emerson)[1]

THE IMMORTALIST IS a visionary, whose high self-esteem and desire to succeed stands as a beacon to their followers. When Don Kendall became chief executive of Pepsi Cola in 1963 it was no more than a modestly profitable soft-drink company with $300 million in revenues. Twenty-three years later, in 1986, Kendall retired as chairman from a hugely profitable $9 billion corporation with powerful interests in beverages, snacks and fast foods. He accomplished all this by stamping his authority on to PepsiCo such that it became imbued with his personality, and his vision. Don Kendall was a constructive immortalist.[2] He was motivated by the same kind of self-confidence that led Dwight Eisenhower to the conclusion that only *he* could lead America out of danger, and which spurred him to take the plunge into the waters of presidential politics.[3] Similarly, it was immortalistic bravura which led Bob Cizik, CEO of the $4.5 billion US corporation Cooper Industries, to assert: 'We're going to be a manufacturing company, one of the best damn manufacturing companies in the world. We're going to get on the pulpit and say manufacturing is not dead in the United States, and we're going to beat the Japanese at this, and the Germans and anyone else.'[4]

The idea that leaders seek to imprint their personality on their organizations is well attested. Leadership commentators Warren Bennis and Burt Nanus have referred to these processes as the *creative deployment of self.*[5] For example, one biographer of Jack Welch has argued that 'More than any other large corporation in

America, General Electric has assumed the personality of its general.'[6] Intel, it has been said, 'is the personal creation of its chief executive, Andy Grove.'[7] The success of the Japanese consumer electronics company, Sony, owes much to the character and perseverance of its founders, Masaru Ibuka and Akio Morita. And the French couturier, Pierre Cardin, so conflates his own persona with that of his organization that he once claimed that his 'is the biggest name in the world . . . It's the most important name in the world. It is number one.'[8] The powerful tendency for people to link personal and corporate triumphs is not restricted to leaders themselves. For instance, at the pinnacle of Harold S. Geneen's achievements at ITT, the business community began to refer to the company as the 'Geneen Machine'.[9]

Others have described the same phenomenon a little differently, stating that 'leaders want to do something significant, to accomplish something that no one else has yet achieved'.[10] The accomplishment is, though, most often a personal one. There are many corporate leaders who would like to be described and remembered in the terms that were once employed for the Turkish Cypriot entrepreneur Asil Nadir and his Polly Peck empire: 'Polly Peck is Asil Nadir and Asil Nadir is Polly Peck, and often the twain shall meet.'[11] Bill Hewlett's comments on the death of his business partner David Packard underscore the importance of embroidering a leader's personality into the fabric of an organization. He said:

> As far as the company is concerned, the greatest thing he left behind him was a code of ethics known as the HP Way . . . [which] . . . includes a deep respect for the individual, a dedication to affordable quality and reliability, a commitment to community responsibility . . . and a view that the company exists to make technical contributions for the advancement and welfare of humanity.'[12]

One aspect of the immortalistic role leaders play is the creation, embodiment and realization of a vision. This vision is intimately tied to a leader's self-concept. *Envisioning* means creating in one's mind an image of a desired future state that can serve as a guide to interim strategies, decisions and behaviour. Such a vision is not merely 'whimsical' but powerfully invested with the executive's own ego. Unsurprisingly, leaders' visions are generally carefully devised to straddle the fine line between over-caution and wild optimism, insipidity and extravagance. The point is that leaders formulate 'vision' statements which have a good chance of success. They need to, because quite often failure of the vision would represent a personal failure for the executive; success, in contrast, produces an organization that is very nearly a hologram of the executive mind.[13]

In a sense, then, organizations are leaders' personal visions transformed into social and economic facts. And, just as vision shapes leadership, so the dreams and aspirations of leaders inform vision. In short, leaders and their organizations are not so much distinct entities but complementary facets of the same persona. As the famous philosopher Karl Popper is reputed to have said, vision is to leadership what conjecture is to science.[14] Leaders' visions tend to have several elements. These include a statement of why the organization exists, that is, its *raison d'être*; an aspiration regarding what the leader wants the organization to become, a view of how the visionary end-state is to be achieved; and motivational appeal. Putting this vision into effect is an immortalistic enterprise. It has to be. Without the single-minded determination that immortalistic projects require, visions will always fail. Fred Smith, the founder and chairman of the $11 billion company Federal Express Inc., did not just envision a future for fast package delivery companies, he worked doggedly to make it a reality. The result: Federal Express employs 120,000 people in 200 nations transporting 2 million packages a day in a $20 billion plus industry.[15]

Of course, not all visions are realistic, credible or attractive. Not all visions are able to mobilize the emotional and spiritual resources of people to generate a formula for success. But neither are examples of this felicitous consonance of factors hard to discern. John F. Kennedy's vision of landing a man on the moon sparked an immortalistic enterprise that energized the greater part of the United States. Bill Gates' vision of 'a computer on every desk and in every home' has become Microsoft's guiding corporate goal.[16] Sir John Egan, head of the British Airports Authority (BAA), likes to reiterate that 'our mission is quite simply to make BAA the most successful airport company in the world'.[17] At their most evocative, expressions of leaders' visions are almost things of beauty. Consider, for example, Henry Ford's delightful articulation of his prescient goal of democratizing the automobile:

> I will build a motor car for the great multitude . . . It will be so low in price that no man making a good salary will be unable to own one and enjoy with his family the blessing of hours of pleasure in God's great open spaces . . . When I'm through, everybody will be able to afford one, and everyone will have one. The horse will have disappeared from our highways, the automobile will be taken for granted . . . [and we will] give a large number of men employment at good wages.[18]

A word of warning. In recent times there has been something of a revolt against the idea that leaders should promulgate statements of visionary intent. As one commentator on corporate leadership has asserted, 'Vision has become a fad, and there are times when visions are only for prophets, not for business leaders.'[19] Leaders themselves have expressed similar views. Lou Gerstner, who took charge at IBM in March 1993, was widely expected to cast a new vision for the ailing computer company. Gerstner's response, which was widely reported, was this: 'There has been a lot of speculation that I'm going to deliver a "vision" of the future of IBM. The last thing IBM needs right now is a vision. What IBM needs right now is a series of very tough-minded, market-driven and highly effective strategies that deliver performance in the market place and shareholder value.'[20] Champions of the need for vision were confounded.

This is a salutary reminder that, like other popular management ideas, the need for leaders to be visionaries cannot be accepted unquestioningly and unthinkingly. Gerstner obviously felt that, at the time, it was more important to set the context for what IBM was going to do in the immediate rather than the long-term future. Given the operational as well as the strategic uncertainties that had then engulfed IBM, he was surely right to do so. Effective leaders, then, are those who can stand back from their immortalistic roles, rather than be engulfed by them. It is also worth remembering that the role of the leader as immortalist, as we shall see, includes far more than just the creation of a personal vision: it means evolving an organization that thinks, dresses and acts according to the precepts of that vision.

Here we consider two broad sub-dimensions of immortalism: *constructive* and *destructive*. Constructively immortalistic leaders have a generally positive influence on their organizations. They play two basic roles, that of

- *rebels*, who build by revolution, and
- *virtuosos*, who make use of some special talent.

Both rebels and virtuosos tend to imprint their personality on their organizations in a detached, reality-adapted manner. Of course, some leaders are fully captured by their immortalistic roles yet may nevertheless exercise an ultimately net helpful influence on their organizations. Such people, although they are still classed here as constructive immortalists, are prone to being reclassified if, for some reason, their visions fail. The borderline between these different role classifications is, thus, in some instances a fragile and a transient one. Make no mistake, destructive immortalists have an overwhelmingly unhealthy impact on the organizations they lead. Two generic role types associated with destructive immortalism are:

- *dramatics*, who are noted for their flamboyance, and
- *conceiteds*, who are blindly driven by pride.

Such leaders face, indeed often create, chronic problems for which they are unable to devise and administer appropriate remedial treatment.

Constructive Immortalists

David Ogilvy was an unconventional Scotsman who, in 1948, founded a US advertising firm which grew, as Ogilvy and Mather, to be among the largest in the world. From the very beginning Ogilvy conflated his own personality with that of his firm and its advertising campaigns. While his company was eventually taken over by the WPP group in 1989 for £864 million, Ogilvy's enduring legacy is twofold. First, he will be remembered as the man who pioneered the fact-based approach to advertising, encompassing serious market research, pretesting and analysis. Some of his marketing principles exemplify this perspective: five times as many people read the headline as read the body copy; speak to readers' self-interest; focus on advice or service; and start adverts with a large initial letter. Second, he will be noted for his immortalism. His book, *Confessions of an Advertising Man*, sold 800,000 copies and made him a celebrity. In fact, it was a self-congratulatory advertisement for himself, notable for the claim that he devised a campaign that altered the image and fortunes of Puerto Rico, and self-aggrandizing comments like 'I doubt whether any copywriter has ever produced so many winners in such a short period.' Ogilvy's place in history as a defining character of the constructive immortalist genre (he won more than he lost!) is assured.[21]

Constructive immortalists always possess a positive self-regard and a secure sense of self, and tend to have the capacity for introspection, radiate a sense of positive vitality, and be empathetic. Such leaders project visions which are sensitive to what is sacred in organizations and what is not, and are able to manage tactfully processes of continuity and change. There is no hint of contradiction, neurosis or schizophrenic uncertainty about these people, but rather a congruence of personality, philosophy and style. Men like the spectacularly successful J. Paul Getty personify this particular dimension of leadership. From Getty's first major success, the purchase of the Nancy Taylor Allotment Lease in Oklahoma in 1915, he determinedly bought up other high profit-yielding oil field leases, and companies, to become one of the wealthiest men in the world.

Roberto Goizueta, sixteen years the CEO of Coca-Cola, also has impeccable immortalist credentials. Goizueta grew Coca-Cola from a $4 billion company into an $18 billion corporate giant, broadening and deepening Coke's presence in almost every country on the planet. The enormity of his achievement should not be underestimated. Before he took over, Coca-Cola had been systematically borrowing money at 16% and investing it at 8%. All the businesses except soft drinks were generating less than 10% profit a year, and between the businesses there was no effective coordination, no central planning, and no strategic thinking. Goizueta focused on the financials, injected a sense of mission, galvanized his senior executives into action, purchased profitable businesses and disposed of those, like shrimp farming and wine production, which could not be made to pay. He forced out or reassigned to dead-end jobs those he considered under-performers, launched the highly successful Diet Coke, and had the presence of mind to recognize that New Coke was a disaster and withdrew it from sale. Hardly surprising, then, that Coca-Cola's stock market value, the measure that meant most to Goizueta himself, jumped from $4.3 billion in 1981 to $180 billion, a staggering 3,500% increase.[22]

The role of the immortalist is not one that all leaders find easy to adopt. A striking example of the difficulties that some individuals find in playing this part is provided by George Bush during the presidential election campaign of 1992. Even though he was the incumbent, and running for a second term in office, his attempt to portray himself as 'the managerial president' was deemed unconvincing by the media. Four years earlier he had been widely mocked by the press for his references to 'the vision thing'. His campaign speeches now featured what he hoped was a more cogent and coherent account of his vision for America. The truth was, however, that Bush always seemed to lack the stature and gravitas of a great immortalist, and rumours that his aides were nervous whenever he was asked about his plans for a second term, underlined this. In retrospect it is clear that the vagueness of his vision, indeed his blind assumption that he did not have to frame the future in very concrete terms, dealt his re-election campaign a severe blow.[23] Bush could have learned valuable lessons from the rebels and the virtuosos.

Leaders as Rebels
Rebels do not simply take risks or merely strike it rich. Rather, they

transform economic activity and build for the future. Some leaders are naturally predisposed to be rebels by their family background, and spend their entire working lives playing out this single role. Such people may never fully realize why they have cast themselves as rebels or what they are rebelling against. A fascinating example here is that of Tiny Rowland, who developed Lonrho into an international conglomerate. Born Roland Fuhrop in a British internment camp for undesirable aliens in India, according to one biographer, 'Rebellion and revenge percolated the character of Roland Fuhrop from the day of his birth.' A brilliant tactical businessman, he desperately craved admiration, money and power. Yet Britain, his adopted country, penalized rather than praised his initiative and wealth creation, further sustaining his natural rebellious tendencies. Says one commentator, 'His is a life of a simultaneous battle within himself and against his adopted country . . . The source of his revolt, its successes and failure, is a reflection upon Britain over the past fifty years.'[24]

Rebel immortalists revolt against traditional ideas of what constitute reasonable principles of organizing, what strategies will succeed, and what is technologically possible – or desirable. For example, if everyone else is talking about the vision thing, then a rebel like Lou Gerstner will say, though possibly disingenuously, that he has not got one for IBM – and that the corporation does not need one. The rebel immortalist Sam Walton founded Wal-Mart because he saw what no one else could: that there was a huge customer base in small towns across America that was being ignored. Herb Kelleher, and his colleagues, created Southwest Airlines based on a then non-standard understanding of what large sections of the American public wanted from a short-haul operator (low fares and no frills). The vision of a rebellious immortalist has the primordial quality of a dream, an imagined possibility that generates excitement and vitality. Theirs is a mind-set of resistance, of a refusal to ally themselves with prevailing norms, and a strident recognition of no authority concerning what is right or appropriate other than their own.

An excellent role model for aspiring rebel immortalists is Philip Smith, the man who founded the company that eventually became

Harcourt General. One of the most far-sighted of those involved in the early movie business, in the 1930s he established a profitable niche with his drive-in theatres. Recognizing the economic significance of large regional shopping centres, in the 1950s and 1960s he developed a national circuit of shopping centre theatres. This strategy gave his company a first-mover advantage so great that within little more than a decade it was the largest national theatre circuit in the USA. From the perspective of history it is clear that Smith has managed to accomplish what so many entrepreneurs fail to do: he established an enterprise that survived him. From its beginnings in 1922, the business that Philip Smith launched has evolved, over more than seventy years, into a major diversified firm, Harcourt General Inc., generating over $3.7 billion in revenues and employing more than 34,000 people.[25]

A good example of a European cast as a rebellious immortalist by virtue of his early personal experiences, is the fashion designer Pierre Cardin. The son of Italian immigrants, Cardin spent his formative years in France. The fact that his family had lost many of their possessions during the war and that he was teased with disparaging names by other children (he was after all an Italian living in France), seems to have affected him deeply. This has led the perceptive management theorist Manfried Kets de Vries[26] to speculate that Cardin matured with 'a feeling of bitterness, a sense of having to get back at his tormentors by showing that he could amount to something, a drive to become the redeemer of the family'. His business success has in fact been remarkable, with sales under his name now amounting to over a billion dollars through 840 licensing agreements in 125 countries. More than this, he has democratized fashion, bringing haute couture to ordinary men and women, something previously unheard of. This said, it seems that Pierre Cardin is not so much playing a role as captured by it, and his continuing need to boast about his achievements is arguably symptomatic of a fragile psychic equilibrium.

Ted Turner, the founder of CNN, is another character immediately recognizable as a rebel immortalist. Turner is a man of incredible vision who could see the future of satellite broadcasting and the many attractions of a twenty-four-hour-a-day news service.

Not just a shrewd businessman, he is also a superb sailor, winning the America Cup in 1977 and the Fastnet race in 1979. He has been described as a man of renegade personality and unbridled ambition who craves both admiration and public respectability. The renaming of his company 'Turner Broadcasting System', and his policy of buying back shares from investors so that he holds 87% of the stock, are testament to both needs. The projection of his personality on to his organization does not, however, stop here. One of his favourite sayings is 'Lead, follow, or get out of my way.' And just before CNN went on air for the first time Turner is reported as having said: 'We're gonna stay on until the end of the world . . . And when that day comes, we'll cover it, play "Nearer My God to Thee", and sign off.' A man of immodest temperament, he drew the names of two of his sons from the 1936 film *Gone With The Wind*, which he purchased together with MGM. One commentator has even argued that 'he saw some of himself in the Clark Gable figure. The square jaw and trim moustache. The rugged individualist. The fighter against all the odds.'[27]

John Sculley, a senior executive at first Pepsi and later Apple, has written a highly entertaining autobiography in which he explicitly casts himself as a rebel immortalist, claiming at one point that 'I was a maverick in a highly standardized world.' He relates how, at Pepsi, winning became an obsession, how he was driven by both competition and the force of powerful ideas, how he always demanded and gave his best, and how while dozens of others had failed before him, he found 'Pepsi was a comfortable home.' There is little evidence of modesty in his account of how, as president of Pepsi-Cola, he was plagued by calls from headhunters of all kinds: 'I had won an enviable and visible place for myself in the corporate world. I was on the cover of *Business Week* magazine in May 1973, at the age of thirty-four. I was frequently quoted in the business columns of newspapers and magazines. And I was having fun running what then was Pepsi-Cola's largest single business.' About his experiences at Apple Sculley is, if anything, still more self-laudatory, asserting that 'At Apple, we are dreamers. We are driven by a passion to change the world, to make it a better, more pro-ductive place for every individual.'[28] The enviable successes of both

Pepsi and Apple during his tenure there perhaps provides some insight into what a rebel immortalist can achieve under favourable conditions.

It is in the world of politics that the role of the rebel immortalist is most often and most interestingly played. Margaret Thatcher's election campaign of 1979 and subsequent years in power were a rebellion against the traditional consensus politics that had dominated Britain since the end of the Second World War. During her period in office conviction dominated over consensus; she stated her goals and mission explicitly; she spoke of 'new beginnings', 'mandates', and 'sea changes'. She was surely aided in this radical transformation of the country by her own immortalistic self-confidence. Like the US President, Eisenhower, in her autobiography she claims to have been motivated by the belief that *only she could save the country*! Highly successful for more than a decade, Thatcher was eventually toppled not by the electorate but by senior members of her own party. These people believed that the mood of the country had altered and that Thatcher's strident rebelliousness was no longer in tune with the voters. A clear example to those naturally inclined to be rebel immortalists that they must learn to discern when it is time to play a new and different role, or succumb.

Less well known outside his own country, but achieving an impact if anything still greater than Thatcher's, is Mustafa Kemal Ataturk, the founder of modern Turkey. Ataturk's immortalistic credentials are in no doubt. Deprived at an early age of his father, and subject to the emotional pressure of his mother, he developed a grandiose sense of himself that led him to try and force the world to conform to his own expectations. The results of this rebellious drive are by any standards remarkable. Between 1919 and 1923 he forged a Turkish national movement that challenged the authority of the Sultan, imposed his will throughout Anatolia thus confronting the western Entente powers of Great Britain, France and Italy, expelled a Greek expeditionary force, and finally concluded at Lausanne a treaty of peace with the Entente powers and their allies, securing the independence and integrity of a newly created Turkish state. Furthermore, once in supreme power, he instituted a series of major reforms which transformed the traditional Islamic structure of Ottoman society, and laid the foundations of a modern, westernized, secular nation-state.[29,30] Such can be the power of those who, in appropriate contexts, play the rebel immortalist with total conviction.

The rebel immortalists constitute a broad category of leaders. There are many different playings of the role. There are leaders who are rebel immortalists by virtue of their family upbringing and who are fully captured by this single role – Tiny Rowland, Pierre Cardin and Mustafa Kemal Ataturk, for instance. Then there are those who, like Lou Gerstner, Sam Walton and Herb Kelleher, play this role among others. There are those whose impact has been confined to one area of commerce such as Cardin. And there are people who have revolutionized a whole country like Thatcher (to an extent) and Ataturk (absolutely). At their most effective rebel immortalists are admirable leaders, and the role is surely one that all aspiring leaders would benefit from learning to play.

Leaders as Virtuosos

With the Second World War over, and Japan a devastated and occupied country, Masaru Ibuka and Akio Morita founded Tokyo Tsuchin Kogyo. While the company initially achieved success manufacturing transistor radios, it is the story of its founders' efforts to produce tape recorders which is in many ways the more instructive. The decision to attempt to manufacture tape recorders was, on the face of it, a remarkable one. Ibuka and Morita knew virtually nothing about tape recorders, having seen only one. Furthermore, while the mechanical and electronic components seemed fairly straightforward, the magnetic tape was a complete mystery. Speaking decades later, one of their colleagues remembered that at the time, 'No one in Japan had any experience with magnetic recording tape, and there were no imports available to us . . .' The task seemed hopeless.

With only inappropriate materials to hand, their attempts to use cellophane and kraft paper coated in various chemical mixes all failed. No real breakthrough was made until high quality plastic became available, but by that time the company, now known as

Sony, had built up enough expertise to be a world leader. A sure sign of success came in November 1965 when IBM chose their magnetic recording tape for data storage. Continuous technological development and shrewd marketing then ensued. Only Ibuka and Morita's vision, persistence and determination in the face of what seemed impossible odds made Sony a success. Indeed, Sony is now known the world over as the company that built the world's first video cassette recorder for home use, invented the trinitron system for projecting a colour image on to the TV tube in 1968, pioneered the world's first CD player in 1982, innovated 8 millimetre video in 1988, and brought out the PlayStation in 1995. Masaru Ibuka and Akio Morita provide us with our first glimpse into the psyche of the virtuoso immortalist.[31]

Virtuoso leaders possess some special gift – such as being an effective negotiator, a convincing salesperson, or a silver-tongued orator – that sets them apart from their contemporaries. Such leaders are often hugely egocentric, believing that they have the *magic formula* or *secret recipe* for success. When describing their accomplishments they like to attribute positive outcomes to their own efforts, and they will often conveniently forget any bad times they have occasioned or poor decisions they may have made. Their capacity for self-aggrandizement is matched only by one other attribute: their glaring and unequivocal success in their chosen field. Like virtuoso musicians, their performances are spellbinding for audiences who, entranced by their charisma and seduced by their record of accomplishment, fail to recall that virtuosos (like rebels) can become destructive if they are unable to adapt to changing circumstances.

Some leaders slip into and out of the role of the virtuoso immortalist with supreme ease. The ability to express the essence of what an organization is about, and where it is going, is one of the defining characteristics of the virtuoso immortalist. Eward Goeppner of the Podestaf Baldocchi chain of flower shops once commented: 'We don't sell flowers, we sell beauty.'[32] Jack Welch, CEO of General Electric, once outlined the future of GE like this: 'A decade from now I would like General Electric to be perceived as a unique, high-spirited, entrepreneurial enterprise . . . a company known around the world for its unmatched level of excellence. I want General Electric to be the most profitable highly diversified company on earth, with world-quality leadership in every one of its product lines.'[33] Who would contest that this vision for GE has all but been achieved?

Such leaders live continuously their virtuoso performances. Bill Gates' relentless drive to dominate the personal computer software industry by setting the industry's standards is a fine example. An older virtuoso immortalist who lived and loved his performance was William Paley of the American television company CBS. When Paley took over the company in 1928, at the age of twenty-seven, it had no stations of its own, was losing money, and was insignificant in an industry completely dominated by NBC. But Paley could see the future, he envisioned an audience at a time when no one else could. Within ten years, CBS had 114 stations and was earning $27.7 million. More than forty years later, with Paley still at the helm, CBS was a dominant force in the broadcasting industry.[34] The virtuoso immortalist is an achiever, someone who creates and perpetuates successful organizations.

An Englishman who has managed to play the role of the virtuoso immortalist with aplomb is Richard Branson. Having founded his company, Virgin, in the music business, Branson's immortalistic virtuosity naturally inclined him to consider other ventures, latterly deciding to start his own airline. Branson's closest advisers were horrified by the idea and tried desperately to talk him out of it. One even told Branson he thought he was a megalo-maniac. Branson, however, not only owned 85% of the company, but was adamant that it was his vision for Virgin that would prevail, and swept all such objections aside. One commentator saw what resulted like this:

> The airline business gave Richard Branson a challenge which, in recent years, the record industry had been unable to provide. And he attacked it with a relish and enthusiasm which surprised even himself . . . Between March and June 1984, he worked harder than he had ever worked in his life. He negotiated the purchase of a plane, and the acquisition of a licence, he flirted

with domestic politics, and international diplomacy. And he thoroughly enjoyed every minute of it . . .

It was from this moment that he put privacy on one side and consciously set out to become 'his company's most visible and effective public relations asset . . . The exhibitionist streak that had been confined to fancy-dress parties . . . now found full public licence . . .'[35]

A particularly beguiling example of a female virtuoso immortalist is Francine Gomez of the French pen company Waterman. Waterman was owned and run by three generations of an aristocratic French family, with Francine Gomez (the third generation), taking charge in 1969. Francine transformed the organization from the struggling business run by her mother into a prestigious company with a 65% share of the French market for non-disposable pens. Outspoken and vivacious, she courted journalists and media interest in herself. Prone to shoot from the hip, she was noted for her very public personal and business rows. Her fondness for herself, for power and success, for activity and excitement, were all indicative of her delight in playing the virtuoso immortalist. She successfully put her own personal touch to the role, however, using her femininity to manipulate others for personal gain. People, it seemed, liked to be with her and enjoyed pleasing her. She had a charming if unsophisticated energy that persuaded others to talk openly and frankly. At the same time she was sufficiently resilient not to be lonely at the helm, and had the strength of personality to dismiss under-performing staff. And while, on the debit side, she excited confrontation and encouraged sycophancy, she represented an unequivocal net asset for Waterman. That is, until changes in French inheritance tax law threatened her majority control, and she sold out to Gillette, finally resigning as president in 1988.[36]

Sir William Siemens was in many ways the archetypal virtuoso businessman who, in partnership with his brothers Werner and Carl, founded the hugely successful German company which bears their family name. Born and educated in Germany, William arrived in London in 1843 where he soon struck his first business deal by selling a patent for a unique electroplating process. His real virtuoso talent, however, was being able to identify practical applications for the many scientific discoveries of the late nineteenth century. Among other things, he pioneered innovative and profitable means of manufacturing steel, generating power, and lighting houses and streets. His seemingly uncanny ability to spot uses and develop products that would find a ready market led *The Times*, in its obituary to Sir William, to note 'how much he individually did to reduce to human servitude the forces of that mysterious power [electricity] of which he was so great a master'.[37]

A more extreme player of the virtuoso immortalist role was Richard Daley, the legendary Democrat mayor of Chicago. Daley stamped his personality on to Chicago in a way few other political leaders have managed. It was his council that controlled the city, and for years it did not defy him on any issue. On entering the chamber he used to look down at the elected officials, bestowing a nod or a benign smile on a few favourites, who would smile back gratefully. This was a man who did not like surprises and did not tolerate complaints. Every word of criticism had to be answered, every complaint disproved, every insult returned in kind. A biographer's comments looking to Daley's eventual retirement give a flavour of the man: 'He'll settle for something simple, like maybe another jet airport built on a man-made island in the lake, and named after him, and maybe a statue outside the Civic Center, with a simple inscription, "The greatest mayor in the history of the world". And they might seal his office as a shrine.'[38]

Our final example of this section indicates the sometimes fine dividing line between the constructive and destructive immortalists. Jan Carlzon was a Swede who aspired to the role of virtuoso immortalist with some short-term success. Carlzon was appointed managing director of the airline SAS in 1981 after the company had lost money for two consecutive years. Using his excellent communication skills and flair for handling the media, Carlzon soon established a reputation as a shrewd operator. Carlzon himself was in no doubt about his abilities, and just in case some people had not noticed, wrote a book, called *Moments of Truth*, which was an explicit effort to 'lecture Americans on how to run their companies'. For others to achieve what he had done, he had this advice:

> It is up to the top executive to become a true leader, devoted to creating an environment in which employees can accept and execute their responsibilities with confidence and finesse. He must communicate with his employees, imparting the company's vision and listening to what they need to make that vision a reality. To succeed he can no longer be an isolated and autocratic decision-maker. Instead, he must be a visionary, a strategist, an informer, a teacher, and an inspirer.[39]

Unlike Ibuka, Morita, the Siemens brothers and Paley, whose success was pretty much unequivocal, and Branson, who continues to impress, Carlzon's ability to play the virtuoso immortalist has been questioned. He at first achieved great things at SAS, turning losses of 7.5 million Danish Kroner into a 1982/3 operating surplus of 620 million Danish Kroner. SAS, it seemed, had been revolutionized from being a technically oriented company to a service-oriented airline ('the businessman's airline'), which in 1982 was recognized as being the most punctual airline by the European Flight Association. In the early 1990s, however, financial difficulties resulted from a depression in the airline business following the Gulf War, preparations for the European internal market, and some poor strategic decisions. The most costly of these failed strategies involved the purchase of a 40% stake in International Hotels, and a share in the American company Continental Airlines. In 1991 SAS cut 3,500 jobs in a bid to reduce operating expenses, a move for which many employees held Carlzon personally responsible. The level of disillusionment with Carlzon was aptly expressed by John Vangen, spokesman for a Danish trade union for cabin crew: 'None of Carlzon's strategies have succeeded since 1984. He has to take responsibility for that. If he cannot make the company run he should leave it. We need a management we can trust.'[40] Such efforts to demonize Carlzon symptomize the fine line between being hailed as a constructive virtuoso immortalist and castigated as a narcissistic agent of destruction.

To summarize, like rebels, virtuosos are not all the same. The role of the virtuoso can be played in multiple ways at various times and in different contexts. Indeed, the injection of one's personality and individuality into the performance is a *sine qua non* for success. While some leaders can convincingly adopt and shed this role at will, the most engaging characters are those who know no other way of working: Morita, Ibuka, the Siemens brothers, Branson, Gomez and Daley are electrifying examples of people who have made a difference. Such virtuosos are uncompromisingly attractive figures, and the world would surely be a less interesting place without them. These are the leaders who breathe life into organizations through their sheer force of personality, and without whom the working lives of many others would be so much more ordinary. When commentators call for more leaders, the sort of people they are thinking of are the virtuoso immortalists.

Destructive Immortalists

Dr Edwin Land invented the polaroid instant camera and founded the Polaroid organization. His company achieved great commercial success, dominating the instant photography market in the 1960s and 1970s. Not content with his achievements, however, Land dreamed of creating a higher quality product, the SX-70, which would be totally automatic, fold to fit into a purse or pocket, possess a single-lens-reflex-viewing system, and focus from less than a foot to infinity. To realize the SX-70 would involve a major strategic shift for the company: instead of subcontracting many activities to outsiders the new product called for integration. Land was not deterred. The total effort cost at least half a billion dollars, but resulted in a design masterpiece. Priced at $180 per camera the company's sales projections were measured in millions for the first year. But by the end of 1973 only 470,000 SX-70s had been sold. Years later, after many design changes and price cuts, widespread market acceptance was gained for the product, but it meant losing many of the camera's original design features.

The problem was that the instant camera market was extremely price-sensitive. As a matter of fact it was well known that consumers wanted inexpensive, easy-to-use, instant cameras yielding good rather than perfect results. Land himself knew this, but ignored it. How do we explain such self-deceit? What happened to Land that made him fail to learn from his and his company's past? Many explanations are possible. For one thing his initial vision of instant photography had been correct; people really did want instant photographs. This initial success seems to have convinced him of the invincibility of his ideas. Second, Land was above all things an engineer; he loved the technology more than the marketing of the product. In short, his very background made him product- and technology-driven, not so much marketplace driven. Finally and most important, Land, like other leaders we will consider in this chapter, came to identify with his vision to an unhealthy extent. He eventually became unable to distinguish between himself and his vision for Polaroid, and this is, perhaps, the ultimate narcissistic conceit.[41] Land's unquestioning self-belief and self-aggrandizing tendencies undermined his vision.

One typical tendency of leaders captured by this role is the compulsion to build monuments as symbols of their achievements. This phenomenon, called an 'edifice complex', can be built into the culture of an organization. Even otherwise admirable leaders and their organizations are prone to excess. Consider, for instance, John Sculley's description of the PepsiCo boardroom, with its abstract paintings, custom-designed carpeting, bronze-plated ceiling and 'high-backed beige leather chairs, so imposing they could have carried corporate titles of their own'.[42] There is no hint of understatement here, and in it we perhaps gain a glimpse into the unhealthy world of the narcissist, and the sorts of organizations they evolve. Walt Disney took great pride in his luxury air-conditioned Burbank studio which opened in 1939, and which he considered 'a reflection of his success'.[43] Even the normally level-headed Henry Heinz, founder of the giant Heinz food corporation, became, in later life, consumed with the design and construction of a grand administration building to hold the company's home offices. Says one biographer: 'It was to have stained-glass windows with designs and quotations. The reception room would have walls of hauteville marble, a fish pool and fountain directly under a central light dome five stories up, four balconies, and twelve mural panels showing Heinz operations around the world . . .'[44]

Closely related to the edifice complex is the tendency of many leaders to engage in profligate conspicuous consumption in order to demonstrate their wealth and power, and so bolster their self-image. Wayne Huizenga, of Waste Management and Blockbuster Video, has a penchant for collecting vintage cars and fast airplanes, symptoms of a less than modest lifestyle. The Australian entrepreneur, Alan Bond, did nothing to forestall the collapse of his empire by amassing $50 million worth of 'toys', including a Falcon 900 corporate jet, a four-masted schooner, expensive artwork, an island, and various properties such as a sixteenth-century estate called Glympton Park near London.

There are two primary types of destructive immortalist roles, the *dramatic* and the *conceited*. Those who play them are often troubled by a sense of deprivation, anger and emptiness. They may also become fixated on issues of power, beauty, status and prestige. Destructive immortalists have an unhealthily grandiose sense of their own importance, exaggerate their talents and achievements beyond what is reasonable, and require excessive admiration from their subordinates. Such leaders have an unrealistic view of their own entitlement to success, may be inclined to exploit people, and lack the ability to empathize with others. These arrogant and manipulative individuals are impulsive and thoughtless in their actions, and the consequences they visit on their organizations are always negative.

Leaders as Dramatics

Leaders who play out their working lives as dramatic immortalists revel in constant sycophantic attention from their subordinates. Such people are highly impulsive and can be dangerously uninhibited in their ventures. The tendency of these leaders is to hoard not share power, and their organizations are over-centralized as a result. Isolated at the top, some dramatic immortalists can become suspicious that a menacing force is out to get them. In these cases leaders are distrustful of everyone and everything, and in extreme cases can create a sort of organizational police state. Ed Artzt, ex-CEO of Procter & Gamble, is a classic example here.[45] What is more, they force their personality on to their subordinates in a way that leads them to either leave or regress to infantile, dependent behaviour patterns. This category of macho leader nurtures their image at the expense of all else, practises debilitating strategies and uses slogans to stymie objective argument. They

> . . . must always be on the alert with sword ready. Like Jesse James, they never sit with their backs to the window; like gunslingers, they always manoeuvre so that the sun is in their opponent's eyes. They suspect that everyone is out to get them, and they protect themselves at all times. They sleep with a gun under their pillow – or, in this case, an updated set of denial memos stashed in the top drawer.[46]

A dramatic immortalist who developed a huge following in his own time, and who still has a certain notoriety today, was General George Armstrong Custer. Custer's habit of charging the enemy, by no means always successfully, but always at the head of his men, endeared him to the public. He was a natural leader with a genius for the flamboyant, especially in terms of his personal appearance. He was particularly noted for his long curled hair, and for wearing a velveteen jacket with five gold loops on each sleeve, a dark blue sailor shirt, red tie-top boots, and a soft Confederate hat that he had picked up from the field. It was not just his appearance that proved Custer's sense of the dramatic. He had some notable military successes too. For example, his division cut General Robert E. Lee off from his supplies, and Custer personally received the white flag from Lee's men. The destructive streak in Custer's character is equally hard to doubt. His legendary death at the Little Bighorn together with all 215 men who were with him at the time continues to ensure his place in popular mythology.

In more recent times, Steve Jobs of Apple has been described as a dramatic immortalist by his ex-friend and colleague John Sculley. A college dropout who in 1972 was designing computer games at Atari, Jobs by 1980 was co-founder of a corporation with sales of $583 million. 'He was arrogant, outrageous, intense, demanding – a perfectionist. He was also immature, fragile, sensitive, vulnerable. He was dynamic, visionary, charismatic, yet often stubborn, uncompromising, and downright impossible.' He was an inspirational leader whom people believed in, an impresario, but also a flawed personality. 'Like everyone else at Apple,' says Sculley, 'I accepted his behavior because Steve was unique. People made exceptions for him. They held him to the standard of a smart, young kid; they didn't really view him as an adult.' But dramatic immortalists, especially those akin to smart young kids, have difficulty cohering organizations and sustaining success. Says one recent corporate biographer, 'Jobs' arrogance, his unwavering conviction that he knew more than almost anyone else, influenced the birth of a culture that saw fit to demean worthy competitors instead of respecting and learning from them.' Little wonder then that Sculley eventually removed Jobs as head of the Macintosh operation claiming that he (Jobs) had lost touch with what consumers wanted – and, incidentally, forever souring the friendship between the two men.[47,48]

An equally fascinating dramatic immortalist was John DeLorean, a man fired with a narcissistic vision of his own abilities. As a young man, he once wrote that: 'Being an engineer is to live in a mean, bare prison cell and regard yourself the sovereign of limitless space; it is to turn failure into success, mice into men, rags into riches, stone into buildings, steel into bridges, for each engineer has a magician in his soul.'[49] Living this dream, he rose to prominence heading up GM's Pontiac division before being fired, and starting his own eponymous car company which ultimately spectacularly failed. During the early part of his career he was the archetypal rebel immortalist, rising through the ranks at GM while refusing to play their game – dressing stylishly, not eating every lunch in the executive dining room, writing critical reports about the company, and courting the media. Even leaving GM was something of a triumph, retaining as he did a healthy salary, a Cadillac dealership worth $1 million, and a public reputation as an articulate campaigner for the rights of minorities and the disadvantaged. The DeLorean Motor Company, however, despite its initial promise, was an unmitigated disaster. He was accused personally of living a jet-set lifestyle at the British taxpayer's expense, and there were dark rumours of misappropriation of funds. At one point he was indicted for smuggling cocaine into the

USA, and while he was found not guilty in a court of law, his reputation was from then on beyond all hope of rescue. More worrying still, at least one commentator thought he could discern in DeLorean the symptoms of paranoia.[50]

A UK-based dramatic immortalist of world renown is Charles Saatchi. Careful self-publicity ensured that Charles Saatchi gained a public reputation as an advertising genius in the 1970s. Those who knew him, however, often described him as extremely mercurial. Behind the scenes he was prone to nightmarish tantrums, feuds, and other lavish displays of temperament. For many employees Charles was powerfully charismatic. But even his closest colleagues conceded that his brilliance was tinged with a dark side. He was notoriously uncompromising and frequently refused to allow a client to reject or accept his work until he was completely satisfied with it. He confined his interest only to those advertisements he believed would make a difference, and was insensitive to others. Such was the violence of his temper that there are reports of him physically attacking his brother Maurice. Says one biographer, he used to 'storm round the office, demanding better ideas and harder work'.[51]

Charles undoubtedly had immortalistic tendencies. It was he who insisted that the company had to be the biggest and the best, who inspired its phenomenal growth, and who was the driving force behind the firm's motto 'Nothing is Impossible'. We should remember here that in 1988 Saatchi & Saatchi was the biggest advertising group in the world. Three years later, of course, its shares had lost 98% of their value. Further, growth by acquisition had led to the brothers' holding in the company being highly diluted, and when the downturn in Saatchi & Saatchi's fortunes occurred, they could not fight off calls for their demotion. Interestingly, the company's downfall was sagely predicted by the advertising man David Ogilvy, who a few short years before had written lamenting 'the emergence of megalomaniacs whose mind set is more financial than creative'.[52]

Leaders as Conceiteds
Conceited immortalists unswervingly pursue strategic visions

which lead to disaster. Their substitution of unrealistic personal goals for reasonable organizational goals is an exercise in hubris. For every Ross Perot, whose success captures the public imagination, there is a Thomas Edison unable to see real problems and opportunities in their environment. Thomas Edison, we should recall, became fixated on the use of direct electrical current for urban power grids. His monomania was such that he was unable to discern the more rapid acceptance of alternating current power systems by America's newly emerging utility companies. The result was the failure of Edison's company. On another occasion he forgot to take out an international patent on his movie projector, and sold copying patents to Mr A. B. Dick for just $500. Edison was able to deny market realities and so mitigate his fears, but in ways that were wholly self-defeating.[53,54] Conceited immortalists have no awareness that fear can sometimes be a friend worthy of embrace rather than an enemy to be crushed. As Andy Grove of the giant computer chip company Intel has said, 'I think fear is your ally in management because it's fear that gets you out of comfortable equilibrium – gets you to do the difficult tasks.'[55]

The conceited immortalist is very often the victim of Lord Acton's dictum that *power corrupts, absolute power corrupts absolutely*. By virtue of the positions they hold, chief executives are particularly prone to the corrupting influence of the sort of power that feeds pride and erodes integrity. The American industrialist Robert Campeau is a good example of this. Campeau made a fortune in real estate only to squander it trying to develop a retail empire, autocratically dictating an acquisitive strategy in the face of overwhelming evidence that he lacked the long-term resources necessary to make the venture a success. Campeau, like so many others before him, destroyed himself. The forces which foster conceit have been admirably described in a *Business Week* cover story:

> Pampered, protected, and perked, the American CEO can know every indulgence . . . It is a job that can easily go to one's head – and often does . . . With each higher step on the corporate ladder, an executive discovers fewer restraints: unlimited expense

accounts, fewer performance appraisals, and the power, in some cases, to make decisions unchallenged by anyone . . . The decreased supervision and increased power that coincide with success only reinforce and confirm the narcissist's already grandiose self-image.[56]

Some of the most common conceits engaged in by leaders include failing to pay adequate attention to external environments (competitive, technological or consumer), a failure to obtain the resources necessary to realize a vision, and misreading the needs of the market. A good example here was Lee Iacocca of Chrysler. In the 1980s Iacocca erroneously believed that automobile style rather than engineering was the primary concern of those who purchased cars. Relying on this theory, he was responsible for Chrysler building new cars on an ageing chassis (the K car) which had been developed in the late 1970s. The consequence was, with hindsight, predictable, and after several initial years of apparent success, Chrysler's sales plummeted 22.8% in 1987.[57]

As we might expect, conceited immortalism has a lengthy pedigree, and has also long been recognized as a failure of leadership. In the sixteenth century, Niccolo Machiavelli[58] counselled princes that their 'behaviour must be tempered by humanity and prudence so that over-confidence does not make . . . [them] rash'. Among John D. Rockefeller's business principles was 'Be sure that you are not deceiving yourself at any time about actual conditions.'[59] The examples of Edison, Campeau, Iacocca, and others like them, have inspired Harold Geneen to name personal egotism as a worse problem than alcoholism. Says Geneen, 'The supreme egotist in corporate life believes that he is smarter than everyone else around him, that he is somehow "ordained" from on high to know the answer to everything, that he is in control and everyone else is there to serve him. To my mind, he is sick.'[60] In a similar vein, Tom Niles, CEO of Cincom Systems, one of the largest privately held computer software companies in the world, has commented that 'Whom the gods would destroy they first make arrogant . . . Therefore, the proper attitude for accelerating and aiding growth seems to be humility.'[61]

It is a peculiar fact about self-aggrandizing conceit, however, that while it is always immediately evident in others, we find it near impossible to recognize it in ourselves. So concerned was J. Paul Getty that leaders should be reality-adapted, that in his auto-biography he advised business executives to periodically make an inventory of their strengths and weaknesses. Yet his advice is couched in the midst of a self-laudatory account of his own and his father's achievements of which Narcissus himself would have been proud.[62] Intel, under Andy Grove, is famous for the slogan (some call it *Grove's Law*), that *only the paranoid survive*, meaning that vigilance, not conceit, is required at all levels. But the Intel that Grove has created, says one biographer, is plagued by arrogance, suffers from the *Not invented here* syndrome, and finds it hard to accept outsiders into its senior ranks.[63]

There are many corporate leaders who, despite managing to engineer years of success, eventually succumb. Ken Olsen, for instance, grew Digital Equipment Corporation (DEC) into a $6.7 billion company in just eight years by offering a wide range of computers in different sizes. Having founded the company in 1957, however, in 1992 Olsen announced that he had stepped aside as head of the company: an enormous loss of $2.8 billion and an obvious need to cut staff were just symptoms of the real problem. Olsen's forced departure from DEC, and the subsequent takeover of the company by Compaq, are an object lesson in conceit. Indeed, part of the legend of Olsen is as the man famous for repeatedly dismissing the personal computer as a passing fad of no great consequence.

Another example of a leader captured by a narcissistic illusion in the computer electronics industry is worth considering here. An Wang, the Chinese-American who built Wang Laboratories into a major supplier of electronic calculators in the 1960s and 1970s, is particularly interesting. Like Ken Olsen, for years Wang turned in a virtuoso performance. At one point Wang even foresaw the imminent arrival of low-cost competitors in the calculator business and reinvented his company as a leading supplier of word-pro-cessing machines. While these were not true personal computers, because they could only handle text, they were appropriate for their time and soon began to replace typewriters in offices around the world. Wang even managed to develop high quality software for his machines. The problem was that this software was proprietarily tied to Wang word processors. Once general-purpose personal computers appeared, machines capable of running a variety of different word-processing software applications, his empire began to contract. Conceit overcame virtuosity. Perhaps the greatest tribute to Wang's ability to play the role of both virtuoso and conceited immortalist has come from Bill Gates in his book *The Road Ahead*. Gates writes: 'If Wang had recognized the importance of compatible software applications, there might not be a Microsoft today. I might be a mathematician or an attorney somewhere, and my adolescent foray into personal computing might be little more than a distant personal memory.'[64]

Learning Points for Leaders

Great leaders are able to impose their will and their personality on to the organizations they lead. In part, this means elaborating a vision that not merely appeals to but inspires others. More importantly, it requires the ability to deploy one's own persona creatively, and to weave it into the fabric of an organization. Most significantly of all, the true immortalist is able to do these things in reality-adapted ways. To succeed in this dimension of leadership a leader must eschew undue flamboyance and unjustified conceit. At their most impressive, immortalistic leaders are, like Jack Welch and Bill Gates, dominating figures who set new standards in contemporary corporate leadership.

The lesson from history is that constructive immortalism is an integral dimension of effective leadership. Napoleon built an empire on the strength of his extraordinary willpower and supreme confidence, once claiming that 'The world begged me to govern it.'[65] And yet, while unquestionably inspired by a vision of his own power and glory, he pursued it with his eyes open to the real world of unobliging obstacles and setbacks. The English Civil War leader, and later Protector of England, Oliver Cromwell, was fired by an unwavering immortalistic conviction in the rightness of the cause of parliament and godly reformation. In the twentieth century, revolutions, coups d'états and civil wars have been fought by immortalists around the world: Lenin in Russia, Chairman Mao in China, Ataturk in Turkey, Castro in Cuba . . .

Successful business leaders too have often proved themselves to share these immortalistic aspirations. Not all have a world profile, though all have their different personal styles. It has been said of Walt Disney that the bright sharpness of his vision compelled his workers to achievement.[66] In Japan, Ryuzaburo Kako likes to describe how *he* turned Canon around, taking it from 867 in the *Fortune* league of top industrial companies in 1975 to 60 in 1995. In contrast, Ken Iverson, the head of America's third largest steel manufacturer Nucor, has undoubtedly imposed his idiosyncratic vision on his company, yet, in attempting to build a company that will last, he insists that 'The credit for most Nucor achievements rightfully belongs to hundreds of people you'd find throughout the company.'[67] J.W. Marriott, Sr, was a remarkable man who built Marriott Hotels into a hugely profitable concern. But, like Iverson, he did so without insisting on the organization being dependent on his daily presence, and consequently his organization has survived him.

Without exception these, and other constructive immortalists, recognize the perils of tangling with the dark side of immortalism. Constructive immortalists have taken to heart the lessons of men ranging from the English colonialist Cecil Rhodes to Adolf Hitler who desired to govern the world, but who lacked critical self-insight. They take to heart Demosthenes' warning that 'Nothing is easier than self-deceit. For what each man wishes, that he also believes to be true.'[68] Furthermore, the most effective leaders realize that just possessing constructive immortalistic aspirations is not enough. One must always strive to avoid role capture, and to be as skilled as possible in all the dimensions of leadership.

To conclude, then, effective leaders are high self-esteem immortalists. As a matter of fact, low self-esteem is not a problem that actual and would-be leaders tend to suffer from. Low self-esteem individuals are more often content to be followers rather than leaders anyway. The more usual problem for leaders is to harness high self-esteem and to use this advantage to best effect.

Some individuals find that trained counsellors can help elicit useful insights on their psychodynamics. For most people, however, no special professional assistance is required: just deep, concentrated self-reflection, and a willingness to learn and adapt. Some specific questions to bear in mind when evaluating your competence in this dimension of leadership are:

As a Constructive Immortalist

- *As a Constructive Rebel.* Are you a successful independent thinker with an original and creative mind? When an orthodoxy has been established, do you like to do things differently? Do others think of you as a 'rebel', a 'maverick', or as someone who is not afraid to be different?

- *As a Constructive Virtuoso.* Do you possess some special talent(s) that sets you apart from your contemporaries? Have you used your abilities to establish an enviable track record of success? Does your organization share at least some of your most important personality traits?

As a Destructive Immortalist

- *As a Destructive Dramatic.* Are you fixated on money, power and status? Do you view others as mere tools for accomplishing your own personal objectives? Are you impulsive, suspicious, and prone to irrational temper tantrums?

- *As a Destructive Conceited.* Are you unwilling to accept information which contradicts your view of the world? Are you certain that you are always right and will always be successful no matter what? Do your subordinates think of you as dangerously arrogant and egocentric?

Don Kendall

Akio Morita

Masaru Ibuka

William Siemens

Five

LEADER AS POWER-BROKER

The leader can . . . be envisaged as a broker who seeks to pull together a socially acceptable leadership dream. (Lessey Sooklal)[1]

LORD HANSON IS the founder and leader of Hanson Trust, the £15 billion international conglomerate employing 80,000 people worldwide. His office, in London, popularly known as 'the furnace', is where he turns his fearsome temper on those subordinates who offend his sense of how his corporation should be run. Tales of senior executives leaving Hanson's office shaking like a leaf after an angry encounter with the chairman are legion. Indira Gandhi was an expertly manipulative politician who wielded her party machine so effectively that she served as Prime Minister of India for four terms between 1967 and 1980. Masaru Ibuka and Akio Morita, the men who founded Sony, were noted for their sensitivity to people, and an ability to develop an atmosphere of cooperation. In the macho world of Japanese business, where the only personality that usually counts is that of the chief executive, their efforts to foster individuality down the line have reinforced their reputation as people with outstanding leadership qualities. Hanson, Gandhi, Ibuka and Morita, illustrate some of the many different facets of the leader as power-broker.[2,3,4]

Leaders deal in power. They accomplish goals by mobilizing others to act on their behalf. But leaders do not possess *all* the power in their organizations. Even the most junior and down-trodden in the massed ranks of the under-achievers have some power – even if it is only to throw a spanner into the production line. According to David Kearns, the former chairman and CEO of the Xerox Corporation, 'In the twenty-first century, every person at every job – at whatever level in the organization – will have access to unlimited information, and therefore power.'[5] Generally speaking, the higher one moves up through the corporate hierarchy the more power individuals possess. A leader's fellow board members may often have very considerable powers indeed. Organizations, then, are political arenas in which individuals and groups attempt to exert influence. They do so to bolster their self-esteem and in the pursuit of their selfish career interests. In extreme cases, as with John DeLorean, who secretly diverted $17 million of DeLorean Motor Company funds into a Swiss bank account, leaders exercise power in purely self-serving ways.[6] Others, such as Jack Welch and Tiny Rowland, broker power in support of their own self-esteem, but in a manner which also profits their organizations.

Leaders, of course, occupy positions of privilege at the apex of the organizational pyramid. From their vantage point they can direct and channel the energies of others, reconciling differences, coaxing and cajoling when possible, directing when necessary. Always listening, ever watchful, effective leaders broker power in their organizations, cutting deals which suit their ends. Rivals may be bought off, demoted or undermined. Those resistant to the leader's strategies can be challenged, subjected to retraining regimens, and, ultimately, coerced into submission. The softly softly approach can always give way to the dictatorial command. A disapproving memo can, if ineffective in modifying subordinate behaviour, be followed up by an ultimatum.

Leadership, then, crucially centres on power. Power is the capacity to listen to others, to resolve conflicts, to persuade. It is also the ability to stifle discontent when it is destructive, to prevent potentially damaging issues from being discussed, and to silence unhelpful critics. A leader's power is bound up with the resources at his or her disposal – knowledge, skills, time, budgets, charisma, energy, even in some instances his or her sexuality. Power is manifested in leaders' attempts to manipulate how their people think, the values and beliefs they subscribe to, and how they behave.

Theoretically, power to the leader is like energy to the physicist: it is the fundamental key, the final explanation to how and why things are. In practice, leaders are power-brokers: they make things happen, they get things done. Just as modern France was the autocratic creation of De Gaulle and modern Turkey was moulded by Ataturk, so with business corporations: Coca-Cola owes much to the pervasive influence of its former leader Roberto Goizueta; EDS, in its creation, was for Ross Perot an exercise in power; GEC was created by Lord Weinstock in his own puritanical image, and Hyundai was brokered into existence and made a success by Chung Ju Yung.

Cecil Rhodes, founder of the De Beers diamond company and the man who gave his name to the country formerly known as Rhodesia, is in many ways typical of those leaders who are at supreme ease with this dimension of leadership. Rhodes travelled from England to South Africa in 1870 with little more than a calculating mind and unrivalled ambition. He soon became involved in prospecting for diamonds, and while making his fortune, was guided by the ideal that 'the English should rule this earth'. Rhodes saw that the key to making this happen was money, for along with the accumulation of vast wealth goes considerable political power. Through clever manipulation, persuasiveness and sheer force of personality he gained control of diamond production in South Africa, leading one biographer to argue that 'None could doubt his moral courage, and he had an inborn power of command.' At the age of thirty-five he financially and politically dominated South Africa and was able to influence both British and American policy. By the age of forty-two he controlled, in Rhodesia, his own private empire. At the end, with his health failing, the man who once asserted that 'I would annexe the planets and the stars if I could', clung with increased intensity, if not scruple, to the illusion that 'My career is only just beginning.'[7]

Naturally, the power that leaders exercise can be brokered in a variety of ways, giving rise to a range of different power-broking roles. Rhodes' genius was his facility to excel in all of them. His example suggests that leaders need to be

- *despots*, whose naked use of raw power attracts both ardent admiration and intense revulsion among followers and commentators.
- *manipulators*, who deal in power rather like the puppeteer controls his or her puppets.
- *conductors*, whose brokerage activities integrate and harmonize the efforts of diverse factions in organizations.
- *empowerers*, who encourage their subordinates to believe that they have the power to make a difference.

As we shall see, leaders, to be fully effective, need to be comfortable and adept with all these facets of the power-broking dimension of leadership.

Leader as Despot

Of the media baron Robert Maxwell it was once said that he could charm the birds from the trees – and then shoot them.[8] Noted as a man who would explode when his instant decisions were not instantly complied with, Maxwell is typical of that breed of leader with naturally despotic inclinations. Such people are frequently colourful, headline-grabbing characters, much beloved by business press journalists. Another of the more outlandishly dictatorial business despots was the US entrepreneur Victor Posner, who built up a business empire that at its peak grossed $26 billion. Having acquired businesses, however, he was not so adept at running them, and many filed for bankruptcy. Indeed, he seemed to excel at destroying both his businesses and his family. Said one analyst, 'His management style was extremely dictatorial and intimidating. Attending a board meeting was like attending an old-fashioned camp meeting: all directors were supposed to say amen to each of his statements, no matter how outrageous they were.' The final outcome was that soon after each of Posner's acquisitions, some of the best executives left, and in the end, asset stripping led Posner and his empire into bankruptcy.[9,10]

Ed Artzt, the ex-head of Procter & Gamble, is one of the most celebrated of recent American corporate despots. Memorably described by one commentator as the *Prince of Darkness*, Artzt was noted for his tendencies to terrorize his subordinates and to seek revenge on those he despised. Rumoured to be an admirer of Attila the Hun's methods of dealing with the disloyal, he was known to keep three spare copies of *Leadership Secrets of Attila the Hun* in his office bookcase. According to one of his subordinates, Artzt was the sort of man who could 'peel the skin off of people a strip at a time and love every minute of it'. Unsurprisingly, Procter & Gamble under Artzt was a fear-filled organization in which junior staff lived in terror of his visits. His performance in one meeting gives clues as to why: unhappy with a particular product development manager's report, Artzt interrupted the presentation with the comment 'You're the sorriest excuse for a manager I've ever seen. How did you get your job?'[11]

While Artzt's despotic inclinations are rarely disputed, the question of whether he was a force for good or ill is. For some, he was a tyrannical maniac who developed a paranoid institution obsessed by secrecy and control. Artzt, it is said, lost more of his senior management team than any other incoming CEO in the company's history. Employees, we are told, were turned into blue-suited 'Proctoids' whose lives were policed by company bullies and spies. These analysts see the company's headquarters in downtown Cincinnati – a grim, brooding monolith – as symptomatic of Procter & Gamble under Artzt.[12] Others, however, point out that Artzt's preoccupation with profit and emphasis on individual accountability had many positive implications. His intolerance of disagreement and freedom of expression may have made him a lot of enemies, but his ruthless cutting of unprofitable brands reinvigorated Procter & Gamble's bottom line.

Probably the UK's nearest equivalent to Ed Artzt was Lord Weinstock. Phenomenally successful in growing GEC from a small producer of electrical goods into Britain's largest industrial firm, Lord Weinstock was also a noted dictator. He had a particularly high need for control, and delighted in exercising his power by contacting subordinates and asking them to explain 'problems' personally. Said one manager of their former boss, 'He's a bully. He bullies people by the use of intellect . . . I have seen fully grown, tip-top men in tears.' Weinstock was obsessive about cost reduction, and once even suggested that every other light bulb should be removed from offices and corridors to reduce the consumption of electricity. He was also always quick to find fault. On one occasion as he toured a factory he spied a workman reading what he thought was a newspaper. 'Look at that man slacking,' he shouted. It was only with great difficulty that his entourage persuaded him that the man in question was in fact reading an engineering blueprint. No wonder then that GEC under Lord Weinstock has been described by one industry commentator as 'a cold, unforgiving place animated by intellect and logic'.[13]

A generation earlier Walt Disney's dictatorial tendencies had been projected not just within his own organization, but throughout the film-making industry in America. From 1940 he became a domestic spy for the US government, believing it his patriotic duty to report on the activities of Hollywood actors, writers, producers, directors, and union activities to the FBI. Within the Disney studio he considered himself the paternal head, and thought his subordinates (his 'boys') should show him unflinching loyalty. Working long hours for low pay, in 1941 his most talented artists engaged in collective strike action. Detecting what he thought was a betrayal of trust, Disney's response was to publicly accuse the ringleaders of being Communists, irreparably damaging their careers. With the strike broken he then turned his attention to the Hollywood system itself, which he believed had conspired to prevent him from achieving the level of success he deserved. His perception was that an 'old boys' club' of mostly immigrant Jews who controlled production, distribution and exhibition needed to be dismembered. Ultimately, he accomplished his ambition as one of the litigants in a landmark Supreme Court case that found the studio system to be an illegal cartel. The public presentation of Disney as a gentle, loving husband and model citizen, masked a private side in which fear and frustration fed despotic inclinations.[14]

Operating in a very different country and cultural context, Chung Ju Yung, the founder and long-time leader of Hyundai, has impeccable despotic credentials, exciting both great fear and respect. The sheer force of his personality coerced his family members and Hyundai executives into 'dumb, often cowering, obedience and subservience'. No one – his six siblings, nine children, wife and his numerous female friends included – argued with the old man and won. One former Hyundai manager remembers how Yung could change his mood in an instant, from benign grandfather-figure to ice-cold menace. As one observer has written: 'In full-dress meetings he could shift from jovial regular guy to gangster-like monster – sometimes even punching or slapping his executives across the face.'[15]

Not all leaders with despotic tendencies are as fully captured by this single role as Posner, Artzt, Weinstock and Yung. Some leaders who have been demonized in the popular business press actually reveal a sophisticated self-awareness in their comments and especially their autobiographical writing. For example, Harold S. Geneen, the legendary president and chairman of ITT, was often described by outsiders as a tough man to work for. The stereotypical view of him from outside the company was as a difficult, ruthless s.o.b. who drove his subordinates to early graves. Yet according to Geneen, his management team stayed with him because they thrived on the fast pace he set, and the action and growth that went with it. At the same time, however, he explicitly recognizes the dangers associated with pressures to adopt authoritarian roles. Says Geneen:

> In the vast majority of large American companies, the chief executive lives in a world of his own. He is sequestered in his luxury executive suite high up in the headquarters building. His word is law. Everyone kowtows to him. They adjust to his moods and to his idiosyncrasies. He runs the company from his inner sanctum . . . Subtly, he changes. It is easier and less time-consuming to be authoritarian.[16]

My argument is that, despite the inherent dangers, the institutional pressures which foster despotism are not wholly negative. Leaders sometimes need to be despots. When Gerstner took over at IBM his strong and decisive actions ripped apart the *rule by committee* mentality that had predominated until his arrival. Gerstner typically breezed into a meeting only when everyone else was assembled and, without any of the usual pleasantries, got started. He would then ask a series of quick, tough, some would say rude questions of his subordinates, winding up the proceedings within fifteen minutes. It was a style that promised results. The problem is that leaders often find it difficult to extract the positive elements of the despotic role without also buying into the negative. For instance, the more extreme side of Gerstner's personality would also be expressed, this being vividly illustrated in his dealings with individuals during his time at American Express. Through the closed door of his office he was frequently heard shouting 'That's the stupidest thing I've ever heard! You're an idiot! Get out of my office!' If those who were in the hall hung around a second, the chances were they would see some angst-ridden employee shoot out the door. No wonder that, according to one subordinate, knees literally buckled and hands trembled when Gerstner walked into a room.[17,18]

Shrewdly calculating leaders who adopt despotic methods to accomplish company objectives are surely the most interesting exemplars of this genre. They are men such as the British leader Lord Sheppard, CEO of the food and drinks conglomerate GrandMet, whose aggressive style he himself refers to as 'management by light grip on the throat'. In Lord Sheppard's organization toughness with people who he thinks do not add value is enshrined in his dictum that 'Either you are making an input, or you are output.'[19] They are men like the celebrity Swiss businessman Nicolas G. Hayek, who rescued SMH (Swiss Corporation for Microelectronics and Watchmaking) from crisis. Describing how he turned around the Omega division of SMH, Hayek said, 'I pushed out practically the entire management at Omega. I fired a lot of people. I got the reputation as a brutal guy. I am not a brutal guy. But the organization was so full of arrogance and stupidity that I didn't have much choice.'[20] And they are men like Jack Welch of GE, who recognized that despotism occupies a useful niche in the chief executive's armoury. According to Welch, 'You've got to be hard to be soft. You have to demonstrate the ability to make the hard, tough decisions – closing plants, divesting, delayering – if you want to have any credibility when you try to promote soft values.'[21]

The value of despotism to leaders attempting to establish their authority and improve the prospects of their organizations has been demonstrated many times and in many contexts. When Goizueta took over at Coca-Cola he turned the budget review process into what was known internally as 'The Spanish Inquisition'. His rationale was that 'Once in a while, to make a point, you have to have a flogging in the town square. There's more to it than just the pain of the lash, it's the crack of the whip that has a beneficial effect on everyone who hears.'[22] At Intel, Andy Grove can be abrupt, aggressive and interrogatory in his efforts to create a culture of 'constructive confrontation'. According to one commentator, he is like a shepherd – signalling with his crook where he wants the flock to go, but keeping a team of dogs to bite the ankles of any sheep that strays off in the wrong direction.[23] Tiny Rowland, who built Lonrho, has been described by his detractors as 'a genius without scruples' who intimidated his critics into silence. Supporters, however, point out that his natural inclination not to tolerate failure may have seemed brutal, but it often made good business sense.[24,25]

In conclusion, then, despotism represents a trade-off. On the one hand it is associated with an ability to move swiftly and decisively, to silence opposing voices when they are hypercritical, and to focus on those issues that really matter. It is an intensely time- and resource-efficient style of leadership, intolerant of wastage and of under-performance. Despotism may not be pretty, but under appropriate conditions, it can generate success. Artzt revitalized Procter & Gamble, Yung created the hugely successful Hyundai, and Welch, Goizueta, Grove and Rowland all skilfully employed this role to create world class organizations. On the other, and more negative side, the despot can fail to hear important messages and, isolated at the top, lose touch with his or her organization and its markets. Robert Maxwell and Victor Posner are object lessons here. Despotism is a role to be adopted when required and shed when expedient. It is to be used effectively by skilled and self-aware leaders; not allowed to capture and control their every act.

Leader as Manipulator

Leading people often involves getting them to do things they would not otherwise choose to do. The manipulative leader does this with considerable skill. Of course there are many subtle variations here. In playing the manipulative role some leaders, like the now deceased UK media baron Robert Maxwell, are devious, underhand and egocentric. By contrast, leaders such as the World War Two US army chief of staff George C. Marshall, are models of integrity. Some leaders, like Wayne Huizenga who developed the Blockbuster Video chain, have a high need for personal control and like to exercise their manipulative powers directly. Others, such as Ken Iverson of the US steel company Nucor, prefer to use less palpable methods. Whatever one's preferred personal style, the manipulative role is one that is central to power-broking successful corporate performance.

Those manipulative leaders who have a strong sense of their own abilities, and a high need for personal control, tend often to be overtly demanding individuals. The lack of subtlety with which they exercise power may not win them many friends, but they can be highly effective. This is especially true when they are motivated not by a need for personal power, but to make their organizations succeed. John Sculley gives some insights into the thought processes of this type of leader in describing how he got to the top of Pepsi. He writes:

> If I was brash or arrogant on my way to the top, it mattered little to me. I was an impatient perfectionist. I was willing to work relentlessly to get things exactly right. I was unsympathetic of those who couldn't deliver the results I demanded. I was driven, not by simple power or raw ambition, but by an insatiable curiosity and skepticism as to business's accepted notions. I considered myself a builder, someone whose success was dependent on building products and markets, on changing an industry's ground rules, not merely competing. I felt as if I were an architect of new ideas and concepts.[26]

One tendency of some leaders who are naturally inclined to manipulation, is to make seemingly arbitrary decisions on the flimsiest of whims. Such leaders, like Wayne Huizenga in his early days at Blockbuster, seek input rather than consensus, and strive to retain total control over decision making. A good example of the results of this style centres on Blockbuster's chief marketeer responsible for store image. He wanted the outlets to fly American flags, and sent out a memo telling store managers where to source poles and flags. Huizenga, who had not been involved in the decision, called his chief marketeer into his office and let him know he could not see much value in the move. Word quickly spread that the idea had been axed by the boss. A few weeks later Wayne noted that McDonald's stores had both a company and an American flag, changed his mind, called his chief marketeer into his office and told him to reinstate the flag policy.[27] There are obvious dangers in brokering power in this way, for while it might get things done, it can also build a culture in which subordinates become dependent and reactive, too scared to think beyond predetermined limits, and unhealthily preoccupied with second-guessing their leader's reactions. Overt manipulation, especially when supported by a cultural infrastructure that favours disciplined obedience, sacrifices the imaginative capabilities of subordinates.

There are, though, leaders who manage to broker their manipulative powers in more disguised ways, and their covert approach has particular advantages. People are often more compliant, less complaining, and even more forgiving of those who manipulate by stealth. This has been recognized by, for instance, Don Burr, who together with two colleagues set up the American low-cost airline People Express. From the start, Burr sought to create a culture and a horizontal management structure that put the growth and development of individuals at the top of the company's list of guiding precepts. According to Gitner, who was People Express's president and one of the original three founders, this culture and structure was little more than a smokescreen that diverted attention from Don Burr's all-pervasive influence. To an extent, Burr himself concurred with Gitner's assessment, stating that he saw his job as setting direction and creating an environment that would make People Express successful: 'Some people criticize that as being manipulative and so forth, and I say, yeah, it is manipulative . . . but it's good manipulation, it's constructive manipulation.'[28]

Still more sophisticated in the manipulative arts are those leaders who have learned to tame their egoism, and who are able to distance themselves from the control mechanisms they develop. Typical of this breed of leader is Ken Iverson, the boss of Nucor, which is the third largest steel company in the US with sales in excess of $3.6 billion. Iverson is the unseen hand at Nucor who manipulates through management principles and practices that set the agenda for work activities. Here employees are supplied with equipment, training, a benefits programme and other support, and then largely left alone to work out how to meet targets they themselves set. Base parameters are naturally determined by Iverson, but few in the company pay much attention to these fundamentals given the apparent latitude and stake in the business they are granted. Ken Iverson, then, provides a fascinating example of the *latent* leader-as-manipulator. As Iverson himself has written, to be successful what one has to do 'is to shape an environment that allows employees to fulfil the goals of the business.'[29]

The capacity for deft yet understated manipulation is not an unduly rare phenomenon among business leaders. Alfred P. Sloan's talents as a manipulative negotiator and bargain-maker at GM are widely known.[30] Ruud Koedijk, in his position as chairman of KPMG in the Netherlands, attracted a *Harvard Business Review* article on his success in manipulating what was a collection of small fiefdoms in which each partner was a lord, into a strategically integrated organization. And furthermore, he did it with such guile and *savoir faire* that a new culture of trust, self-confidence and self-fulfilment evolved.[31] In Japan in the 1980s Tsutomu Murai achieved a national reputation as a turnaround specialist following his exploits at Mazda and Asahi Breweries. Murai's technique was to tackle conflicts head on by discussing them in the light of overall corporate goals, often at small night-time gatherings. These sessions allowed him not just to keep in contact with managers at all levels, but to direct their thinking on a more personal basis. Murai's gift was to guide and mould, yet be thought of as someone who merely 'ignites the middle management' by preparing 'a positive environment'.[32]

In the field of politics, Napoleon is celebrated as one of the most sophisticated of manipulators. Napoleon was, perhaps above all things, consumed by the need for power, on one occasion telling a follower 'Power is my mistress . . . I have worked too hard at her conquest to allow anyone to take her away from me or even covet her.' As emperor of France and its annexed territories Napoleon was intellectually shrewd, socially adept and politically astute. Intensely realistic regarding what it would take to secure his authority, he set about ensuring the support of a cadre of pro-fessional loyalists. He did this by offering them the sort of careers and promotional prospects that would bind them more closely to him, and by lavishly bestowing honours and material rewards on many of them. In this way, he aimed to establish a system in which the professional and propertied classes would more firmly associate their interests with his regime. He even allied himself with the pope (Pope Pius VII), in 1801, on the calculation that this would further endear him to the traditional Catholicism of his subjects. Such overt and considered manipulation naturally comes at a price. As Napoleon himself is reputed to have said, 'Although you say that power came to me of its own accord, I know what it has cost me – the sufferings, the sleepless nights, the scheming.'[33]

To conclude, leadership in organizations is inevitably intimately concerned with the manipulation of people, their minds and their behaviours. Manipulation can not only have both positive and negative consequences, but it can also be exercised both more and less competently. At their most destructive, manipulative leaders verge on the megalomaniacal. Typical in this regard was Steve Jobs, who while at Apple was known to have darted in and out of operations causing havoc by 'dictating designs with little or no knowledge of whether or not the technology even existed to make his ideas work'.[34] At their most effective, however, manipulators like Harold S. Geneen of ITT, realize that power is best brokered by inspiring and convincing subordinates. As Geneen the arch-manipulator asserts, 'So, as far as I can see, the best way to inspire people to superior performance is to convince them by everything you do and by your everyday attitude that you are wholeheartedly supporting them. You have got to mean it and demonstrate it. Deep down they have to feel that support . . .'[35]

Leader as Conductor

Great leaders share many of the characteristics that have been attributed to great orchestra conductors. They deploy power subtly rather than overtly. They coordinate without being overly imposing or egocentric, and they show sensitivity and respect for the members of their group. Conductors recognize that they are involved in a reciprocal power–dependence relationship, and that while they act as the central decision-maker and nerve centre of activities, coercion will be counterproductive. As the leadership commentators Daniel Bradford and Allan Cohen[36] have argued, business leaders are like musical conductors who 'follow complex, separate strands of music and weave them into one whole, co-ordinated performance'. And just like musical conductors, leaders of organizations succeed 'through careful preparation, knowledge of what is needed, and exact control', which means that the conductor can see 'that every player is doing his or her share as needed and is in proper harmony'.

Perhaps the best evidence of the close parallels between musical conductors and business leaders is that the descriptions of the great conductors could equally fit many effective business leaders. For example, the well-regarded English conductor Simon Rattle is notoriously unpretentious and professional, always dedicated to the musical job in hand, but also possessed of a creative good humour. Just as the best business leaders naturally attract adherents, so with Rattle musicians find that they want to play for him, and strive to give their best. As one biographer of Rattle has written, 'He always knew the right thing to say to people at the right time, a word of encouragement or appreciation or even mild but firm complaint, and it always had whatever result he wanted. Not that he was calculating or smooth: it all just came naturally.'[37] Much the same things have been said about leaders as diverse as Lee Iacocca, Alfred Sloan and Richard Branson.

Another good indicator of the links between musical conduct-ing and leading organizations is that business leaders themselves often use the conductor/orchestra metaphor in describing their own behaviours. Lord Sheppard of GrandMet has expressed his opinion that the role of those at the helm of organizations is to take full and complete responsibility for 'the strategy, the people, the products, the rules, everything' and then 'orchestrate it all'.[38] Harold S. Geneen has gone still further, and suggested that 'the process of conducting business is fascinating, demanding, and creative, worthy of being classed with the higher arts, worthy also of the greatest personal commitment for self and society, and yielding the greatest satisfactions'.[39] Roberto Goizueta of Coca-Cola liked to emphasize to reporters that he believed he was 'the conductor of Coke's orchestra'.[40] And Napoleon once claimed that his love of power was akin to the love of an artist, saying 'I love it [power] as a musician loves his violin . . . I love it for the sake of drawing sounds, chords, and harmonies from it.'[41]

The role of the leader as conductor requires an ability to achieve balance and harmony throughout an organization. The best conductors are good listeners who can also stimulate their subordinates with well-chosen prompts, and who broker power by building consensus. Like the jazz musician and composer Duke Ellington, these are people with charisma, intensity and charm, who avoid being seen as devious, but who are nevertheless very much in control.[42] In striving for a consensus the conductor always has in mind his or her ideals and objectives. They do not merely *go with the flow*, but shape and steer the eddy currents in their organizations so that subordinates' thoughts and actions flow in particular directions. As has been noted, rarely will such a leader explicitly favour given solutions or strategies; 'rather, the Conductor style calls for some indirect but active manoeuvring to lead members to arrive at the Conductor's solution on their own'.[43]

Foremost among the skills needed to be a conductor is the ability to listen. Conductors require a keen ear and a special talent for discerning variations in tone and motifs. They must be able to distinguish unusual and significant information against a some-times deafening background noise of banality. Played to its maximum potential the conductor role demands the sort of audio acuity that few possess, but which many leaders recognize as vital.

Mary Kay Ash, for example, believes that 'Listening is an art.' She knows that to be an effective listener one needs to give the other party one's 'undivided attention'. Further, she claims to put this tenet of good leadership into practice such that 'When someone enters my office to speak with me, I don't allow anything to distract my attention . . .'[44] Michael Dell, founder and CEO of Dell Computer, has made a similar point, arguing that a good leader has 'to keep an ear cocked for what's being whispered in the pews'.[45] And J.W. Marriott Jr[46] has asserted that 'After more than forty years in business, I've concluded that listening is the single most important on-the-job skill.'

Good listening skills are also prized by Lawrence A. Bossidy. When he became Chairman and CEO of AlliedSignal, the $13 billion industrial supplier of aerospace systems, automotive parts and chemical products, he quickly asserted that 'First, we want to create an environment in which people will speak up. Every question is interesting and important. When I conduct interactive sessions, I don't walk out after three questions. I make it clear that I'm going to be there until the last question is asked.'[47] For leaders of large organizations with a diverse spread of activities the ability to listen is all the more vital because it is practically impossible for one person to have a detailed knowledge of all the issues which impact on the business. As Derek Wanless, Group Chief Executive at the UK-based financial services group NatWest has said, 'My personal style is to analyse issues out, to ask questions of detail, to get views on the table. It's not the quickest way of doing things, but in a group of this size and diversity I can't know everything about every business and its market. I'm much more about testing people out so that we have as much information as possible.'[48]

As Derek Wanless recognizes, conducting an organization is not just about listening. It also involves stimulating interesting and helpful ideas and behaviours in others. Further, a good conductor encourages subordinates to develop themselves in ways which benefit the organization as a whole. A crucial aspect of this is to ensure that people do not feel trapped or coerced, but rather *buy into* and hence *own* self-developmental ideas and strategies. As Paul Fentener van Vlissingen, who became head of the Dutch company

SHV Holdings in 1984, has said, 'It's very important all the time to tell people to do it themselves . . . We have very talented people. You don't have to stimulate an athlete who is running the thousand metres. You don't have to tell them they have to win. They know that. But you can ask them, "Have you checked your diet? Have you got the best trainer?" That you can do . . . You can ask them questions, but they find out themselves.'[49] These sentiments echo those of Alfred P. Sloan, who by the time he left in 1956 had led GM to become the richest corporation in the world. Sloan believed that it was best to exercise power with discretion and to treat people with respect. As he once stated, 'I got better results by selling my ideas than by telling people what to do.'[50]

One last example will serve us well here. When Brian Baker became hospital commander of Raymond Bliss Army Community Hospital in Arizona he found an organization in disarray. Morale was low, and conflict between doctors and nurses was endemic. Within two years Baker changed the culture of the hospital so profoundly that all the fear, hostility and tension were gone, and he did so largely without hiring and firing staff. Instead, he listened and mentored. He did not try and tell people what to do, but made sure they understood what needed to be done without infringing their discretionary powers. As Baker himself said, 'You never assume control of the issue. They own it, not you. You coach and you mentor, but you make them decide and act. If it's their plan, they're most likely to make it happen. I helped add what I consider the most important ingredient: mutual respect and a feeling of togetherness. After that, everything just came together.'[51]

If being an effective leader sometimes means playing the role of a conductor, then the most appropriate image here is quite possibly that of the jazz band maestro. As the management academic Mary Jo Hatch has written:

> In jazz bands the leader's role is not only to be a featured artist but also to select musicians for the 'gig' and to bring out their best qualities during the performance. Knowing the abilities and preferences of the selected musicians allows the leader to choose tunes and set up solos at appropriate moments during the

performance. Keeping everybody fully engaged and enjoying themselves promotes the overall performance of the band and gives the audience the greatest chance for satisfaction. (Duke Ellington and Miles Davis were particularly well-known for these leadership skills.)[52]

To conclude, then, the leader as conductor is, like John Pepper, chief executive of Procter & Gamble, a 'gentlemanly consensus-builder'.[53] This is in no way meant to imply that conductors stifle all conflict. On the contrary, they often foster it. But they then broker it in astutely constructive ways. As the ex-head of the UK chemicals company ICI, Sir John Harvey-Jones, says, a degree of constructive conflict is essential in making progress. The point is, asserts Sir John, that 'The seeking of business success is far too difficult and serious a matter to be done in a cosy way. Of course one wants to avoid situations where the conflict reaches excessive levels and actually gets in the way of running the business, but if the right decisions are to be taken it is essential that conflicting views are heard and thrashed out.'[54]

Leader as Empowerer

As we have seen, no leader can possibly control all aspects of his or her organization. All leaders delegate some decisions to their subordinates. Even the most dictatorial and despotic leaders with high needs for personal power and control also, in part, lead by empowering others. Time constraints and the sheer size and complexity of big corporations force this expedient upon them. As Jim Renier of Honeywell has said, 'At some point you've got to loosen the reins, delegate.' Renier likens being CEO of a big corporation to a military commander whose battlefield is shrouded in fog: 'It's too much to ask the commander to describe the terrain as if the fog wasn't there. I don't have all the answers, but we've got to be willing to listen and say, well, someone else has seen through part of the fog so we'd better listen carefully to that person.'[55] Jan Carlzon of SAS has expressed a similar view, arguing that in a changing business environment 'You must give people authority far out on the line where the action is.' Only by doing this will a CEO have immediate information on changes in markets, and so 'be in the best position to gain a competitive edge'.[56]

More than most other facets of the power-broking dimension of leadership, there is a resurgent emphasis on empowerment. Ross Perot, founder and chairman of the Perot Group and 1992 presidential candidate, has preached that leadership is centrally concerned with 'empowering a group of people to successfully achieve a common goal'. Reuben Mark of the Colgate-Palmolive Company has argued that 'One of the essentials of leadership in business, in government and any sector is to practice empowerment by getting everyone's involvement.' Bill Gates, chairman and CEO of Microsoft, has asserted that 'It's really up to leaders to pull the group together, get the best talent out of that group, get the group thinking about the greatest possibilities, and think how each person can contribute as a leader.' The point is, as Jack Welch of GE has explicitly recognized, that 'empowerment is really about involvement', and starts only when a leader truly believes 'that everyone counts'.[57]

To empower someone is to authorize or license them to do something. The importance of empowerment in modern business organizations is indicated by its prominence in influential management texts such as Tom Peters and Robert Waterman's *In Search of Excellence*.[58] In their book, Peters and Waterman cite numerous examples of 'excellent' organizations which are led by people who value autonomy and cherish individuality. For example, Thomas Watson of IBM has argued that respect for the individual is the company's most important value, while Mark Shepherd of Texas Instruments has asserted that workers should be seen as a source of ideas not just a pair of hands. Such people have recognized the benefits of an empowering style of leadership: it encourages creativity and innovation, fosters mature, well-rounded (rather than sycophantic) subordinates, and harnesses energy and enthusiasm. What is less generally recognized are the many different roles of empowering leaders: they must foster partnership relations with their subordinates, non-directively facilitate activities, concern themselves with the development of their staff, and even learn to be good followers themselves. The skilled leader-as-empowerer will do all of these things with finesse.

Empowerers seek to build a partnership with their board colleagues and subordinates. Mike Walsh, who took over the faltering conglomerate Tenneco in 1991, sought to turn the organization around by encouraging employees to think of themselves as empowered mini-CEOs.[59,60] Michael Edwardes, in his efforts to rebuild the automotive manufacturer British Leyland, insisted that every major decision would be debated, and that where possible important decisions would be made by consensus. Said Edwardes, 'People need to feel part of an overall strategy and feel they have some responsibility and involvement in decisions which affect them. No amount of table-thumping in the boardroom will achieve optimum performance from senior executives, middle managers or the shop floor if they do not understand the reasoning and accept some responsibility for their own actions.'[61] The same sort of philosophy has been succinctly described at Apple, where a central management tenet is 'Along with the privilege to make a difference goes the responsibility to make a difference.'[62]

Leaders who effectively empower their staff tend to be good facilitators, who are confident in their choice of subordinates. They are men like Richard W. Sears who founded the mail order company that bears his name, and who insisted that the secret of business success was to 'Select your men carefully and at the right time – then give them a free rein within certain well-defined limits.'[63] More contemporary examples include Percy Barnevik of ABB, Ken Iverson of Nucor and Lawrence A. Bossidy of AlliedSignal. Barnevik has become one of Europe's most eminent businessmen with his philosophy of liberation and empowerment.[64] Iverson has set up a management infrastructure in which all important decisions are decentralized.[65] Bossidy is noted as the CEO who, in an interview with *Harvard Business Review*, quoted Teddy Roosevelt's dictum that 'The best executive is the one who has sense enough to pick good men to do what he wants done, and self-restraint enough to keep from meddling with them while they do it.'[66]

Leaders who are outstanding empowerers do not merely show

care and concern for their employees, they are inspiring developers and coaches. They need to be if they are to avoid their organizations becoming dustbins of what Jack Welch has referred to as 'wasted minds' – people who are uninvolved, bored, and who may harbour feelings of anger. Welch counsels that leaders should think constantly about how to make 'every person more valuable'.[67] Sir John Egan, of the British Airports Authority (BAA), has argued that continuous improvement in organizations requires every single person to 'bring their brains to work'.[68] Richard Sears advised every senior manager to 'encourage his men to take the initiative and make mistakes' because only then 'can they gain experience'.[69] Harold Geneen of ITT claims to have made such sentiments the bedrock of his approach to leadership, asserting that 'I've had men come into my office and admit they goofed, that the mistake cost the company several millions of dollars, but then they presented a plan by which they would rectify the situation. As long as they came in with a plan to remedy the disaster, they had my support.'[70]

Particularly talented and insightful empowerers realize that one of their most important tasks is to assist in the development of other leaders. In the eighteen months before becoming CEO of PepsiCo in early 1996, Roger Enrico spent nearly a third of his time in remote off-site settings cultivating a new generation of company leaders. Jack Welch of GE, Lew Platt of Hewlett Packard, Larry Bossidy of AlliedSignal and Andy Grove of Intel all devote time to developmental activities. Larry Bossidy has stated: 'You won't remember when you retire what you did in the first quarter of 1994 or the third. What you'll remember is how many people you developed.'[71] So significant are these sorts of behaviours, that some theorists of leadership have even built the idea of nurturing others into ideological programmes. For example, Robert K. Greenleaf coined the phrase 'servant-leadership' in 1970 to refer to that type of leadership perspective which particularly values helping others to grow and flourish.[72]

Perhaps most importantly of all, the skilled empowerer recognizes that leading and following are not polar opposites but two sides of the same social coin. This point has been confirmed by Robert Kelly's intriguing study which demonstrated that effective followers shared many of the salient characteristics of excellent leaders.[73] It was, thus, not without reason that the business leadership analyst Warren Bennis wrote, 'Good leaders must also be good followers.'[74] For leaders derive their power from those they lead, and paradoxically, '*we become the most powerful when we give our own power away.*' [75] By empowering others, leaders rescind only the rather limited power to direct individuals and their projects. At the same time they gain the much broader and often more potent power to exert influence over vast organizations. This, doubtless, is part of what the ancient Chinese sage Lao Tzu had in mind when he wrote that 'A leader is best when people are hardly aware of his existence.' It is testament, too, to the view of the late Wilbert L. Gore, founder of W.L. Gore & Associates, that the real skill of the CEO is in 'making heroes of other people'.[76]

To conclude, the leader-as-empowerer has, like the soft-spoken and unpretentious Toru Hashimoto of Fuji Bank, learned that sometimes things that are said softly are easier to hear.[77] Playing the role effectively is, however, never a simple matter. Part of the problem is often the expectations of those who surround the leader, and who because of their lack of imagination and experience, insist that he or she dominate proceedings. Another aspect of the problem is that most leaders actively enjoy the business of managing at least as much as they do leading, and must learn to stand back from the fray. Penny Hughes' comments on becoming the commercial director of Coca-Cola and Schweppes Beverages in the UK are instructive here. She relates how at the age of thirty she was trusted with a much bigger job than she had been accustomed to, with a team of more than 1,300 people and a budget of £650 million. Says Hughes: 'I really had to stop doing and begin coaching and influencing, creating the environment and the organizational structure to make the thing work. It was quite tough because I love actually seeing the results of things I do and I love "playing" in the game, being on the pitch.'[78] Hughes' case is interesting not just because she consciously recognized the need to switch roles, but because she evidently succeeded, and a few years later was appointed president of Coca-Cola in the UK.

Learning Points for Leaders

In many ways organizations are like political arenas, and their leaders prominent politicians. Great leaders are intensely aware of the power resources at their disposal and are able to exploit them with sensitivity and skill. To be fully effective in this dimension of leadership means being a despot, manipulator, conductor and empowerer as and when required. The key to success is not to be captured by a single role, but to be flexible and adaptable. For example, allowing oneself to be wholly seduced by the role of the despot might be psychologically satisfying, but it can also be self-defeating, as Victor Posner discovered. The best power-brokers have profound self-understanding and are insightful analysers of their subordinates' motives. The most admirable leaders are those who, like Ken Iverson and Sir John Harvey-Jones, order, cajole, persuade, discuss and empower with equal facility in appropriate circumstances.

If this chapter has been in any way provocative perhaps it is in the importance accredited to despotic and manipulative roles. There are leaders who will protest that they have little need to play the role of the despot, and that manipulation has too many negative connotations to be a useful description of what they do. Objections of this ilk are either disingenuous or naive. In *The Prince* Niccolo Machiavelli[79] famously observed 'that a man who wants to act virtuously in every way necessarily comes to grief among so many who are not virtuous', and that therefore 'if a prince wants to maintain his rule he must learn how not to be virtuous'. While Machiavelli may have overstated his case, he has a good point. There are people who respond more positively to autocrats than to coaches, and there are high-threat business situations where coercion rather than request is needed to get things done quickly. Vested interests may often threaten to undermine rational decision making, thus calling for behind-the-scenes manipulation by leaders. Few individuals other than the leader have the long-term good of an organization as their over-riding goal. Effective power-brokers will therefore tend to be not just charismatic conductors and sensitive empowerers, but calculating despots and savvy manipulators as well.

Brokering power is the dimension of leadership that comes most naturally to most leaders. Juggling the different roles effectively, however, is less common. There are relatively few leaders who, like Ross Perot, can be trusting and empowering of subordinates, comfortable with cooperation and teamwork, but also autocratic when required.[80] Not every business leader can, like Alfred Sloan, coax and cajole, and manipulate and placate with the subtlety and sensitivity required to build a successful corporation.[81] Fewer still can engage and disengage from these different roles in a mature and confidence-inspiring manner. The charge once levelled against John DeLorean that 'He sheds personalities as a snake sheds its skin'[82] is one that should obviously be avoided. To do so requires that the leader be supremely at ease with him or herself and in the company of others. It means being able to integrate the different power-broking roles into one's personality to create a seamless web of nuanced role-change as and when circumstances dictate.

Of course, a leader can only broker power effectively if conditions permit it. Chief among these conditions are the talents and ambitions of their subordinates. Effective power-brokers are shrewd assessors of the merits and abilities of others, and able to deploy power to good effect in part because they place appropriate subordinates in appropriate positions. An excellent example here is the expatriate Scotsman Andrew Carnegie, who developed a dominating interest in the US iron and steel industry in the nineteenth century. An eminent manufacturer once said of him, 'He exceeded anyone I ever knew in his ability to pick a man from one place and put him in another with the maximum effect.' Carnegie himself explained his talent by claiming that it stemmed from a realization that 'You must capture and keep the heart of the original and able man before his brain can do its best.'[83]

It is during periods of intense change that the multiple roles of the power-broker are most required. Gerhard Schulmeyer's performance in transforming the culture at Siemens Nixdorf Informationsysteme (SNI) is an object lesson here. In just four years (between 1994 and 1998), Schulmeyer reformed SNI from a serious loss-maker into the largest European player in data processing and the continent's number two in software services and mainframes. He did this by instating a radical programme of change on the corporation designed to make it an entrepreneurial 'ideas factory' focused on customers. He initiated a series of meetings in which he listened to employees, explained the difficulties the organization was facing, and then empowered key opinion-formers within the organization to help create the future. Emotional buy-in from the workforce was manipulated through the introduction of a matrix structure which decentralized activities to local business unit entrepreneurs. It was reinforced by making individual workers (in consultation with managers) responsible for constant improvements to processes, which also helped promote a virtuous circle of success. Behind it all stood Schulmeyer, the architect and conductor of this vast and complicated plan for sustainable culture change.[84]

A generation earlier Konosuke Matsushita, founder of Matsushita Electric Industrial (MEI), developed a vast multibillion dollar corporate on the strength of his power-broking finesse. At one extreme, when he detected incompetence, he yelled at his key executives, 'occasionally becoming so angry that his face would turn a deep red'.[85] Despotism was, however, mixed with a generous blend of the conductor's charm and guile. Rather than bully his divisional heads he most often queried, listened and counselled, asking them, 'How are you? Are there any problems? Have you considered this idea?' Manipulation too was evident in many guises: employees were required to recite company mottos and the company song, and managers at all levels were inculcated with the Matsushita philosophy of profit through service. Perhaps most importantly of all, Matsushita grew MEI through the empowerment of the various divisions, and the trust he placed in senior managers. A classic epic hero who rose from humble origins, Matsushita's special talent was in successfully harnessing the power-broking dimension of leadership.

To conclude, then, effective leaders are shrewd power-brokers. This is the dimension of leadership most readily recognized by leaders themselves. Yet this does not mean that it is easier to succeed in this dimension than any other. Self-reflection and careful analysis of how you handle difficult people and complex situations will help reveal to you your strengths and weaknesses. If you harbour doubts regarding your abilities, then there are many 'how to' (negotiate, deal with people, resolve conflict situations, etc.) seminars, conferences and workshops available to you, which may be of assistance. To improve in this dimension of leadership, however, your first step might valuably be to reflect on these critical questions:

- *As a Despot.* Are you unafraid to let others know when they are underperforming, and to tell them in straight, no-nonsense terms? Do you effectively employ your strength of will to impress others and reinforce your authority? Do others agree that you can be coercive and dictatorial, but in ways which tend to benefit your organization?

- *As a Manipulator.* Are you able to get others to do the things you want them to do while retaining their respect? Can you read the intentions of others and predict their behaviours, and then use this information for your advantage? Are you the unseen hand that guides your organization's activities?

- *As a Conductor.* Do you think of yourself as working with people to accomplish organizational goals? Are you a sensitive coordinator of people and activities who generally manages to achieve balance and harmony? Do your subordinates think of you as a talented consensus-builder, who listens, mentors, and moulds?

- *As an Empowerer.* Do you effectively delegate authority to reliable individuals right down the chain of command? Are you a convinced facilitator of others, secure in your knowledge that organizational success depends on involving your subordinates? Do your followers agree that you allow them to develop and have sufficient self-restraint to permit them to do their jobs without interference?

Lord Weinstock

Andy Grove

Indira Gandhi

Cecil Rhodes

Six

Leader as Ambassador

The effectiveness of his group will be very largely determined by the way the leader performs his role as ambassador. (Charles Handy)[1]

OPERATING A BUSINESS while the Japanese occupied Korea was no easy task for Chung Ju Yung. Despite many restrictions, Yung nevertheless fostered a cordial relationship with the Japanese, and developed a profitable line repairing their cars. Later, when the Japanese had been expelled from Korea and the Americans took over, Yung embraced them warmly, won many lucrative construction contracts, and thrived. Later still, as Korean independence blossomed, Yung courted good relations with Korea's leader, Chung-hee Park. Hyundai's rapid expansion of its operations into the Middle East and Europe also had much to do with the effective ambassadorial talents of Yung and his senior management team. Within Korea itself the success of Hyundai was intimately tied to the wrangling, bribery and influence-peddling – all norms of the Korean construction industry at the time – of which Yung was an impressive exponent.[2] In short, Chung Ju Yung grew Hyundai into a hugely successful Korean conglomerate largely because of his ambassadorial skills.

The point is that organizations are not closed systems. All firms are subject to government legislation, prone to swings in public opinion regarding the utility of their products and services, and susceptible to the vicissitudes of markets. Leaders need a sophisticated understanding of the extent to which the health of their companies is dependent on such externalities. They also need to interface effectively with significant individuals and institutions on behalf of their organizations. Leaders need often to build and maintain relationships, acquire and disseminate information, and negotiate deals. In short, corporate leaders must be their organizations' principal ambassadors.

A key task of the leader as ambassador is to establish a positive public profile for their organization, sometimes referred to as 'legitimacy'. As Louis B. Lundborg of Bank of America has written, 'Legitimacy – the public perception that business is serving a societal need – is the charter under which business must operate in a democratic society. Without it, corporations will be strangled by legislation, regulation, or in the extreme, nationalization.'[3] There is considerable research to suggest that corporations that are widely thought of as benefiting society have far fewer problems securing access to resources and markets, and their environments tend to be less volatile and more predictable.[4] Little wonder, then, that Edmund W. Littlefield, as CEO of Utah International, once claimed that 'It is necessary to create a new level of business acceptance and legitimacy that is attuned to the socio-political demands.'[5] Such sentiments have been reiterated by B.F. Biaggini, of Southern Pacific Company, who argued that it was only by building good relations with the entire public that business could regain 'a proper measure of total credibility'.[6]

The boundary-spanning roles of corporate leaders have, of course, been widely commented upon, not least by astute business leaders themselves. John Neill, head of the world renowned auto parts supplier Unipart, has publicly committed himself to building relationships with dealers, politicians, other business people and the media.[7] Penny Hughes, ex-president of Coca-Cola UK, has commented that 'As the world grows smaller and the relationships with preferred suppliers and customers stronger, it is critically important to know how to influence and encourage relationships across the business.'[8] Playing the ambassadorial role with real flair, however, entails more than just sensitivity to external environmental factors and relationship building. It means achieving a more substantial stature in society. As the ex-CEO of General Motors, Thomas A. Murphy, has said: '. . . the inescapable fact is that today's chief executive officer, too, must be a public figure. He must be ready to assume all of the risk and all of the difficulties that up-front visibility entails . . . [I]t is the individual – the flesh-and-blood man who exhibits such qualities himself – who must humanize the corporate image . . .'[9]

Rupert Murdoch is famous for having spent all his adult life restlessly flying around the world, forging relationships and building an international empire. But in attempting to build the most powerful media company in the world, by 1990 Murdoch had massively overstretched his News Corporation. He was forced to work with Citibank in a desperate attempt to reschedule $7.6 billion of debt and restructure the company. Faced with the daunting prospect of persuading 146 different creditors to give him breathing space, Murdoch began a swift series of global 'roadshows'. It was then that his ambassadorial prowess was put to possibly its greatest test. While much helped by his highly professional team, Murdoch's own impressive relationship-building performances were crucial. Speaking with quiet persuasiveness about his business, he was instrumental in saving his own skin. Looking back at a time when Murdoch again seems all-powerful, it is hard to believe that News Corporation, and all Murdoch had worked so hard for, had teetered on the brink of collapse.[10]

The business leader's ambassadorial roles are not restricted to external liaison work. The leader also acts as a sort of internal ambassador, collecting information from, and disseminating information to, more junior employees. In addition, organizational leaders must develop a rapport with their workforce, even if it is one that is based largely on their reputation rather than personal contact. More than this, as the management guru Charles Handy has said, the role of the leader as ambassador is to help the organization by filtering out stresses and strains, so facilitating the process of work.[11] A similar point is made by the US Marine Corps Manual, which directs leaders to act 'as a *buffer* to protect subordinates'. In these ways leaders can help to shape a more coherent and consistent organizational identity. Indeed, those leaders, such as Lord Weinstock of GEC, who are unable to fulfil this role effectively, often evolve organizations in which there prevails an unhealthy climate of fear.[12]

Elizabeth Dole, ex-senior civil servant and president of the

American Red Cross, is a good example of a leader who has excelled in her ambassadorial roles. According to one biographer she has been practising networking since childhood, and has made getting to know other people with similar interests an important part of her professional life. It was, in part, Dole's ambassadorial skills that persuaded President Reagan to appoint her head of the White House Office of Public Liaison, a job that involved trying to 'sell' the president's policies to special interest groups. She was widely regarded as having a remarkable ability to build bridges with critical constituencies, gather opinions, and then feed them into decision-making processes in the White House. Reagan was so impressed he appointed her Secretary of Transportation, a Cabinet post, where she championed a range of car and air safety measures. Later on President Bush appointed her Secretary of Labor, giving her charge of a department with 18,500 employees and a $31 billion budget. She resigned on 24 October 1990, and in 1991 joined the American Red Cross where she believed her talents could do most good.[13]

Failure to engage in internal ambassadorial duties can have career limiting consequences. For example, Ken Iverson, boss of the steel company Nucor, tells a parable about an outstanding individual with an advanced degree in metallurgy, and an MBA, who was recruited into the organization. His prospects for advancement looked outstanding. He did not last long, however, when he surrounded himself with lieutenants whose primary function was to insulate him from his employees.[14] This individual could have learned a great deal from George C. Marshall, who gave his name to the US plan for reconstruction in Europe after the Second World War, and who travelled around the country and the world to see officers and front-line soldiers in the belief that one should prevail by cultivating respect, not by engendering fear.[15] He could also have learned much from the example of Thomas Watson Jr, son of the founder of IBM and later himself chairman. Watson Jr was so good at playing the ambassadorial role on behalf of IBM that President Carter made him America's ambassador to Moscow.[16]

In this chapter I identify four roles which leaders as ambassadors play. Ambassadors must be

- *relationship builders*, skilled in forging and maintaining external relationships with constituencies such as politicians, bankers and the general public.
- *salespeople*, who not only court good relations with customers but are deal-makers too.
- *melders*, who operate internally within their own organizations, cohering and integrating them, and creating corporate character.
- *information acquisitors*, highly sensitive to their environments, able to absorb significant information which is then relayed to others in their organizations, and which informs corporate strategies.

Leader as Relationship Builder

Building and maintaining relationships with stakeholders is a key leadership role. John D. Rockefeller's huge success owed much to his ability to make friends when face to face with people. Says one biographer, 'He went into the field to win friends for his business and won them. He went to bankers to explain his firm's need for funds and won loans.'[17] More recently, corporate leaders, such as Tiny Rowland of Lonrho and the Australian entrepreneur Alan Bond, constructed vast empires largely on the basis of their relationship-building skills.

As Lundborg, the former CEO of Bank of America, has pointed out, '. . . even the most internal concerns, when examined, prove to be largely a response and reaction to changes in the environment and climate in which today's corporation is operating'.[18] In such a world, business leaders need to forge external networks of allies and sympathizers on whom they can rely for support, and through whom they can exercise influence. This is why, in his efforts to extend Coca-Cola's reach into Eastern Europe in the early 1990s, Roberto Goizueta paid visits to both the Czech Prime Minister, Vaclav Klaus, and the Polish Prime Minister, Hanna Suchocka. Just two weeks after his trip to Poland in the Spring of 1993, the Poles agreed to Coca-Cola being sold in their country for the first time, vividly illustrating the potential pay-offs of high-level relationship building.[19]

Some of the most important external interfacing that leaders of large corporations must engage in is with elected government officials and their civil servants. Ex-CEO of General Electric, Reginald H. Jones, believed that corporate leaders had to 'participate actively in the formation of public policy affecting business', and claimed that he personally devoted half of his available time to this 'either in preparation or in actual spokesmanship and personal representation in Washington'. According to James R. Shepley, the ex-President of Time Inc., 'The Battle of Washington is as important to the CEO as anything on his agenda – personnel, finance, litigation, production, marketing – you name it.'[20] The importance of political links is certainly not a uniquely American phenomenon. In the UK, the significance of senior political contacts is exemplified by James Hanson. Hanson grew Hanson Trust into an international conglomerate while cultivating friendships with Prime Ministers such as Harold Wilson and Margaret Thatcher. Such was the strength of his influence with Thatcher that she made him a lord in 1983.[21] Similarly, the success of Sir Colin Marshall and Lord King in securing British Airways as a business had much to do with their shrewd international diplomacy, and strong links with Margaret Thatcher's government.

One of the most impressive relationship-building corporate ambassadors of our age is Tiny Rowland, who grew Lonrho into an 800 company conglomerate with 160,000 employees spread over 82 countries. Tiny purchased and developed enormously profitable companies in the often troubled African continent with the assistance of various heads of state whose friendship he assiduously cultivated. It was on the strength of his relationships with the politically influential that when his company's assets in Tanzania and Zaire were nationalized, they were then returned. Tiny's love of his roving ambassadorial role, and the strength of his influence in Africa, saw him assist in bringing Israel and Egypt together to sign the Camp David Agreement, and help to sustain Kenneth Kaunda in power in Zambia. Reciprocally, political contacts of this exalted kind, presented in public as efforts to bring peace and prosperity to Africa, reputedly bolstered his business affairs.[22,23]

Further examples of individuals who have relied heavily on

networks of political friends to grow and sustain their businesses are legion. The Turkish Cypriot Asil Nadir was a small-time businessman involved in the UK clothes industry until the Turkish Cypriot government asked him to help market their citrus fruit abroad.[24] This was the big break that allowed him to build Polly Peck into a hugely profitable international corporation. The now disgraced media tycoon Robert Maxwell developed and protected his empire for so long through personal contacts with world and national leaders ranging from Deng Xiaoping, President Reagan and Mikhail Gorbachev, to the King of Spain, and the presidents of France and Portugal.[25] The importance of low-level political contacts can also be considerable. In the US, Wayne Huizenga, together with his partner Dean Buntrock, built Waste Management by acquisition of smaller waste companies into a billion dollar (now a $10 billion) business. The US waste industry has frequently suffered from a bad press, and it was Huizenga's considerable ability to talk round local politicians worried about the effects of having a corporate giant involved in the waste business in their neighbourhood, that made Waste Management a success.

In addition to establishing personal relationships with politicians, many leaders have found that it pays dividends to establish a positive profile with the general public. Ross Perot had already disbursed millions of dollars to worthy causes and achieved celebrity status as a businessman before launching his presidential campaign.[26] The British public's sentimental attachment to the eccentric founder and owner of Virgin, Richard Branson, means that when his companies fail to deliver good service he is able to escape much of the blame. A particularly interesting case from the world of politics is that of the French general, De Gaulle, who during the Second World War found himself exiled in England following the German invasion of France. Needing to build relations with the Allies, he sought to gain leverage over his powerful patrons (the British and American governments) by manipulating their own publics against them. That he succeeded in gaining the affections of ordinary people in the UK and the US despite having no previous experience of either country, speaking at best rather stilted English, and in the face of systematic attempts by the governments of both countries to influence press coverage against him, is testament to his ambassadorial talents.[27]

In developing a rapport with the public, business leaders are pivotally dependent on journalists and the mass media. De Gaulle was greatly assisted in his efforts to establish himself as the leader of the French in exile by influential friends in the British and American press. Similarly, some of the most effective and insightful corporate leaders have invested great efforts in courting the media. For instance, Marconi went out of his way to cultivate good relations with newspaper journalists. On one occasion, in January 1898, he was in Bournemouth when a heavy snowstorm hit the south coast of England, bringing down telegraph lines. Newspaper men there were much concerned because of their inability to communicate news of the dying William Ewart Gladstone to London. Hearing of the reporters' problem, Marconi sent their messages by wireless to the Isle of Wight, where they could be communicated to London by telegraph. Says one commentator, 'The incident was widely reported, not only giving Marconi some excellent publicity but making some good friends for him in the newspaper world.'[28]

Corporate leaders must also often invest considerable resources in evolving good relations with those who head important financial institutions. Many fledgling entrepreneurs owe the early growth of their businesses to their abilities to charm, cajole and persuade bankers into lending them substantial sums. An excellent example of this is the US industrialist Henry Clay Frick, who prospered in partnership with the expatriate Scotsman Andrew Carnegie. At an early age Frick became interested in manufacturing coke (central to the manufacture of steel), and wanted to set up a company with fifty ovens. In 1871, needing finance, and at the age of just twenty-one, Frick approached Judge Thomas Mellon, a sharp-featured austere man, and a stickler for formality in business attire. Frick turned up unannounced but fortunately for him, immaculately dressed, and proceeded to talk Judge Mellon into a $10,000 loan, a large sum in those days. So impressed was the old judge that he sanctioned another $10,000 loan before the first was paid off or the ovens built. Not that the judge's confidence was unjustified, for

Frick was a millionaire by the age of thirty, and later expanded his coke operations to the point where he had a virtual monopoly on its production in the US.[29]

Alan Bond is a more recent (and transient) example of an individual with an amazing ability to charm bankers into financing his deals. For example, at the time he bid $36 million for a stake in Burmagh Oil, Bond not only did not have the money but seemingly had no prospect of raising it. Massively in debt in Australia, and with no Australian financial institution willing to lend him more, Bond flew out to China where he negotiated a new source of finance from the Hong Kong & Shanghai Bank. He then persuaded other international banks to take part in a consortium to raise another $600 million. The chief executive of the Hong Kong & Shanghai Bank, Michael Sandberg, was so impressed by Alan Bond that he personally played a large role in the promotion of him as a reputable international businessman. Bond proceeded to build a mighty empire which reached its zenith around June 1988 when the Bond Corporation reported total assets of $9 billion. But it was an empire built on enormous amounts of what was eventually unsustainable debt, and the smooth-talking Bond and his corporation soon crashed.[30]

Ambassadorial relationship building is a particularly vital role for corporate leaders seeking to grow their businesses. While Philip Smith founded the company that became Harcourt General, it was his son Richard Smith who did much to develop the corporation, negotiating most of the crucial shopping centre leases himself.[31] Wayne Huizenga not only helped to grow Waste Management, but then went on to develop the Blockbuster Video rental chain by making 110 deals – buying video chains, music stores and Hollywood studios – in just seven years. Said one colleague, 'Wayne is a relationship guy . . . He's great at setting up an acquisition. He sets it up like an artist sets up a painting.'[32] Mike Markkula used his relationship-building skills to make the Apple computer company a success and turn Steve Wozniak and Steve Jobs into high-tech heroes. Before Markkula there was no US distribution system for personal computers. But as one of Silicon Valley's Wise Men, with an intimate knowledge of venture capitalists and an extensive array of corporate friends, Markkula, together with a sales vice president, initiated the country-wide network of computer dealers (and independents who developed Apple-related products) that helped the company to grow so quickly. The critical importance of this network to the success of Apple was thrown into relief much later on when things started to go wrong, and the third party companies who developed Apple software and peripherals abandoned them to work with IBM.

The benefits of playing the relationship-building role with finesse are, perhaps, best illustrated by a couple of relationship-building disasters. In 1991, with GE's Electrical Distribution and Control (ED&C) division in trouble, a mid-ranking but fast-track executive persuaded the Japanese corporation Mitsubishi to consider merging its ED&C businesses with those of GE. The result would be a dominating world player with annual sales of $3.5 billion. Extensive strategic analysis suggested that the deal made good financial sense, and also opened up the possibility of further lucrative GE-Mitsubishi alliances. Both sides agreed to settle the deal over a five-month period, and a get-acquainted meeting was set up between Jack Welch of GE and Moriya Shiiki of Mitsubishi in September 1991. It was designed as a protocol meeting in which both leaders would exchange pleasantries and pronounce their mutual respect and admiration.

Things started well, but then Welch said (through an interpreter) '. . . let's not let the bureaucracies get in the way. Let's agree to do this deal right now.' This push for an immediate commitment was not only alien to Japanese business culture, but contravened the prior agreement to a five-month time scale. Says one commentator, 'Shiiki and the Mitsubishi contingent recoiled, pressing their spines to the back of their chairs.' Things went from bad to worse when Shiiki insisted that he would have to tell Westinghouse, with whom Mitsubishi had a long-standing relationship, of its intentions with regard to GE. Welch was appalled, misread classic traditional Japanese caution for lack of inclination to carry the deal through, and considered that he had been embarrassed by the meeting. Negotiations broke down, and the subordinate who had helped put the Mitsubishi deal together for GE, plus another more senior executive, were subsequently fired.[33]

Even the most naturally gifted of relationship builders can make catastrophic mistakes. For example, in attempting to purchase Blockbuster's biggest competitor in the US, Major Video, Huizenga called a meeting with the Major Video franchisees in Dallas. The idea was to sell them on the idea that a takeover would be good for all. Huizenga bombed. The Major Video franchisees had always looked upon Blockbuster as the enemy, and needed to be sweet-talked rather than goaded. Huizenga, however, made a pitch which focused on Blockbuster's superior system and support, meaning that he was not going to budge on conversion costs, higher royalty rates, stricter development schedules or other requirements. The franchisees felt they were being coerced into not only conceding, but capitulating, leading to the reaction, 'Who were these arrogant s.o.b.s anyway?' The result was that lawsuits were filed by some franchisees which delayed the Blockbuster deal going through. And while the deal was eventually realized, it was with additional legal costs that might have been avoidable. Huizenga had mis-assessed the situation – this was not just a business deal for franchisees, but an emotional calculation. In fact, says one commentator, the 'legacy is still so bitter that many former Major Video, now Blockbuster franchisees, won't discuss Huizenga or that time period'.[34]

In summary, it is clear that leaders of organizations need, as William S. Sneath, the ex-CEO of Union Carbide, has said, to spend a 'good bit of time dealing with outside activities'.[35] What is more, these external relations need to be handled astutely and with sensitivity. The Andrew Carnegie philosophy of demanding the complete surrender of others to his demands might have been highly successful in the late nineteenth century,[36] but now seems somewhat old-fashioned. For many modern leaders it is better, perhaps, to strive for the epithet awarded to Lord Hanson, who in one biography is described as 'the consummate politician'.[37] As such diverse examples as Marconi and Frick in the late nineteenth century and Goizueta and Tiny Rowland in the late twentieth century show, shrewd ambassadorial relationship building is a key component of effective corporate leadership.

Leader as Salesperson

When President Johnson promoted Medicaid after the death of JFK, suddenly US states needed to process vast numbers of medical claims. After all, Medicaid was now relevant to one in six Americans. Ross Perot's staff at EDS soon invented an efficient computer programme to process these claims and payments. Mindful of the huge business opportunity that presented itself, Perot went out on the road, selling EDS as if it were a new wonder drug that could cure the benefits claims blues. Within twelve months he won contracts for running Medicaid billing operations in eleven states, and soon after signed up another thirteen. With twenty-three state Medicaid contracts under his belt, EDS had achieved its first major breakthrough.[38] Ross Perot, like many other admirable business leaders, proved himself a highly proficient salesman. If there is a lesson for us here, it is that excellent ambassadors do not merely forge strong relationships, they are also often their company's most effective salesperson.

Convincing salespeople need a deeply felt conviction that customers matter. Eminent corporate leaders such as Jack Welch, Lawrence Bossidy and John Connelly have all realized this, and spoken publicly about their role as salesmen. Looking to the future, and his likely successor, Jack Welch at GE has stated that 'Anyone who is too inwardly focused, who doesn't cherish customers . . . isn't going to make it.'[39] When, in 1991, Lawrence A. Bossidy became chairman and CEO of AlliedSignal, he immediately made strenuous efforts to talk to customers, encouraging them to come forward with problems and issues for discussion. Says Bossidy, 'I made an effort to talk to customers early on, but that's something you need to do all the time.' John Connelly saved Crown Cork and Seal Company from bankruptcy in 1957, and a story told by one visitor to the company illustrates one part of how he did it. According to this visitor, he was in Connelly's office when a complaint came through from the manager of a Florida citrus packing plant. Connelly assured him the problem would be taken care of immediately, then casually remarked that he planned to be in Florida the next day. Would the plant manager join him for dinner? He would indeed. As Crown's president put the telephone down, the visitor mentioned that he had not realized Connelly was planning to go to Florida. 'Neither did I,' confessed Connelly, 'until I began talking.'[40]

The most skilled ambassadorial salespeople are those who open up totally new markets. Akio Morita, one of the founders of the Japanese corporation Sony, is a shining example. In the mid-1950s Sony was a minnow of a company with almost zero international sales or marketing expertise. At this time, export-oriented Japanese companies relied on giant trading companies to represent them in what were perceived to be fantastically difficult foreign markets. Says Morita, 'I think it is ironic that American businessmen now complain about our complex Japanese distribution system, because when I was first planning to export to the United States I was astonished and frustrated by the complexity of marketing in America.' Not that this perturbed him, and armed with samples of Sony's first transistor radio he went to New York and made the rounds of possible retailers. Morita soon realized that the US was a ready market for Sony products, but that to be really successful he needed a better understanding of the American way of life. As Morita, reflecting on his early experiences, has said, 'To make the company name more common in the US was one thing; to understand Americans would be more difficult.'[41] Sony's incredible success worldwide indicates that this understanding of alien cultures has been more than adequately achieved.

At about the same time that Morita and Sony were learning how to penetrate the US market for consumer electronics, the French couturier Pierre Cardin was busy promoting his work in Japan. Cardin realized at an early stage that in order to turn his name into a designer brand he would have to be a very public salesman on his own behalf. Typical of how he did it was his trip to Japan in 1957, when he spent six weeks travelling with his entourage between Tokyo, Osaka and Kyoto. With characteristic panache he staged a sparkling fashion show at Tokyo's fashion school, Bunka. It was the first time that a French couturier had come to Japan with a collection, and he created a sensation. Hardly surprising, then, that Cardin became the first French fashion designer to earn Japanese loyalty and awareness. Equally cognizant of the importance of the US market, in 1958 Cardin engaged in an eight-city tour of America. Here Cardin played his role as the fey couturier to perfection, endearing himself to the American public with claims such as 'I think this tour will help me get better acquainted with the American woman . . . She is an inspiring creature.'[42]

One of the most outstanding of all those corporate leaders who have cultivated new markets is Richard Warren Sears, the co-founder of the legendary mail order company. As a young man he purchased watches from wholesalers and sold them on to agents at a healthy profit. From watch sales he moved into the watch repairs business, employing a skilled watch repairer by the name of Alvah Curtis Roebuck. Sears' good relations with the wholesalers allowed him to expand operations into Canada, and then to add other products to his business repertoire – diamonds, watch chains and jewellery. In 1891 Sears issued his first catalogue. In 1893 the 'Sears, Roebuck and Company' name first appeared, heralding a new 196 page catalogue. By the Spring of 1894 it became a 507 page book. The product lines were expanding all the time, and Sears' first large department store was opened in Chicago in 1895. Sales rose year on year, even through the depression, and by 1906 gross sales were $50,861,763. Sears' remarkable business acumen and foresight are aptly described in one biography like this:

> It may have been true that rural folk needed a system of distribution like Sears's; but making them realize that they needed it was something else. The great task was to win their confidence in numbers and to manage to retain that confidence by keeping enough customers satisfied to offset the number who were dissatisfied. Sears the man was perfectly equipped for the job. His spellbinding advertisements exerted a telling effect on farm readers. His compelling messages pulled the reader into his copy and kept that reader's attention to the end. That end was usually the dispatching of an order to Richard Sears for merchandise.[43]

The best leaders are not just great strategic salespeople, they are also persuasive one-on-one deal-makers. Masayoshi, founder and

CEO of the Japanese company Softbank, and Richard Branson of Virgin, have both been successful because of their salesmanship skills. Masayoshi succeeded by first signing up manufacturers of software, and then persuading the president of Joshin Denki (the third largest home electronics dealer in Japan), to give him an exclusive contract to supply software. Says Masayoshi,

> After I got Joshin Denki, I went to many other department stores and electronic shops. Have you seen Joshin Denki? They're the largest PC dealer in Japan now. And do you know why they are so successful? Because they have the software! And I have the exclusive on that software. So if you want to succeed, please talk to me. And they all opened accounts with me very quickly. In one month, I got most of the biggest dealers in Japan as my customers.[44]

Richard Branson is, in his own way, equally remarkable. Branson might still be unknown outside the UK if his personal negotiating style had not impressed American buyers in the late 1970s and early 1980s. According to one biographer, to US music executives 'more accustomed to the slick, desk-pounding, hustling and screaming school of salesmanship, Branson's gauche, schoolboy manner and his abashed confessions that "actually, I'm not sure who produced this one" proved appealing . . .'[45]

Not all big business leaders are comfortable and competent playing the role of the ambassadorial salesperson. Andy Grove of Intel, despite many virtues, is legendarily poor in this respect. Grove abhors the fast cars, Dom Perignon, and expense-account entertaining style of doing business. According to one analyst, Grove's sales instinct is to visit a customer, put his product on the table, state the unit price for orders of 10,000, and if the customer is not interested then not to waste time arguing but pack up and move on to the next call. A story that exemplifies this approach tells of the time that an Intel team met a major potential client in a restaurant to massage his ego and convince him that Intel valued his custom. Atypically, Grove arrived late, and when he did get there launched immediately into an interrogation, 'utterly oblivious to the human subtleties of the situation'. Predictably, the Intel team came away from the meeting empty-handed. Fortunately for Intel, they had a particularly talented sales team working under Ed Gelbach, and Grove's lack of diplomacy has not proved too costly or damaging.[46]

Salesmanship skills are just as important to politicians as they are to corporate leaders. It is not just products and services but ideas and policies that need to be sold in the global political marketplace. A recent example of this was Tony Blair's efforts to set out a new doctrine of 'international community'. Taking the initiative he flew out to America for a NATO summit in April 1999, arriving well before any other national leader. He proceeded to give a lecture in Chicago outlining his views, and then appeared in a succession of prestigious television shows – NBC's 'Today', CNN's 'Larry King Live', and NBC's 'Meet the Press' – to reinforce his message. According to one journalist, Blair made such excellent use of his presentational skills that 'he managed this weekend to fill the gap created on the international stage by the relative eclipse of post-impeachment Clinton'.[47]

In summary, we can say that for those able to play the role of the ambassadorial salesperson, the benefits can be immense. DeLorean charmed and connived the UK government into giving him a package worth an estimated \$160 million to set up his automotive company in Northern Ireland after just forty-five days of negotiations.[48] In a different context, Eisenhower, as supreme commander of NATO, did such an admirable job as public salesman of the alliance to US politicians and the public, that it strengthened his political hand. And while, as the case of Andy Grove proves, not all leaders are effective salespeople, skilled commercial practitioners of salesmanship have – as leaders as diverse as Perot, Sears and Cardin illustrate – a significant edge.

Leader as Melder

Especially in big, spatially dispersed organizations, leaders need to take on the role of a sort of internal ambassador on behalf of the board. The role of the leader as melder is to forge an empathic relationship with ordinary employees, to be sensitive to their views while attempting to shape them through various information disseminating fora. Percy Barnevik of ABB speaks to 5,000 of his employees every year.[49] Jan Carlzon, when head of SAS, made communicating with employees a top priority. During his first year at the helm he claims to have 'spent exactly half of my working hours "out in the field" talking to SAS people'.[50] Farmland Industries, which is the thirty-fourth largest food company in the world, is owned by 1,650 member cooperatives representing 250,000 farm families in twenty-two US states. It therefore presents particularly difficult coherence problems. No wonder then that its CEO, Harry Cleberg, spends about 200 days a year meeting with cooperative members and Farmland employees: his purpose in these trips is getting to know the people and listening.[51]

As an intra-organizational ambassador, the role of the leader is primarily to cohere the company by creating a consistent corporate identity. A major part of this involves being visible to ordinary employees. As James L. Ferguson, ex-CEO of General Foods Corporation, has said: 'If the first job of the chief executive is to see that the corporate identity and direction are established and understood, the second is to take the lead in defining the obligations that emanate from that and to spark the action necessary to meet those obligations.'[52] For example, J.W. Marriott Jr of Marriott Hotels clocks up 150,000 air miles a year visiting Marriott locations. Says Marriott, 'I want our associates to know that there really *is* a guy named Marriott who cares about them, even if he can only drop by every so often to personally tell them so. I also want to show our team in the field that I value their work enough to take the time to check it out.'[53] While the Marriott organization is particularly highly dispersed, even leaders responsible for just one factory cannot afford to remain invisible to their staff.

Pierre du Pont helped to form the vast consolidated Du Pont Powder Company controlled by members of his extended family, and then did more than anyone to keep it from falling apart. Family loyalties and traditions were vital concerns to Pierre, and he was always sensitive to the feelings and prejudices of his family members. He worked hard to keep the many different branches of the family informed, and gave many of them real or nominal jobs.

In return, they permitted him and his senior executive team to exercise real decision-making authority in all their best interests. Valuable non-family members were incorporated into the company through stock and pension plans. For more than a decade his efforts as melder were successful, though in the end not even Pierre could prevent a disastrous family split.[54]

One reason why Ken Iverson of Nucor claims to have been so successful is that he has always kept in touch with the people in the plants he runs. By making managing by walking around a priority he says, 'I always knew what people thought. I had a strong sense of who they were, what they could do, and what they cared about. They knew the same things about me. I can't imagine staking my success on a group of people and *not* knowing them. It would be like trying to fly a plane with one wing.'[55] Furthermore, by being visible and appearing interested, the leader can bolster the morale of those they direct. For instance, on Christmas Day during Desert Shield, while preparing for Desert Storm, General Norman Schwarzkopf made a point of going down to the war room and shaking hands with every officer and enlisted person on duty. He then went to two separate encampments and shook hands with everyone he saw. Says Schwarzkopf:

> Next I went out to Escan Village where there were three huge mess halls in tents. At the first a long line of troops stretched out the entryway. I shook hands with everyone in the line, went behind the serving counter to greet the cooks and helpers, and worked my way through the mess hall, hitting every table, wishing everyone Merry Christmas. Then I went into the second and third dining facilities and did the same thing. I came back to the first mess tent and repeated the exercise, because by this time there was an entirely new set of faces. Then I sat down with some of the troops and had my dinner. In the course of four hours, I must have shaken four thousand hands.[56]

Engaging in internal ambassadorial duties also allows a leader to defuse those tensions which inevitably develop within any organization. Sometimes this means accepting that you will be a target for criticism as well as adulation. Iacocca remembers a time during 1980 when Chrysler workers were becoming increasingly agitated because their terms and conditions of employment were so much worse than those at Ford and GM. Says Iacocca, 'I gave them my pitch, and they hooted and hollered, and some of them applauded and some of them booed.'[57]

Key to a leader's efforts to meld an organization, is the ability to communicate effectively at all levels. Often, good leaders combine listening to others with attempts to shape their subordinates' understanding of what the organization is and should be, its strengths and opportunities for improvement, its strategies, and future challenges. Michael Dell, founder and CEO of the US company Dell Computer, likes to roam around his organization asking questions. He also spends time ensuring that employees have a clear understanding 'of what our strategy is and where the company is headed'.[58] Sir John Egan, who was chairman and chief executive of Jaguar cars before becoming chief executive of British Airports Authority (BAA), seeks to meld BAA by going 'round the company each year on "roadshows" to debate our mission with all our employees and to see whether managers are indeed managing in the way that the mission statement suggests they should'.[59]

The significance of this role has been singled out for special mention by countless leaders with impressive track records. When Anders Lindstrom became head of the diversified and overstretched Swedish-based tools and equipment manufacturer BAHCO, he 'travelled almost continuously . . . and when I wasn't meeting face-to-face I made a series of videos to report on the situation and lay down challenges'.[60] BAHCO was turned around within two years. Al Zeien, CEO of Gillette, a 34,000 employee company, says that he spends so much of his time travelling around his organization 'because that's where the people are. I travel because I want to be sure that people who are making the decision in, say, Argentina, have the same reference base as I do for the company. I want to make sure they are all using the same ground rules I would use. I want to see if they have the same objectives. I travel because you can only find these things out on the home ground.'[61]

Playing the internal ambassador and bringing coherence to a company is, perhaps, most important when the organization is in crisis. When appointed head of the nationalized British car company British Leyland, Michael Edwardes was faced with the daunting task of trying to accomplish massive restructuring, changing outmoded work methods, and initiating job losses as smoothly as possible. To make his views known in the face of what he saw as the disinformation and trouble-making of union representatives was no mean feat: to this end, he handed out summary proposals to workers in each of his thirty-six factories and offices, wrote to employees at home, placed newspaper advertisements, held face-to-face meetings with the workforce on the shop floor itself, and set up briefing groups.[62]

Lawrence Bossidy is another corporate leader appointed in difficult times. When Bossidy became chairman and CEO of AlliedSignal the corporation was haemorrhaging cash alarmingly. Intuitively understanding the need for employees to comprehend why it was necessary to address the problem, in his first sixty days he journeyed around the country talking direct to about 5,000 employees:

> I travelled all over the company with the same message and the same charts, over and over. Here's what I think is good about us. Here's what I'm worried about. Here's what we have to do about it. And if we don't fix the cash problem, none of us is going to be around. You can keep it simple: we're spending more than we're taking in. If you do that at home, there will be a day of reckoning . . .[63]

In summary, leaders are ambassadors not just on behalf of their organizations to external stakeholders but on behalf of senior executives to more junior employees. As such, their role is to mould organizational culture and identity by gathering and disseminating information, and motivating, and defusing tensions. In these ways, leaders promote coherence and consistency that, as Wayne Calloway, CEO of PepsiCo has said, can 'create a virtuous circle of behaviours that lead to "continuous improvement"'.[64] According to Calloway, what he is trying to do is to model integrity in order to generate honesty, and so confidence and trust. These in turn will, he argues, prompt creative risk-taking and problem-solving behaviours and improve the company's operations: success will lead to happiness and so back to integrity. Idealistic? Well, maybe. But a little immortalistic idealism, projected internally by a competent ambassadorial leader, may go a long way towards achieving an excellent organization.

Leader as Information Acquisitor

The leader's roles as relationship builder, salesperson and melder, afford plentiful opportunities to acquire valuable commercially relevant information. Some leaders, like Alfred Sloan of GM in the 1920s and early 1930s, use their ambassadorial time mostly to learn.[65] It has been said of Pierre du Pont that before acting he always tried to obtain the best possible information.[66] The iron and steel magnate Andrew Carnegie was a boss who was always prodding his subordinates for better quality information about his business, and progress reports on its operations.[67] Bill Gates is particularly noted for his in-depth industry knowledge, detailed memory, and his voracious reading capacity.[68] Even Lee Iacocca, who was renowned for shooting from the hip, once claimed that 'Whenever I've taken risks, it's been after satisfying myself that the research and the market studies supported my instincts. I may act on my intuition – but only if my hunches are supported by the facts.'[69]

Journeying around one's own organization permits the leader to put various aspects of its operations under the microscope. When J.W. Marriott Jr visits his Marriott hotels he gets down on the floor of the hotel rooms and checks under the beds. He not only opens drawers, switches on faucets, showers and lamps, but peeks in closets to see if there is an iron and ironing board and sufficient hangers. Neither are his visits limited to the public areas: the laundry, accounts rooms and kitchens are all inspected. Commenting on the value of such activities he asserts: 'I can't think of a single tour in all the years I've been on the road that didn't teach me something . . . Visiting Marriott locations year in and year out has also provided me with a strong knowledge base for making decisions.'[70] Much the same sentiments have been attributed to the ex-CEO of Coca-Cola, Roberto Goizueta, who spent a good deal of his time travelling between different parts of the far-flung Coca-Cola empire. As one commentator has described his job: 'During busy periods, he spent more than a third of his time on the road, a kind of soft-drink missionary carrying the Coca-Cola product and way of life to the farthest reaches of the globe.'[71]

Lord Weinstock joined the somewhat ailing UK engineering giant GEC in 1961 and assumed control in 1963. Amazed and frustrated by the complete lack of intelligible management information, he set about putting in place systems and structures that would provide him with the information he needed. From a situation in which operating units used to jot down any figures that seemed reasonable and pass them on to the board, Weinstock initiated a set of procedures with a hard-driving emphasis on managerial accountability and quantifiable performance. This centrally involved working out which set of ratios relating to sales, costs, stock-turn, debtors and margins would yield the most useful picture of what was happening in the company, and then insisting that the information needed to produce them was presented by each operating unit every month. Said Weinstock:

> This gives us [a] snapshot every month of each operating unit, expanded with a commentary by its management. It can be misleading if you are not told the truth, but generally it has worked. At the end of each month, for over thirty years, I have taken home two bags of these monthly reports to break the back of this rather onerous but necessary chore.[72]

Weinstock's healthy reliance on high quality management information combined with an emphasis on cost reduction and the stockpiling of cash and growth by acquisition, meant that within eight years of taking over at GEC he was in charge of the UK's largest industrial company with a labour force of nearly a quarter of a million.

Skilled leaders also garner useful information from their external contacts. When Allen Paschal of the Gale Group (which is part of Thomson) was asked about his strengths as a leader he replied: 'I can see the whole industry. And it's not magic; I listen to the customers pretty hard.'[73] In his search for new ideas Jack Welch says he likes to 'hop on an airplane and visit something like seven countries in fifteen days'.[74] For some leaders the search for information that can make a difference to their business verges on the obsessive. A classic example here is that of Robert Wood Johnson, the ex-president and CEO of the US corporate giant Johnson & Johnson. At the helm for thirty-one years, Johnson increased sales from $15.2m in 1932 to $462.4m in 1963. He was doubtless assisted by his compulsive need to know what was happening in the retail stores on which his business was so crucially dependent. Says one biographer, 'He'd spend hours in super-markets and drugstores, gauging how much shelf space his company had compared with the competition, how the products were moving, how they looked.'[75]

Ray Kroc, the man who constructed the vast McDonald's corporation, was fixated on having the right information at his disposal. His early career as a paper cup and milk-shake equipment salesman yielded him a vast knowledge of the restaurant industry in America. Armed with this information he was able to spot the McDonald brothers' winning formula for success and then further refine it into a phenomenally successful profit-generating corporate. Key to this process of refinement was calculated information. For example, all his hamburgers had to weigh 1.6 ounces, measure 3.875 inches in diameter, contain no more than 19% fat and be served in a 3.5 inch bun. In his restaurants, a hamburger, shake and french fries had to be served within fifty seconds.

Not that Kroc was just fixated with the micro-details of his restaurants. From an early stage he went out on the road identifying likely sites for new franchises, mostly at crossroads and busy neighbourhood intersections. As the company grew he took to the air in a rented plane, the better to identify new opportunities for his organization. Kroc was not merely a mass merchandiser with an eye for the main chance, but a shrewd and calculating businessman whose roving ambassadorial role helped elicit the information base that made McDonald's a success.[76]

Learning Points for Leaders
Great leaders are their organizations' most valuable ambassadors.

They realize that to survive and thrive their organizations need to be thought of as useful to society and therefore legitimate. They are people who understand the vital importance of forging, maintaining, and, where necessary, repairing relationships with crucial stakeholders. At their best, they are also skilled negotiators and deal-makers who directly add value to their firm's bottom line. Those who excel in this dimension of leadership are discerning absorbers of information which they then deploy to best effect. In some ways most significantly of all, they are people who can meld, integrate and cohere their organizations, building corporate identity and culture.

The roles of the leader as ambassador are crucial to the success of the modern corporation. As Michael Edwardes of the old British car company British Leyland has said, 'It is no longer sufficient for companies to concentrate on internal efficiency and merely to shelter as far as possible from any adverse influences in their external environment.'[77] His challenge to leaders 'to be outward-looking, to get in amongst these so-called external influences and try to bring about beneficial change' is one that all need to take up. The benefits of playing these ambassadorial roles well, both for the individual and his or her organization, are worth recapping. Asil Nadir's preoccupation with obtaining good information on the countries in which he did business facilitated the growth of his Polly Peck corporation worldwide.[78] It was Martin Luther King's skills and dedication as an ambassador for the cause of civil rights that raised civil rights issues to the top of the political agenda in the US in the 1960s. In 1963 alone, King made more than 350 speeches and travelled 275,000 miles.[79] And it is only because J.W. Marriott Jr is so much involved as an internal ambassador in his organization that strategic decisions can be made so quickly there.[80]

It is, perhaps, in the realm of international statesmanship that the importance of the ambassadorial dimension of leadership is most evident. The examples of Adenauer in post-war West Germany and Gorbachev in the old Soviet Union provide valuable lessons here. At the end of the Second World War Germany was a desert of ruins and guilt. In these inauspicious circumstances Alfred Adenauer, one of the few leading pre-war German politicians not to be tarnished by association with Hitler, or killed by him, became West Germany's Chancellor. He recognized that the economic and security interests of Western Europe depended on close co-operation between Germany, France, Belgium, Luxemburg, Holland and Britain. His Europeanism and democratic beliefs, combined with his impressive statesmanship, made him an ideal figure to rebuild relationships with the rest of Europe and the world. He was particularly adept in his dealings with America, which responded with massive inward investment in the form of the Marshall Plan.

Adenauer's ambassadorial prowess was such that the Allies which controlled West Germany agreed to the recreation of a sovereign German state far more quickly than might otherwise have occurred. His skills as an ambassador-leader were marked by his signing of the Peace Treaty between Germany and the three Western Powers and membership of NATO in 1955, the signing of the Treaty of Rome for the European Economic Communities in 1957, and that of the Franco-German Treaty in 1963. These agreements helped to fulfil his vision of a strong and peaceful Europe, and continue to ensure West European security today.[81]

A more recent example of a national leader excelling in the ambassadorial dimension of leadership is Mikhail Gorbachev. With his policies of *glasnost* (openness) and *perestroika* (recon-struction) having done much to alter, but little to cohere, the Soviet Union, Gorbachev recognized a need to build stronger relations with the Western democracies. His willingness to engage the traditional enemies of Russia was also prompted by a realization that, as he himself wrote, 'all countries are more interdependent than ever before'. Gorbachev's 1989/90 meetings with Prime Minister Thatcher, President Mitterand and Chancellor Kohl were all largely successful. It was his trips to America, however, that yielded the most tangible results. Indeed, at least one commentator has gone so far as to suggest that his talks with President Bush in June 1990 might come to be considered by future historians as the concluding act of the 'cold war'.[82]

To conclude, then, effective leaders are astute ambassadors. Excellence in this dimension of leadership requires a sophisticated understanding of the dependencies of organizations on their environments. To be even just a competent ambassador also means being a skilled and sensitive listener. As we shall see in the final chapter, these abilities require both maturity and wisdom. Some specific questions to reflect on when evaluating your competence in this dimension of leadership are:

- *As a Relationship Builder.* Do you make friends easily? Do people you do not know well nevertheless tend to like and to trust you? Have you developed good networks of friends and acquaintances on whom you can call for assistance and advice?

- *As a Salesperson.* Do you passionately believe that customers matter? Are you a persuasive one-to-one deal-maker? Do you have a track record of successfully courting new, and retaining existing, customers?

- *As a Melder.* Do you make a point of speaking and listening to large numbers of your subordinates? Have you made active and successful efforts to build and manage your organization's culture? Do your followers think of you as the person who brings coherence to your organization, and who gives it its individuality?

- *As an Information Acquisitor.* Are you able to absorb and understand large amounts of information quickly and easily? Are you constantly on the look out for new ideas that you can introduce into your organization to improve its processes and strategies? Do your followers tend to look to you as the person most likely to hear first about innovations happening outside the organization?

Mikhail Gorbachev

Rupert Murdoch

Jack Welch

Tony Blair

Seven

LEADER AS VICTIM

The role of victim falls to many people whether or not they choose it. (Klapp)[1]

IN THE 1990 BURMESE elections Aung San Suu Kyi's party won 82% of the popular vote. Daughter of the Burmese political figure Aung San, the woman who drew her inspirational beliefs in democracy, respect for human rights, non-violence and personal and collective discipline from Mahatma Gandhi was not to enjoy the fruits of her victory. The military nullified the electoral results and placed her under house arrest. Today she is a victim of the state: she is under strict surveillance, suffers from extreme restrictions on her freedom of movement and communication, and needs special permission to receive visitors. Aung San Suu Kyi is willing to continue to live in Burma, rather than retreat to the West, in the belief that her commitment will ultimately lead to political change. As she once said, 'I think one has to be committed all the way in politics to bring about really revolutionary change. I suppose the primary role of leaders is to persuade people to develop that kind of commitment.'[2]

Aung San Suu Kyi is on the one hand a political leader and moral crusader, and on the other, a victim. Not just a symbol of important values, she is a realistic visionary, fearless in the face of repression and violence. In what sense is the story of Aung San Suu Kyi an illustration of another dimension of leadership? Some clues are evident in the oration delivered by Professor Sejersted, the Chairman for the Norwegian Nobel Committee on the occasion of the award to Aung San Suu Kyi of the Nobel Peace Prize in 1991. He said:

We ordinary people, I believe, feel that with her courage and her high ideals Aung San Suu Kyi brings out something of the best in us. We feel we need precisely her sort of person in order to retain our faith in the future. That is what gives her such power as a symbol, and that is why any ill-treatment of her feels like a violation of what we have most at heart. The little woman under house arrest stands for a positive hope. Knowing she is there gives us confidence and faith in the power of good.[3]

Like Suu Kyi, corporate leaders are often willing, indeed talented, victims. They need to be in order to ensure their continued health and survival and that of their organizations. While at first this claim might seem strange, it is only because the social value of victims to corporations is less often discussed than other dimensions of leadership. Business leaders such as Andy Grove, Ken Iverson, Jan Carlzon and Harold Geneen, and political leaders like Fidel Castro and Bill Clinton, have all shown themselves to be admirably sensitive to this dimension of leadership.

Many leaders are naturally reluctant to accept that they sometimes need to be victims, and this reticence is not difficult to understand. Victims are often the prisoners of their enemies' intrigues, or of inescapable circumstances, or even their own self-destructive impulses. As such, victims excite both our pity and our contempt. Victims are generally thought of as underperformers who have lost out in the race for survival and success. Yet however painful it may be to acknowledge that there are losers in business, it is nevertheless a fact of corporate life. Leaders are frequently ousted by their boards, sometimes hounded by the media, and occasionally work themselves into early graves. Even those who experience considerable success may also go through phases when problems multiply, followers lose faith, and self-doubt creeps in. This is the unwelcome, the unwilling facet of victimage.

There is, however, a less frequently recognized and positive aspect of victimage. Self-confident leaders, sure of their abilities and their authority, are often willing to take the blame for problems even when they were not directly responsible for them. This self-victimage turns them into useful organizational scapegoats, as leaders such as John Sculley and Rupert Murdoch have explicitly recognized. For example, when Rupert Murdoch faced the task of persuading his many creditors to reschedule his debt in 1990, part of his strategy involved admitting his mistakes, and promising to put a stronger management team in place.[4] Conversely, those leaders unable or unwilling to make personal sacrifices are more likely to be victimized by others. Lord Weinstock, for example, delighted in making victims of others at GEC for more than thirty years, but was in the end 'hounded out' by those who considered him too old and no longer effective.[5]

To summarize, in this chapter I identify two facets of this dimension of leadership: willing victims and unwilling victims. Willing victims make a sacrifice on behalf of their organization in order to facilitate learning and evolve a healthier culture. As I illustrate, the sacrifice they make not infrequently strengthens their authority. Unwilling victims are forced to accept victimage by others, by external circumstances beyond their control, or as a result of some internal psychological dysfunction. The examples of unwilling victims we will consider are a fascinating and salutary warning of the dangers associated with failing to handle this dimension of leadership effectively.

Willing Victims

When a flaw was discovered in Intel's flagship product, the Pentium chip, Andy Grove initially sought to avoid taking any corrective action other than to agree to replace a few chips for scientists and mathematicians. Public anger flared, and the company that had brought computing power to the desks of hundreds of millions of people was derided in the media. Seizing the moment, Andy Grove issued a grovelling public apology for the irritation that his previous stance had caused. A no-questions asked exchange policy was set up, and $475 million set aside to finance it. Says one commentator, 'Once Intel backed down, the bad publicity went away almost instantly. Within weeks, public confidence in the corrected Pentium chip began to return . . . and Intel, scarred and chastened by the experience, began to return to . . . building microprocessors for personal computers.'[6]

As the case of Andy Grove illustrates, there are times when to be an effective leader requires a sacrifice – of one's self-esteem, one's public reputation, or sometimes even one's career. In giving his public apology, Grove made a short-term concession of some of his personal stock of goodwill and aura of invincibility in exchange for longer-term gain: Intel was ultimately seen to have done the right thing, and Grove himself was strengthened by association. This sort of personal sacrifice on the part of leaders, which I refer to here as self-victimage, is often vital for the wellbeing of organizations. There are two principal sets of benefits. First, the ability of a leader to cast him or herself as a victim is central to attempts to build *learning organizations*. Second, leaders able to accept victimage are better equipped to *humanize* their organizations, and therefore to build more person-respecting corporate cultures. One aspect of this worthy of particular mention is that those leaders with the capacity to constitute themselves as victims can, when crisis threatens, offer themselves as the vehicles for *collective catharsis*, and hence tend to lead healthier organizations.

Leader as Victim-learner

J. Paul Getty once wrote that 'There isn't a human being who can be right about all things at all times – and this is at least as true of businessmen as it is of bartenders, biologists or bus drivers.'[7] Given this inexorable feature of the human condition, successful leaders need to learn how to make a virtue of the errors they commit. One way of making mistakes more acceptable to followers is to offer explanations for them that emphasize their centrality to processes of learning. The most skilled self-victimizing leaders are able to do this in ways which neutralize organizational tensions, reduce follower hostility, and even strengthen their authority. People are generally, after all, very forgiving of those they believe have gained something positive out of problematic situations – even if they were the original authors of them.

For example, when Jan Carlzon at SAS came under fire from people with safety concerns, he asserted that 'When we made the transition from a product-oriented to a market-oriented company in 1981, we had pushed the service orientation so vigorously that we lost our footing a bit on the technical and operational side. I point a finger at myself alone for this shortcoming.'[8] By taking full and unequivocal personal responsibility, and later on by initiating safety committees and commissioning external safety consultants, Carlzon was able to quell anxieties and deflect critical media attention. Carlzon turned round a difficult situation because he skilfully self-victimized: he listened, admitted errors, offered a reason for them, acted to address perceived problems, and convinced his followers and external commentators that he had learned from his experiences.

Ken Iverson, of Nucor, tells another salutary tale of self-chastisement in the cause of personal learning. In his attempt to make his steel manufacturing plants more egalitarian he implemented a corporate policy that all hard hats worn by employees would be green, and those of visitors white. Previously, individuals at different levels wore different hat colours to indicate status – topped by the gold hats of senior executives. While grudging acceptance of the policy was gained over a period of months it soon transpired that maintenance people, who needed to be instantly recognizable when problems arose, had become much less visible. In his haste to eliminate a symbol of hierarchy, Iverson had lost sight of a very good reason why some people needed to wear a different coloured hard hat. In retrospect, comments Iverson, 'One of my favourite sayings is, "Good managers make bad decisions." Forgetting to set apart maintenance people was a mistake. When it was pointed out to me, I admitted as much and agreed the maintenance crews could wear yellow hats.'[9] Here again, Iverson managed to retain the respect of followers through self-victimage.

The advertising maestro David Ogilvy has explicitly recognized the importance of self-victimage, asserting that 'It is important to admit your mistakes, and to do so before you are charged with them.' Ogilvy relates how on one occasion he was cajoled into devising an advertising campaign for Lever according to parameters set by the client. The result was what Ogilvy terms the 'silliest copy in the history of advertising' – a verse designed to be sung to the tune of 'Boys and Girls Come Out to Play':

> Rinso White or Rinso Blue?
> Soap or detergent – it's up to you!
> Both wash whiter and brighter than new,
> The choice, dear lady, is up to *you*!

Says Ogilvy, when this dreadful doggerel duly appeared 'I lost more face than I could afford; my staff thought that I had gone mad, and the working levels at Lever concluded that I had no conception of what kind of advertising was required . . .' Not only was Ogilvy fired by Lever, but for years afterward it was more difficult for him to recruit serious marketing personnel. But Ogilvy and his company had learned a valuable lesson: 'This episode taught me that it does not pay to appease clients on matters of grand strategy.'[10]

As John Sculley has made clear, leaders cannot just cling to anachronistic images of themselves as tough, macho and aloof, and expect to succeed. Part of the reason why Sculley survived for so long at Apple was that he habitually accepted victim status. He publicly held himself personally responsible for many of the problems faced by the company in the mid-1980s. Yet he did so in a way that emphasized not just his own culpability, allowing others to feel better about themselves, but also the importance of trial and error learning generally. Commenting on his own leadership performance, he particularly identifies the empathic and relationship-building benefits of error admission. Says Sculley, 'The new-age leader almost has to show his fallibility. Making mistakes is a very real and important part of succeeding . . . If you fail to convey the idea at the top that you can make mistakes, you can send the wrong message, isolate yourself from the people.'[11]

Perhaps the best way for leaders to mitigate the negative consequences of their errors, is to present them as signs not just of personal growth but of organization-wide learning. This is not simply a matter of deflecting criticism. Organizations, to survive, need to experiment, and when things go wrong a leader who is willing to take the blame takes the pressure off those further down the hierarchy whose positions are less secure. Innovative behaviour is naturally encouraged when the threat of sanction is removed; even more so, when 'mistakes' are attributed elsewhere. Self-victimizing leaders are thus more likely to evolve learning organizations than those who are uncomfortable with this dimension of leadership. As Peters and Waterman have said in their memorable book *In Search of Excellence*, excellent companies 'encourage practical risk taking . . . They follow Fletcher Byrom's ninth commandment: "Make sure you generate a reasonable number of mistakes".'[12] It is up to leaders to ensure that this commandment is followed.

David Kelley, founder and CEO of the multi-award winning US industrial design firm IDEO Product Development, is an exemplary case here. Asked to explain how his organization has succeeded in designing everything from the first Apple computer mouse to the 25 foot mechanical whale that stars in the *Free Willy* movies, one of Kelley's main points is that organizations must destigmatize failure. Says Kelley:

> Organizations that don't tolerate some mistakes, breakdowns, or detours take too long to plan and replan where they're going. In contrast, we do our pioneering largely by enlightened trial and error. Allowing people to fail – indeed, expecting them to learn a great deal from falling or stumbling forward – is part of the IDEO culture.[13]

The importance of leaders owning errors and then deploying ownership of them in ways which encourage organizational learning is aptly illustrated by J.W. Marriott Jr of the Marriott Hotels group. In addition to the many laudable strategic moves Marriott has made, the corporation has also committed its fair share of mistakes. It unwisely diversified into theme parks and home security systems, neither of which it could make succeed. Worse still, when in 1990 the market for new hotels collapsed, it was left with a billion dollars of unsold property sitting on its books. While many leaders who have faced difficulties of this magnitude have sought to disown or downplay them, Marriott exemplifies a more constructive approach. First, he sought to own the problem, saying, 'I felt like I had single-handedly let . . . the company down.' Then he looked for learning points, claiming that from every disaster 'we've tried to learn something', whether it is the importance of letting people develop new ideas or the perils of trying to manage too many unfamiliar businesses.[14]

A fascinating example of a political leader employing the techniques of self-victimage to good effect, is that of Fidel Castro. On 26 July 1970, with the Cuban economy a shambles, Castro rose before an immense crowd to deliver what was to be a vital speech. Without warning or preamble, he launched into an astonishing criticism of the management of Cuban society over the previous decade. At one point he stated 'We are going to begin by pointing out the responsibility of all of us [leaders] and mine in particular for all these problems.'[15] Castro's speech captured the imagination of the people. It was a *tour de force*, at once highly personal, didactic and visionary. He explicitly revealed his own shortcomings and failures, but in ways which suggested that the future was bright. With this single coruscating performance, Castro was able to turn seeming defeat almost into a virtue. Just as the myth of his infallibility looked like being eroded he was able to encourage Cubans to look for collective solutions and preserve his authority.

In some ways the most politically adroit politician of our times, President Clinton is equally skilled at self-victimage. The first time he used this strategy to further his political career was after he had lost the governorship of Arkansas, and was fighting for the Democratic nomination in order to run for Governor again in 1982. Realizing that the citizens of Arkansas viewed him 'as a prodigal son who had grown too big for his britches', Clinton and his team saw the value of a public apology.[16] A television advertisement was devised in which Clinton announced his comeback bid by saying he was sorry. This simple act of contrition, asking for what amounted to Christian forgiveness, seemed highly risky at the time. Indeed, the immediate result was that Clinton's support fell from 43% to the mid-20s. But in the highly negative campaign which followed Clinton appeared to have been immunized from attack. The prevailing mood seemed to be: it is a rare man who can admit his mistakes, and he should be respected for it. Not only did Clinton win the Democratic nomination and the governorship, but he filed away a useful political tactic. Years later when, as president, he was embroiled in a scandal involving Monica

Lewinsky, the *mea culpa* strategy got its most famous public airing. Shrewd self-victimizing again saved Clinton's political career.

To summarize, successful leaders are sufficiently psychically robust to take responsibility for errors and problems. They do so, in part, to stifle recriminations and limit criticism of themselves, but also to promote action-learning behaviours in their followers. Sir John Egan was not afraid to fault himself for failing to understand the lessons to be learned from Japan's approach to design process in time to prevent Jaguar cars being taken over by Ford in 1989. And perhaps these candid admissions partially account for him gaining the top job at British Airports Authority (BAA), where he has used Japanese design processes to halve construction costs.[17] When at Airco, a large US industrial gas company, Richard Giordano expanded into the graphite business just when the world markets for the product were contracting. Airco wrote off $117 million. Undeterred, Giordano did not lose confidence but sought to learn and reinvest, claiming that 'One of the measures of a good leader is that when he makes a mistake and the company suffers for it, people still follow him.'[18] Giordano went on to become chairman and chief executive of the BOC group. The point of being a victim today is to triumph tomorrow.

Leader as Victim-humanizer
Leaders who are willing and able to cast themselves as victims can be instrumental in creating healthier and more humane organizations. When problems arise and mistakes are made, those individuals and groups associated with them are often troubled by feelings of guilt and anxiety. The self-confident leader, who is willing to own such problems, provides a convenient target for criticism. Followers who might otherwise expend valuable time and energy engaged in bitter feuding and recriminations between themselves, can be encouraged to purge their fears by attaching blame to a single and unassailable figure, the leader. There are, of course, obvious dangers for a leader in accepting the role of the victim too often or in unpropitious circumstances. The skilled leader must learn when and how to adopt and deploy victim status to best effect, and when and how to avoid being victimized by others.

There are not just organizational but personal advantages to be gained from efforts to regulate the psychological health of followers through self-victimage. As Noel Tichy and Eli Cohen[19] have made clear, it is only by admitting mistakes and showing themselves to be vulnerable that leaders can serve as effective role models for others. Paragons of perfection are much less favoured as role models than those with human frailties, because of the seemingly impossible standards they set. Moreover, self-victimizing leaders reduce the psychological distance between themselves and their subordinates, easing two-way communication. A leader's personal standing, information, and range of influence may thus be increased by skilful self-denigration. The personal advantages of adroit self-victimage that accrue to a leader are most palpable when his or her authority is threatened. Casting oneself as a victim of not just one's own errors, but of circumstances such as an economic recession or restrictive government legislation, or underperforming lieutenants, can create a symbolic advantage. It tends to quieten criticism for a time, whether or not critics actually feel sorry for the victim, because they do not want to appear to be 'hitting a man when he is down'.[20]

The advantages of exposing weaknesses are best illustrated by reference to legendary heroes such as Achilles, Siegfried and King Arthur who retain our interest and our sympathy in part because of their vulnerabilities. Such characters derive much of their heroic status from being victims. In contrast to them are those who adhere to grandiose self-images, whose confidence surpasses their abilities, and who rely on themselves alone for self-validation. My argument is that such people, by detaching themselves from those they would lead, are not just naive, but self-destructively career-limiting. In failing to appeal to the emotional sensitivities of their followers they stand (and fall) alone. Unable to make victims of themselves, they are more likely to be victimized and scapegoated by others. When problems and difficulties occur they are less likely to be forgiven, and their pleas of mitigation are less likely to be heard.

Robert Wood Johnson, at the helm of Johnson & Johnson for thirty-one years, recognized the importance of highlighting his own shortcomings, claiming that 'Doing so shows you're human and makes others more receptive to your advice.'[21] Harold Geneen has been remarkably candid regarding the mistakes he made while head of ITT, and the benefits that accrue to leaders who are unafraid to admit to mistakes. Says Geneen,

> I admitted them [errors] at General Managers' Meetings, often with the expression 'I guess I pushed the wrong button,' and then outlined my plan to save as much as could be saved from the situation. Usually such *mea culpas* were well received. Anyone who has goofed gets a little enjoyment out of seeing the Man Up There admit to a mistake. There's nothing lost and much to be gained by admitting that you're human.[22]

In those situations where an organization is experiencing particularly acute trauma, the leader can cast him or herself as victim in the hope that perceptions that they have suffered may purge and renew the social order. In art this is called *catharsis*, and in religion *purification*. Whatever the label, the process refers to a sort of ceremonial cleansing of guilt, pollution or defilement. Jeff Campbell of Burger King, desperate to have franchisees understand his programme for reform, went out to face them knowing they were unhappy with the way things had been run in the past. Part of his solution was to offer himself up as a target for franchisees' anger. Says Campbell, 'When I came on board I had enough of a reputation in the system so that they felt excited but they still needed to beat me up. I had to go out there and give them a forum in which they could spill their guts.'[23] Such events can often be cathartic for those involved, allowing frustrations to be vented, and a more helpful and fruitful atmosphere to develop.

In extreme cases, when mere suffering is insufficient to purge guilt and extinguish sin, catharsis may require the dethronement of the leader. While Julius Caesar provides the most famous historical example, the corporate equivalent of this most extreme form of scapegoating has been much observed in recent times. John Akers was fired by IBM after its market value plunged nearly $50 billion. Kay Whitmore was fired in 1993 from Eastman Kodak after the company failed to gain the lead in digital imaging technology. At American Express, Jim Robinson was fired in 1993 after the company's market share began to drop – from 26% in 1985 to 15% in 1996.[24] Leaders need to realize when they should voluntarily depart, before they are ousted.

In terms of my argument, knowing when to take the final bow is as much a part of being an effective leader as being a skilled ambassador or fine actor. One of the best examples here is that of Pierre du Pont, who twice sacrificed his power-wielding career in what he thought were the best interests of his organizations. As the man in charge of the Du Pont Powder Company, between 1911 and 1919 he quadrupled assets, led a seven-fold increase in profits, and diversified and expanded the corporation into a broad-based chemical firm. When he bowed out in 1919 he gave way to a younger generation of highly trained and professionally competent family executives he had helped to develop. He then took charge of General Motors, resigning in 1928 when his friend and colleague, John Raskob, was forced out by Alfred Sloan, the man to whom he had already ceded the presidency. Growing small family-run businesses into large enterprises in a rational, calculated manner, and designing them to cope with the challenges of expansion and diversification while ensuring effective planning, coordination and control is fantastically complex. Knowing when the time is right to move on is more difficult still. Say the great business biographers Alfred Chandler and Stephen Salsbury, 'Few American business-men have handled this almost inevitable crisis in the growth of the modern corporation more effectively than Pierre S. du Pont.'[25]

Unwilling Victims

There are pathologies that leaders need to guard against, some internal, and some externally located. Just as there is sometimes a thin dividing line between immortalism and narcissism, so there is between constructive self-victimage and damaging victimization. Successful leaders constitute themselves as victims as it suits them: they have the power, they make a choice, and they are in control. But there are many instances where they are manipulated by others into the role of victim, and the consequences for leaders then are generally negative. There are also cases where leaders themselves lose their way, only to be overcome by their own self-destructive impulses. Leaders as victims are not just positive learners and humanizers, but, potentially, the subjects of conspiracies and the consequences of their own fragile psychic equilibrium.

Some leaders, such as Cecil Rhodes, founder of Rhodesia, succumb to a complex mixture of their own psychology and external circumstances. Part of his motivation, and what made him so desperate for quick results and so utterly unscrupulous, was his omnipresent fear of death. Rhodes' rush to achieve great things in a politically unstable and fractious part of the world (nineteenth-century Southern Africa), ultimately limited his success. More recently, Prime Minister Thatcher's 'manner of exercising her leadership, like "a tigress among hamsters" in John Biffen's striking phrase, was bound in the long run to make her vulnerable to the fate of Julius Caesar'.[26] The examples given in the next sections illustrate leadership traits and pitfalls to be avoided.

Leader as Victim of Conspiracy

King Henry VIII was manipulated by members of his court into having the woman he loved, Anne Boleyn, beheaded, and their daughter (later Elizabeth I) declared illegitimate. He, as much as she, was a victim of a conscious conspiracy, although the consequences for Anne were clearly more serious. The downfall of Anne Boleyn had been plotted for some time by a shrewdly calculating alliance of conservative peers and courtiers, friends of Henry's divorced (and deceased) first wife Catherine of Aragon, and the Imperial ambassador. They had carefully selected and coached a new candidate for the king's hand, Jane Seymour, to first attract his attention, then frustrate his desires, and finally turn him against his queen. Once captivated by her, Henry forced 'his' decision on his subjects. Writes one eminent historian,

> Henry VIII had been able to enforce his wish to dispose of Anne – but he had been manoeuvred by councillors and courtiers into wishing to dispose of her. No matter how great the formal power of the King of England, it was exercised under the informal influence of the politicians who surrounded him. By control of access to the King's presence, by selection of the documents he

was to see, by the doctoring of reports and the whispering of half-truths, those about Henry had the opportunity to manage him.[27]

How many CEOs, we may wonder, are, similarly, victims of such pernicious conspiracies?

Machiavelli[28] once argued that 'the prince's chief fear must be a secret conspiracy'. Some anti-leader conspiracies are highly generalized. Warren Bennis, writing of his own experiences as president of the University of Cincinnati, describes his realization that 'I had become the victim of a vast, amorphous, unwitting, unconscious conspiracy to prevent me from doing anything whatever to change the university's status quo.'[29] Other anti-leader conspiracies are located outside the leader's own organization, and are highly focused. Martin Luther King, for example, was assassinated on 4 April 1968 in Memphis, by a right-wing drifter called James Earl Ray. Some leaders become the deliberate target of one or more among their own followers. Gandhi, for instance, was killed by a Hindu, Nathuram Vinayak Godse, in January 1948 as he was walking to a prayerground. Corporate leaders provide no less remarkable or interesting examples.

Alan Bond, founder of the Bond Corporation, once the ninth largest enterprise in Australia, was mercilessly victimized by Tiny Rowland. Bond and Rowland were on the best of terms until the exuberant Bond sprung a buying raid on Tiny's organization, Lonrho. Acquiring 20% of the stock for $655 million, Bond became Lonrho's largest shareholder. Rubbing salt into Rowland's wounds, Bond, whose yacht was moored just three berths away from Rowland's at Antibes, had his captain ask Rowland to move his yacht so he could go alongside the quay. Rowland was furious: 'It was so embarrassing,' he said. 'It's such a small community down there, everyone must have heard about it. It was then that I decided to destroy him.'[30] While there had always been rumours concerning the asset values and profit valuations of the Bond Corporation, they had until then been muted. Rowland recognized where Bond was vulnerable, and went for his jugular. He commissioned a stream of documents and circulars claiming that

Bond's companies were technically insolvent, leading to intense scrutiny of the Bond Corporation. Deals began to go wrong for Bond, and the group was hit by a liquidity crisis from which it could not recover. Towards the end it was paying about $1 billion a year in interest, soaking up every dollar of its cash flow. The group was by then mortally wounded, and eventually dismembered. Of course Bond had a big hand in his own demise, but Tiny Rowland's enmity was in many ways the prime cause of disaster.

While Bond was victimized by his 'friend', David Thieme was a victim of his bankers. In 1981 Thieme was arrested in the boardroom of the Crédit Suisse bank in Zurich on charges of fraud and embezzlement of $4.5 million. The bank also claimed he owed them another $40 million. Thieme was an American who made a fortune at the age of thirty before starting the company Essex Overseas Petroleum, which transported, refined and marketed petroleum products with leased shipping and refining capacity. He was flamboyant with his money, holding expensive parties and sponsoring the Lotus racing car team. In the late 1970s he made a lot of money – maybe as much as $120 million. But in 1980–1 the markets turned against him and he spent a lot of time with his bankers, Crédit Suisse, working out how to reschedule debt. The bank got nervous when it heard he was going to watch his Lotus formula 1 team in Argentina, and arranged for his arrest at their offices where Thieme was in a meeting with them. 'Word immediately went out to the press that Thieme had been stopped on his way to South America.'[31] He was refused bail, but with no strong evidence against him he was released thirteen days later. Thieme then spent seven months cooperating with the authorities investigating the case. Eight months after his arrest all charges against him were dropped. A year of legal wrangling followed, with Crédit Suisse appealing against legal decisions that favoured Thieme. The case hit Thieme's business hard in the years after his victimization – but, unlike Bond, he survived.

A large number of corporate leaders become the victims of negative media campaigns. In January 1914, when Henry Ford announced that he would pay his workers five dollars a day, thereby doubling wages overnight, many questioned whether his 'generosity' was wise. The conservative *Wall Street Journal* declared that Henry Ford was a menace who had 'in his social endeavours committed economic blunders, if not crimes . . . [which] . . . may return to plague him and the industry he represents, as well as organized society'.[32] At the other end of the political spectrum, the socialist *New York Daily People* attacked the plan as a $10 million dust-raising scheme designed to ruin competitors. Few in the media understood the assembly line technology that made the new wage possible, and even those who did not believe that the move would undermine capitalism, or wreck the lives of workers, thought Ford was likely to ruin himself. It was not until Ford's high profits were seen to match the high wages that he paid that public opinion altered and he came to be seen as an American hero.

At the height of his powers at the turn of the twentieth century John D. Rockefeller was both feared and openly criticized everywhere. Newspaper editors denounced him. Church ministers preached against him. Businessmen condemned him. Says one commentator, 'Foes and apologists alike commonly referred to him as "the most hated man in America".' Viciously attacked as 'the ogre of business' and a 'malefactor of great wealth' he was quite probably the most cartooned man in the United States. Thirty years later, following a wealth of positive publicity associated with his philanthropy, Rockefeller's negative reputation was 'as lost as the palaces of the Pharaohs under Egypt's sands'. Commenting on this transformation in his public profile in 1926, one newspaper described how: 'Once it was the fashion to denounce him as an evil force in the business community. People have now come to perceive that he was an advance agent of new and better ways of doing business. The future will regard him as one who contributed greatly to the labor-saving devices upon which the prosperity of this civilization is partly based.'[33]

Another noteworthy victim of the media is Larry Tisch, who in 1986, together with his family, purchased 25% of the somewhat ailing US TV network CBS, and installed himself as head. At first Tisch was hailed as a hero. But then, when he threatened to cut $50 million out of a $300 million budget, perceptions altered. In October 1986 *Fortune* magazine described him as '. . . this short, bald dumpling of a man'. Press stories depicted him as a miser who drove his late-model Pontiac station wagon to the front door of Paley's classy 'Black Rock' skyscraper in search of anything that could quickly be converted into cash and reinvested in anything that might yield a safe, respectable return. The portrayal of Tisch as greedy and insensitive was, arguably, a gross oversimplification. Unsurprisingly, Tisch began to feel picked on, and it certainly was not how he, then aged sixty-five, had hoped to be remembered. Even when cost-cutting looked like it was paying dividends, in February 1990 Kenneth Labich's piece in *Fortune* carried the headline: 'Has Tisch Lost His Touch?' Tisch himself claimed that he was not greatly hurt personally by such criticisms, but that they did 'pose a threat to his ability to lead'. Even so, by 1994 perceptions had altered once again, and he was widely hailed as a successful leader of CBS, having altered the culture from one that rewarded loyalty to one that rewarded performance.[34]

As the case of Tisch shows, even the most successful corporate leaders can be victimized by the media and regarded with suspicion and concern by the public. Harold Geneen had a somewhat similar experience. Taking over ITT in 1959, Geneen transformed the corporation's financial position: sales of $765.6 million and a profit margin of only $29 million became $16.7 billion and $562 million respectively by 1977. He had bought, merged with, or absorbed some 350 different businesses in eighty countries and fashioned them into 250 different profit centres. But he did so much so quickly that a large segment of the population thought that there must be something malevolent behind such rapid success. A variety of accusations and charges were made against him, but none resulted in corrective action being taken because investigation revealed that there was nothing to correct.[35] To an extent, Geneen contributed to his own victimization by failing to associate with the business community, much of which considered him a maverick. But more than anything he was a victim of the times, for his rise to prominence occurred against a backdrop of congressional investigations into the power wielded by conglomerates and anti-trust suits.

Just as democratically elected leaders can always be voted out of office, so leaders of publicly held corporations can be ousted by shareholders. One of the most spectacular shareholder interventions of recent times occurred on 16 December 1994, when Maurice Saatchi was demoted from the top job at the advertising agency Saatchi & Saatchi, which he had helped to found. The victimization of Maurice Saatchi was accomplished by an influential group of shareholders led by the thirty-three-year-old David Herro. This is not to imply that Saatchi was not in part author of his own demise. He had, after all, achieved a justified but unenviable reputation as spendthrift at his company's expense, and presided over a share price plunge from over £50 in 1987 to 89p in 1991. Even so, Maurice had difficulties coming to terms with the advice of the corporation's professional advisers, which included S.G. Warburg and the Union bank of Switzerland, that it was time for him to go. Says one biographer, 'He saw himself as the victim of an aggressive takeover, as a chairman of the board who had lost out in a skirmish between the Men in Suits and the real talent.'[36]

Leaders who become the victims of powerful conspirators have few options available to them. When the conspiracy is managed with secrecy and guile then, like Henry VIII, a leader may not even be aware of what has happened. In those instances where the position of the leader is fundamentally weak, such as with Alan Bond, there may be little that he or she can do to avert disaster. Leaders whose reputations are unjustly tarnished by legal action, such as Thieme, can do nothing other than place their confidence in judicial processes and hope. Only when the leader, like Tisch, has both a secure position and extreme self-confidence, can he or she wrest back control of the situation. And even here there are costs – to self-esteem and public reputation – to be incurred.

Leader as Victim of the Self

That leaders often contribute to their own downfall, making tragic victims of themselves, is widely acknowledged by artists, sociologists and psychologists. The novelist and poet Thomas Hardy believed that individuals tended to be either self-preserving or self-destructive. In his work *The Mayor of Casterbridge* Hardy illustrates for us how a man can rise to a supreme position of leadership, only to frustrate and undermine his success. The academic, Hugh Duncan,[37] has similarly argued that 'There are victims within us too, inner victims locked within the dark regions of the self.' Some will no doubt object that leaders are also prisoners of circumstances beyond their control which both prescribe and proscribe their action repertoire. But few leaders are solely victims of circumstance. Most also make some contribution to their own fall from grace. Mark Anthony was defeated by Caesar in part because he allowed himself to be distracted by Cleopatra. King Lear authors his own dethronement by dividing his kingdom among his daughters. Like Hardy's self-destructive protagonists and Shakespeare's tragic heroes, CEOs sometimes engage in self-defeating, self-victimizing behaviours.

A large number of the figures who have featured prominently in this book have, at one time or another, become tragic victims of their own egos and excesses. John DeLorean's self-destructive tendencies were apparent to observers even before he became embroiled in a drugs scandal. Of DeLorean's time at Pontiac an aide said, 'You had to wonder whether John didn't have a suicide wish or something. He went so far out of his way to insult people who didn't fawn over him or approve of everything he did.'[38] Wayne Huizenga negotiated a deal to merge Blockbuster with Viacom in 1994 which ultimately led to his being marginalized and then forced out of the company he had done so much to build.[39] On his own admission, J.W. Marriott Jr's three heart attacks were the result of his own disabling lifestyle: 'I had been the walking stereotype of the workaholic executive: too little exercise and rest, too much work, and too many heavy dinners too late at night.'[40] Walt Disney's total immersion in his work contributed to his nervous breakdown in 1931.[41] De Gaulle in the late 1960s finally seemed to lose touch with the French people, initiated a referendum he could not possibly win, faced the ignominy of having to resign, and shortly after in 1970 died a deeply depressed man.

While few opt to play the role of the tragic victim by conscious choice, it is one that many, maybe most, corporate leaders experience at some point in their career. Almost no one has an unblemished track record of upwardly spiralling success and advancement. Nearly every leader has to admit defeat at some point in his or her working life, has to stare into the abyss of total failure, and is forced to reflect whether his or her past triumphs were more illusory than real. For example, Henry Heinz's first attempt to create a food business ended in bankruptcy in 1875.[42] During the early phase of his career, Walt Disney's cartoons made money for others but not himself, and it was not until the last decade of his life that his financial situation radically improved.[43] The tragic victim is one overwhelmed by obstacles or opponents who occupy the high ground and appear unassailably strong. Whatever the precise combination of reasons, the victim of the self often stands at the helm of an organization in decline: lack of adaptability, sclerotic rigidity and limited imagination mean a senile and degenerative order. The organization might die, be taken over, or a boardroom coup might merely displace the leader and allow change.

An extreme example of tragic self-victimage is Eli Black, who at 8.00 a.m. on 3 February 1975 at the age of fifty-three jumped from the 44th floor of New York's Pan Am Building. Black had been chairman of United Brands Company (a conglomerate of his own creation) and the United Fruit Company. Reasons for his behaviour were not hard to find. 'United Brands,' said *The New York Times*, 'had incurred heavy losses in Central American banana plantations from Hurricane Fifi, had undergone new burdens with export taxes on bananas imposed by Central American republics, and had sustained losses in its meat-packing division as a result of increased costs of feeding cattle.' Moreover, a subsequent investigation by the Securities and Exchange Commission disclosed that Black had authorized the payment of more than $2 million to government officials in Honduras to obtain a tax reduction on the export of bananas, something which was directly contrary to his external self-image as a morally irreproachable philanthropist.[44] With his world closing in on him, Eli Black jumped.

Few exemplars of the tragic genre are quite so dramatic. More typical in many ways is Robert Campeau, who amassed a fortune as a US real estate developer. Despite knowing little about the retailing business, he then proceeded to expand into this sector in the mid-1980s with a staggering $13.4 billion worth of purchases.

The price of expansion was massive debt, much in the form of high-interest junk bonds. His view was that the right combination of consolidation, selling off of assets to pay debt, and motivation of management through stock options would be a recipe for success, not least because synergies between different parts of the business could be exploited. Campeau's rosy projections could not prevent his kingdom from unravelling within a few short years. The crushing debt load meant that his retailing operations ran out of cash in August 1989. What is more, his own personal fortune of $500 million was said to have all but evaporated by February 1990. According to one observer, 'Campeau's tragic error in this case was tied as much to blind ambition as it was to poor strategic and financing decisions.'[45]

A more ancient but particularly interesting example of a seemingly heroic figure beset by self-victimizing tragedy is Robert Morris. Born in England in 1734 he moved to the USA as a young boy, and by the age of twenty had became involved as a partner in a trading company called Willing & Morris. In later life he became a central figure in the American Revolution: a delegate to the Continental Congress, a signer of the Declaration of Independence, and a member of Benjamin Franklin's elite Council of Safety. His rise to fame began when the US engaged Britain in a war for independence with no money to pay for it. To help fund the war Robert Morris was appointed Superintendent of Finance, whereupon he set up a national bank, reorganized the Treasury Department, established the US mint, and marshalled resources to pay the army. On one occasion he is reported to have personally paid the troops one month's salary in order to induce them to march from Washington to Yorktown. He also personally backed up the paper money issued with his own gold. So important was his role that when in 1783 the Treaty of Peace with Britain was ratified and he resigned his position, he was widely regarded as having 'saved the nation'.[46]

Despite going on to nominate George Washington as the first president and becoming a senator for Pennsylvania, and in spite of having accumulated vast wealth, Morris's downfall was breathtakingly swift. He proceeded to invest in huge amounts of land, eventually accumulating eight million acres to become the country's single largest landowner. Disaster then struck when, exhausted of cash, a downturn in land values led to his being pursued by his debtors. Once the richest man in the United States, on 14 February 1798, he was arrested for nonpayment of debts and placed in a debtors' prison. He was sixty-three years old. He remained in prison for three years. On his release he never again held high office or engaged in any meaningful business.

Chung Ju Yung, the founder of Hyundai, decided in his old age to run for president of Korea. He started his own political party, the United People's Party, and used Hyundai employees and funds to campaign. For all his billions he only won 16.1% of the votes against Kim Young Sam's 42%, the ruling Democratic Party Leader. He was even pushed into third place by Kim Dae Jung. The worst was yet to come. He was barred from leaving the country and brought to the prosecutor's office where he was grilled about the illegal syphoning of funds from a Hyundai company to finance his campaign. A minor official in the corporation eventually took the blame, and Yung promised to repay the $65.2 million in question. The prosecutors were not impressed and launched renewed charges of financial mismanagement against him. Hurt and upset, Yung nevertheless avoided prison, quite probably because the prosecutors feared a backlash against their apparent persecution of an old man who had done so much to assist Korea's economic progress. He did, though, resign as party chairman of the UPP, admit to 'many mistakes' and offered 'a sincere apology' to his political opponents for personal attacks he had made on them. Says one commentator, 'In the tortured agony of abject surrender, Chung Ju Yung had worried most about the future of a business empire, a dynasty that he had nurtured to live on after him.'[47] He feared the game was lost. Facing trial and with the break-up of Hyundai looking a real possibility, Yung experienced his worst moment – a victim of himself and his political ambitions.

There are important lessons to be learned from those who have made tragic victims of themselves. Those who would lead would do well to pay close attention to William C. Durrant, who formed General Motors in 1908 and who was so utterly unable to administer it that he lost control of the company in 1910 – a fact that led Alfred Sloan Jr, a subsequent leader of the organization, to claim 'That he [Durrant] should have conceived a General Motors and been unable himself in the long run to bring it off or to sustain his personal, once dominating position in it is a tragedy of American industrial history.' There are lessons too from the tragic civil-war like intrigues that afflicted the Gucci company from the time of the death of the company's founder Guccio in 1953, and which intensified so tragically in the 1980s and 1990s. Just why do so many leaders end up playing a tragic role? Jack Welch, the former chairman of General Electric, suggests that it might have something to do with individuals' reliance on what they think they know, the speed at which change has to be handled, and their vanity: 'Why do newly made heroes so quickly fall back into incrementalism?' he asks. Because, he says, 'People [leaders] want to come out for the second bow when the world is waiting for the second act.'[48] These sentiments are echoed by Percy Barnevik of ABB. He says: 'You can never rest on your laurels, you have to improve your position every year, every month, and every day. Just two or three years of complacency can destroy a strong and successful company.'[49]

Of course not all leaders who are cast in a tragic victim role are forever tarnished. Some, indeed many, bounce back. For every Margaret Thatcher ousted by her own party at the seeming zenith of her powers, there is a Nelson Mandela who goes from the tragedy of being a political prisoner to president of his country. The temporary resort to a tragic role can even be a longer-term benefit to some. A leader who is seen to have failed may play the penitent and gain sympathy for his or her plight by blaming others or circumstances. The point is that what looks like failure can be redefined by canny leaders as merely a temporary phase in an epic struggle. As long as the people are with you then from the depths of despair a new vision can be forged. From tragedy stems hope.[50]

Learning Points for Leaders
Some of the most widely esteemed leaders in all fields and from all historical ages have accepted victimage, either more or less

willingly. By so doing they have often shown themselves to be exemplary leaders, reinforced their followers' belief in their right to lead, and written themselves into our history books. Jesus Christ was crucified, St Joan was burnt alive and St Sebastian shot with arrows. In politics, President Nelson Mandela was imprisoned, and Mahatma Gandhi, Leon Trotsky, Rosa Luxemburg and President Kennedy, among many others, were assassinated. Like religious and political movements, organizations need victims, and great leaders are sometimes willing to play this role in the best long-term interests of their firms and themselves. For many otherwise admirable leaders this is, in many ways, the most difficult dimension of leadership to excel in. Yet leaders who are willing to cast themselves as victims, in controlled ways, can usefully promote organizational learning and evolve healthy cultures. Moreover, failure in this dimension can have profoundly negative consequences. This is because when extreme situations arise non-self-victimizing leaders are more likely to be made scapegoats against their will. It is also the case that leaders unable to self-victimize are more prone to the sort of psychic frailties that cause them to self-destruct. At their best, leaders are those who, like Fidel Castro and Bill Clinton, are able to accept victimage in ways which reinforce their authority.

In their most positive incarnation leaders as victims are both learners and humanizers. Furthermore, they play these roles in ways which have at least four felicitous consequences. First, through self-victimage they permit their followers to feel good about themselves. This is an important point. As Irwin Fedeman of Monolithic Memories has said, 'Making another person feel good in the unspectacular course of his daily comings and goings is, in my view, the very essence of leadership.'[51] Leaders as victims achieve this by placing themselves as targets for blame and acting as the vehicles for vicarious atonement. Second, leaders are often able to do this in ways which strengthen their moral authority. To constitute oneself as a victim is to communicate that one has the power, the strength of will and position, to 'own' errors. Third, it can sometimes serve a leader to accept victim status on his or her own terms as a means of deflecting more intense and damaging criticism. More than one leader has argued, as has William Smithburg talking about two key mistakes he committed while chairman of Quaker Oats, that 'If you're not falling down, you're not learning.'[52] Finally, being prepared to engage in self-victimage occasionally can be a useful means of defusing antipathies: 'our leader never takes the blame for anything' can be a very dangerous charge, and as Machiavelli has made clear, 'A prince must try to avoid, above all else, being despised and hated.'[53]

Leaders who fail to engage effectively in this dimension of leadership will be more prone to being made the victims of conspiracies. Lacking strength of character, they are also more likely to make victims of themselves. Cecil Rhodes is a classic example here: author of his own decline, even in defeat he excited little sympathy in others.[54] The general point is that leaders who are uncomfortable admitting errors publicly, or to themselves, are less likely to be psychologically resilient.

Of course we all have a tendency to externalize internal problems, projecting our discomforts and fears on to others. In many instances this is functional, because it allows us to deal with anxiety-provoking situations. But in those leaders where this tendency becomes exaggerated, and serves as their predominant reaction to stressful situations, it is intensely problematic.[55] Leaders who experience little sense of personal responsibility, distance themselves from problems, and deny and rationalize away responsibility are, in a real sense, victims of themselves. One classic and well-recognized symptom of this is executive stress and burnout.[56] The organizations such people create are most often blighted by warring factions, political infighting and myopia, which, in a vicious circle, may then contribute to the victimizing of the leader by others.

There are good reasons why for most leaders this is the most difficult dimension of leadership to cope with effectively. Even in those instances where a leader deliberately constructs him or herself as a victim for the good of the organization, the trauma of being thought ill of can be acute. The only real consolation is that being victimized by others is a still more painful experience. Consider, for example, the comments of Henry Heinz on the failure of his first business venture: 'I feel as though people were all pushing us down because we are bankrupt. Such is the world . . . The majority of friends are seemingly so as long as it costs them nothing or they have no sacrifice to make. This I could not have believed . . . People talk terribly . . . I feel sad and constantly worried . . . It is hard to bear.'[57]

To conclude, then, effective leaders are, when necessary, willing victims. The difficulties inherent in openly admitting errors and becoming the target for accusations and negative feelings need little further elaboration. At least occasionally playing the role of the victim is, however, just another aspect of what it means to take responsibility for (i.e. to lead) an organization. To perform well in this dimension of leadership means being able to recognize when tensions are building up, and having the strength of character to defuse them at some small personal cost. Obviously, there are risks involved here, and as with the other dimensions of leadership there is little other than profound self-reflection that can help you to improve. Some specific questions to bear in mind when evaluating your competence in this dimension of leadership are:

As a Willing Victim

- *As a Victim-learner.* Are you willing to take responsibility for problems in order to help build a culture that is tolerant of mistakes? Do you believe that one important way in which people learn is to commit errors? Would your followers agree that you admit mistakes and take responsibility for things when they go wrong, and in so doing encourage them to do the same?

- *As a Victim-humanizer.* Are you willing to take the blame for problems in order to make others feel good about themselves? Do you believe that by showing yourself to be less than perfect you can be a more appealing role model for subordinates? Would you be prepared to sacrifice your job in the best interests of your organization?

As an Unwilling Victim

- *As a Victim of Conspiracy.* Do you think that leaders should always make victims of other people rather than themselves? Do other people tend to blame you for problems even when you have no direct responsibility for them? Do others unfairly criticize your knowledge, abilities or track record?

- *As a Victim of the Self.* Are you afraid to adopt victim status? Do you tend to encourage others to criticize you in unhelpful and destructive ways? Have others remarked that you seem to have a self-destructive side to your character?

Aung San Suu Kyi

Mahatma Gandhi

Margaret Thatcher

Eight

THE MULTI-DIMENSIONAL LEADER

Leadership has to take place every day. It cannot be the responsibility of the few, a rare event, or a once-in-a-lifetime opportunity. (Heifetz & Laurie)[1]

As J. Paul Getty has written, 'Few, if any, of our modern-era business executives are born. Virtually all of them are made – in the sense that they are produced by various processes of education, training and experience.'[2] In other words, it is possible to learn how to be a more effective leader by gaining appropriate education and helpful experience. Furthermore, as Marvin Bower, the so-called spiritual leader of the management consultancy company McKinsey & Co. has said, leadership does not require vastly superior or unusual qualities.[3] What it does require fundamentally is an understanding of what it is that effective leaders *do*. Of course, as Harold Geneen has written, there is no one guaranteed way to teach another individual how to lead: 'Everyone reads the same books and yet one manager will get a 40 per cent effort out of his management team and the other will get 80 per cent.'[4] Quite why this is so has a lot to do with a person's previously acquired or accumulated maturity, wisdom, integrity and courage.

This said, it is now time to review what can be learned from the previous six chapters, and, most importantly, what it takes to become a multi-dimensional leader.

Learning From the Six Dimensions of Leadership

Being a constantly successful leader requires excellence in most, if not all, of the six dimensions of leadership. Ideally, leaders should be believable heroes, fine actors, high self-esteem immortalists, astute power-brokers, sensitive ambassadors and, on occasions, calculating victims. If this sounds difficult and demanding, then that is because being an effective leader in our contemporary world is a challenging business. The complicated and exhausting demands on those who would lead help to account for the many observations that leaders and leadership are currently in short supply. By the same token, having recognized what it means and what it takes to be an exemplary leader, makes it easier to live up to the world's expectations. The examples of effective and flawed leaders in the previous six chapters do more than just entertain: they provide clues as to how actual and aspiring leaders might usefully modify their behaviour.

The most effective leaders are honoured heroes. At their best they are people like Walt Disney, Henry Ford and Andrew Carnegie, whose devotion to their organizations spurs on and inspires others. They are people with whom subordinates can identify and whom they can use as templates to assist in developing their own leadership personas. Such people recognize that by casting themselves in one or more heroic genres – epic, symbolic, playful or warrior – they can reinforce their authority and help ensure the survival and continuity of their firm. They are liberators, role models and creators. They achieve against the odds and become icons to be revered. They often use humour to break down barriers with subordinates, to make employees feel more involved in their organizations, and to spark creativity. During times of difficulty they may seem as warrior heroes, whose courage and determination rally the spirits of those they lead. Most importantly, true heroes are not seduced by fantasy images of their abilities, but are realistic about their personal achievements and generous in their recognition of others.

The best leaders are skilled actors. They are people like Steve Jobs, Lee Iacocca and Richard Branson, who recognize the need to deliver authentic leadership performances that convince others of their right to command. Such consummate actors are gifted with the ability to explain organizational actions and events in ways which are deeply meaningful to others. Leaders as actors recognize that leadership is exercised not merely through formal systems and procedures but through words and deeds. They are poets, rhetoricians, storytellers and showpeople. They are sensitive, persuasive, didactic and, most of all, alive to the dramatic potential of their privileged positions. As actors, they frequently and consistently deploy their key messages to followers. And as political leaders ranging from Winston Churchill and JFK to Fidel Castro illustrate, the best acting is an exercise in power.

Great leaders are self-confident immortalists. They are people like Bill Gates, Margaret Thatcher and the founders of Sony, Masaru Ibuka and Akio Morita. These are people whose high self-esteem has propelled them to achieve at the highest level. They are individuals who have written their personalities into the organizations and countries they lead. Often marked by both a rebellious need to create something new and a virtuoso ability to fulfil their ambitions, immortalists are realistic visionaries. They are self-assured, prescient and dominant. Of course, there are those whose immortalistic aspirations transgress the fine dividing line into narcissism. Edwin Land, founder of Polaroid; Ken Olsen, founder of Digital; and An Wang, founder of Wang Laboratories, are all examples of the dangers here: what they teach us is that immortalism, to be effective, must be tempered with a capacity for introspection, empathy and realism.

Admirable leaders are shrewd dealers in power. They are world historical figures such as Napoleon and Cecil Rhodes, and hugely successful corporate leaders like Alfred Sloan, Jack Welch and Andy Grove. Talented power-brokers know that to accomplish their goals they must mobilize their followers, and that this often involves cutting deals and building alliances as well as issuing directives and manipulating outcomes. Power-brokers have a sophisticated understanding of the various forms of power, and an intimate knowledge of human nature. In particular, they have an impressive ability to choose appropriate subordinates through whom they can most easily exercise their power. What is more, they can skilfully adapt themselves and their techniques to be despots, manipulators, conductors and empowerers as circumstances alter. They are subtle when subtlety is called for, and act with the force of a sledgehammer when coercion is required.

The most able leaders are diplomatic ambassadors. They are people like John D. Rockefeller, Richard W. Sears and Chung Ju Yung, founder of Hyundai. These people are highly skilled diplomats who use their interpersonal abilities to build coherent organizations, and who develop networks of external supporters. Ambassadors understand the importance of *legitimacy* (the feeling that something is right, proper and appropriate), and effect it for themselves as individuals and for their organizations. They are socially adroit, and instinctive psychologists. Such people know that to survive and prosper they must be proficient relationship builders, convincing salespeople, empathetic melders, and sensitive information acquisitors. They grow organizations that are not just secure in their environments, but with a secure sense of their own cultural identity and place in the world.

Impressive leaders are those who, when required, are prepared to cast themselves as victims. They are political figures of the calibre of Aung San Suu Kyi and Bill Clinton, and business people like Harold S. Geneen, Ken Iverson and Jan Carlzon. These people are supremely at ease with themselves, and unafraid to make short-term sacrifices in the best long-term interests of their careers and of those they lead. They are willing to accept their victimage in order to promote healthy and learning-adapted organizations. They are calculating, perceptive and tolerant of their subordinates' needs to project their neuroses on to someone else. As with the other dimensions of leadership, failure here can have severe career-limiting consequences. Those leaders unable or unwilling to engage in self-victimage are more prone to being victimized by others seeking retribution. Alan Bond, Larry Tisch and the Saatchi brothers provide salutary examples. Psychically fragile, such leaders, like John DeLorean and Robert Campeau, are also more likely to destroy themselves.

Six Dimensions – or Many?

In this book I have focused on those six dimensions of leadership that I believe are most helpful in broadening and deepening our understanding of what makes leaders effective. But my decision to focus on these six dimensions is in no way meant to imply that there are not other dimensions of leadership. Indeed, it is my hope that my exploration of what it is that exemplary leaders do well will stimulate debate on what these other dimensions might be. As a first step in this direction I would like to point out a few of the many images/roles that have been elaborated by other leadership analysts. Whether they constitute full and significant dimensions of leadership requires, I think, a personal and subjective evaluation. They are mentioned here in order to promote reflection on the insights into leadership they reveal, and encourage the sort of lateral thinking that might lead to the discovery of other valuable dimensions.

Leader as Sorcerer

Graham Cleverley[5] has argued that management, and we might add leadership, is about magic. Cleverley's argument is that people in organizations live in a world of insecurity and fear, and feel intensely vulnerable to ill-understood forces. In order to exercise the illusion of control we invent myths, establish creeds, cling to rituals, and search for incantations, potions and spells. Shareholders are treated as deities to be appeased and are ascribed supernatural powers to intervene in the running of organizations. Leaders are like sorcerers or perhaps high priests whom ordinary folk look to for reassuring explanations. They are credited with arcane knowledge and skills not possessed by lay people which give them special powers. They are the guardians who exorcize evil (such as under-performers, outdated technologies, unhelpful unions), and deploy powerful medicines (in the form of programmatic change, mergers and acquisitions, and new equipment). They engage in ritual planning and strategic exercises using all forms of bizarre assumptions, and foretell the future using 'sophisticated' forecasting methods available only to the chosen few. Leaders use mantras and incantations (such as profit maximization and shareholder value) to establish orthodoxy, and ostracize, excommunicate and expel those who fail to observe it.

While Cleverley's analysis might at first sight seem an unhelpful parody of leadership activities, I think there is more than a glimmer of truth in it. Fear and insecurity are endemic in organizations and must somehow be attenuated. Most commentators now agree that organizations have cultures, and from this insight it is only a small step to recognizing that these cultures have magico-religious significance. Furthermore, it is not just Cleverley who has detected this aspect of how organizations work. Business school academics have long been fascinated by the importance of seemingly irrational myths and their power to dictate behaviour in organizations,[6] while Edwin Hollander[7] has commented on 'the apparently magical powers of the charismatic leader'. The idea that leaders are sorcerers, with sub-roles as, perhaps, priests, gurus, prophets and shamans, is certainly one that deserves some attention.

Leader as Anthropologist

Max Boisot[8] has suggested that managers, and again we might argue leaders, can usefully view themselves as anthropologists. The leader as anthropologist is sensitive to issues of national cultural differences, and to the tendency for organizations to develop distinctive customs and traditions of their own. Leaders need to be anthropologists to navigate around the global village, to deal with the subtleties and complexities of different ways of organizing, negotiating, marketing, and so on. To play the role effectively means being able to decode the intricate structures of other cultures and to communicate effectively with those socialized into other belief and value systems. More than anything else, the leader as anthropologist is able to interpret objects, actions and events not just from his or her own perspective, but from the vantage point of others. In a global economy leaders need not just to understand with the cold logic of rationality but to empathize with other cultures with an emotional intensity. Such is the strength of, and necessity for, the leader as anthropologist.

Culture is, of course, currently a major focus of interest, and a lot of energies are being expended by business academics attempting to solve inherent problems of culture-clash. It is now reasonably well established that what counts as being a good leader in, say, Japan, may be very different from what is expected in, for example, Sweden. A good instance of this has been demonstrated by André Laurent,[9] who has shown that in response to the statement *It is important for a manager to have at hand precise answers to most of the questions that his subordinates may raise about their work*, 78% of the Japanese sample agreed, 46% of Germans agreed, 27% of Britains agreed, 18% of Americans agreed, and only 10% of Swedes agreed. That international cultural differences really do matter is an important argument in favour of viewing the 'leader as anthropologist' as another dimension of leadership.

Leader as Moralist

In a world in which more than 60% of executives admit to feeling under pressure to compromise their personal standards to achieve company goals, commentators such as John Gardner and John Schermerhorn have argued for a view of leaders as moralists.[10] Says John Schermerhorn, 'Leaders have an undeniable responsibility to set high ethical standards to guide the behavior of followers.'[11] Furthermore, Schermerhorn argues that not only should leaders serve as models for appropriate ethical behaviour for their subordinates, but they must also communicate similar expectations throughout their organizations. According to John Gardner,[12] leaders have a moral obligation to remove obstacles which prevent their staff from achieving their full potential. His hypothesis is that moral leadership of this kind will be beneficial because it will encourage motivation and lead to people feeling a sense of ownership of their work. Similar views have been expressed by high-profile leaders in other fields, such as Desmond Tutu, Archbishop of Cape Town, South Africa. Writing in *Fortune* magazine he told business leaders:

> You can make this world a better place where business decisions and methods take account of right and wrong as well as profitability . . . You must take a stand on important issues: the

environment and ecology, affirmative action, sexual harassment, racism and sexism, the arms race, poverty, the obligations of the affluent West to its less-well-off sisters and brothers elsewhere.[13]

The importance of the moral dimension of leadership is symptomized by the exponential increase in organizations taking ethical issues seriously in recent years. Environmental concerns are now so prominent that a large corporation like Walt Disney Productions has a vice president responsible for environmental issues, while at Du Pont line managers are annually evaluated on how well they manage their environmental responsibilities. Anita Roddick runs The Body Shop with a strong commitment to human and social rights. Corporations such as Goodyear and Procter & Gamble have commented with pride on their programmes for increasing the diversity of their workforces. The Pittsburgh-based Aluminum Company of America (Alcoa) has set up what in 1990 was the largest permanently funded philanthropic corporate foundation in the USA, with $232 million in market value. The idea that effective leaders are often moral crusaders is one that appears to have taken root in our global business culture.[14]

Leader as Servant

Robert Greenleaf and his followers have sought to outline a view of leaders as servants.[15] Says Greenleaf, 'The servant-leader is servant first. It [leadership] begins with the natural feeling that one wants to serve.' The essential idea that true leadership emerges from a primary motivation to help others has been embellished by Greenleaf and his acolytes into a whole ideology. Some of the ideas that have been co-opted into the servant-leader perspective are that: leaders should listen to and be responsive to the will of others; they should strive to understand and empathize with those they lead; they should be a force for healing in organizations; they should be self-aware; they should rely on persuasion rather than coercion; they should be strong conceptualizers of organizations and the issues they face; they should possess great foresight and be able to work through the consequences of actions; they should realize that they are stewards who hold organizations in trust for others; they should be committed to developing their subordinates; and they should focus on building community.

The notion that leaders need to be servants just as much as they need to be heroes and immortalists has attracted some notable adherents. Prime Minister Blair famously provoked his MPs with the thought that 'we are the servants now'. The businessman and author Max DePree has said: 'The servanthood of leadership needs to be felt, understood, believed, and practised.' The noted management scholar Peter Senge, author of *The Fifth Discipline*, has described Greenleaf's book *Servant Leadership* as 'the most singular and useful statement on leadership I've come across'. Two of America's largest grant-making foundations (Lilly Endowment Inc. and the W.K. Kellogg Foundation) have incorporated elements of the servant-leadership approach into their policies. Whether or not one sympathizes with the ideology of servant-leadership, the paradoxical conjunction of the words 'servant' and 'leader' opens up a new angle on business leaders worthy of close consideration.[16]

Becoming a Multi-Dimensional Leader

The most able and successful leaders are those who excel in the many dimensions of leadership. They are flexible, sensitive and empathetic, but also directive and controlling. They are self-confident, charismatic motivators, persuasive, and yet reality-adapted, psychically secure, and capable of modesty. In short, they are multi-faceted or, in the terminology of this book, multi-dimensional individuals. They succeed because they have managed to incorporate and integrate a wide range of different behaviour repertoires into their self-concepts. In other words, such people know how to respond effectively in different situations to achieve their multiple goals. This is no mean feat. The different dimensions and sub-dimensions of leadership demand very different talents, some of which are not naturally compatible. Success requires an ability to reflect on one's own strengths and weaknesses, and to act in ways consistent with one's own sense of self and moral conviction.

A lack of self-insight will severely limit the extent to which an individual can cope with a leadership role. Acting in an incoherent and inconsistent manner can, over time, lead to the development of neuroses. The true multi-dimensional leader does not merely understand the different leadership roles, but accommodates them with maturity, wisdom, integrity and courage.

Maturity

Maturity is a state of becoming. It is an ideal for which a leader ought constantly to strive. In the case of a business, maturity is the phase when wealth creation is maximized, when the most surplus cash is generated and when the business achieves its position of greatest power and influence.[17] In terms of individual leadership, maturity refers to a stable but open, well-integrated and altruistic personality. These are characteristics associated with what Daniel Goleman has termed 'emotional intelligence'.[18]

The sort of maturity that is important to a leader is not physical or biological, but associated with one's intellectual and emotional being. In this sense, maturity means being autonomous – not a slave of one's past, but able to reflect on one's own biography with a degree of detachment. It means being perceptive in relationship to others, appreciating the strengths of diversity, and not allowing one's understanding to be corrupted by prejudices and stereotypes. It means having an altruistic attitude towards others to the extent that they are not treated merely as instruments for the accomplishment of personal goals. Being mature means avoiding unnecessary and damaging conflict. It is also associated with being able to appreciate one's own motivations governing choices, decisions and behaviour. This in turn implies a capacity to gain a full and unfalsified picture of oneself, which means learning to cope with, and mitigate, one's natural ego-defences, and accept oneself complete with limitations.[19,20]

Wisdom

According to the management scholar Ian Cunningham,[21] 'The exceptional CEOs who seem to be able to cope with overloads of information and activity and yet make wise strategic decisions cannot usually say how they do it.' The point is that while we all have an intuitive understanding of what is meant by 'wisdom', it is far from easy to define. Wisdom is not just a simple matter of possessing knowledge. It is an intuitive process by which excellent leaders know what to do. As the author Edward de Bono[22] has said, 'Wisdom is the operating system of "perception".' The people we credit with wisdom are not always those with encyclopedic minds. Rather, they are those leaders who recognize, as George Bernard Shaw once said, that 'success comes from taking the path of maximum advantage instead of the path of least resistance'.[23]

Wisdom is a composite of curiosity, a willingness to learn and an openness to new stimuli. Wise individuals accept the need to explore ego-challenging matters. They do not shield themselves from criticism and blindly attribute failures to the actions of others. Rather, they engage critics in constructive dialogues in an effort to learn more about themselves and how others see them. Wise leaders are not afraid to change, and may even encourage it through processes of profound self-questioning. Wisdom implies an ability to perceive the broader picture, particularly in terms of how things are interconnected. Wise leaders seek to understand how they relate to others in their organizations, and the consequences of these relationships. They recognize their own limitations and, importantly, make sure that they do not build their personal failings into the cultures of the organizations they lead.[24,25,26]

Integrity
As the management scholars Suresh Srivastva and David Cooperrider[27] have written, 'Executive mind is impotent without power, power is dangerous without vision, and neither is lasting or significant in any broad human sense without the force of integrity.' Integrity concerns more than just morality, it is intimately bound up with wholeness. Leaders with integrity show a consistency between their visions and their actions, between what they say and what they do. The problem is that we live in a highly competitive world, and as David Sarnoff has noted, 'Competition brings out the best in products and the worst in people.'[28] As long ago as 1985 the *Wall Street Journal* published over 400 articles reporting illegal or unethical corporate behaviour, and all the signs are that lack of integrity is a problem that is growing still worse.[29] In recent times,

the Shuttle *Challenger* disaster, the meltdown at Chernobyl, the poison gas leak at Bhopal, and the sinking of the *Exxon Valdez* are all indicative of a general failure of leadership integrity.

The scarcity of people with integrity means that it is one of the most prized of all leadership traits. Robert Lutz, ex-president of Chrysler, has rhetorically questioned, 'Does it really matter that the leader have impeccable integrity?' To which Lutz replies, 'You bet it does!' The reason is that people want to follow a superior who genuinely is *superior*.[30] Wayne Calloway of PepsiCo saw it as part of his primary mission to promote virtuous circles of corporate improvement based on a bedrock of integrity.[31] The US army chief George Marshall was particularly effective leading up to and during the Second World War because he 'served as the ultimate model of integrity' for America.[32] These sentiments have perhaps been best expressed by Pearl S. Buck, the only American woman to date to win the Nobel Prize for Literature. She has said: 'Integrity is honesty carried through the fibres of the being and the whole mind, into thought as well as action so that the person is complete in honesty. That kind of integrity I put above all else as an essential of leadership.'[33]

Courage

In July 1944, in New Guinea, Staff Sergeant Gerald Endl saw through a clearing of the Kunai grass that the platoon he led was about to be hopelessly trapped by an enveloping movement of Japanese troops.

> In the face of extremely heavy fire he went forward alone and for a period of approximately ten minutes engaged the enemy in a heroic close-range fight, holding them off while his men crawled forward under cover to evacuate the wounded and withdraw. Courageously refusing to abandon four more wounded who were lying along the trail, one by one he brought them back to safety. (COVA 1973: 548)

He was killed as he carried the last man back in his arms. For these actions, Endl was posthumously awarded the Congressional Medal of Honor.[34] Endl's story is one of extreme courage. It aptly illustrates that courage is more than Ernest Hemingway's 'grace under fire', it is a heroic quality that tilts dangerous situations away from potential catastrophe and toward good. This sort of courage is vital in leaders, and for the continued success of the organizations they lead. It takes courage to lead others, to pursue worthy objectives, to face up to critics, and to remain true to oneself.[35] As the perceptive management scholar D.M. Wolfe has made clear, what most often undermines executive integrity is lack of courage:

> It takes a special kind of courage to stay in tune with your feelings when those feelings conflict and seem to work against you. It takes courage to speak the truth in many situations, especially when the truth is unpopular and may bring down the wrath of others who would rather see the world differently. And it takes courage to live fully by one's beliefs and values – to persist in actions that run the risk of failure or the hostility and rejection from others.[36]

To sum up, being an effective multi-dimensional leader requires maturity, wisdom, integrity and courage. To an extent, of course, these are overlapping qualities. Part of what we mean when we say that a leader has maturity is that they have (at least some) wisdom. Similarly, when a leader is described as a person of integrity this implies that they have at least the courage of their convictions. This said, these overlaps are partial only. All four qualities are important. And what is more they are not the simple traits that early theorists thought were associated with good leadership. IQ measures of intelligence, decisiveness, determination and all the other traits that have been investigated mean nothing when divorced from an understanding of the total personality of an individual. Individual traits are only meaningful when understood in terms of a leader's maturity, wisdom, integrity and courage – and these qualities are largely resistant to measurement by psychometric tests. Leaders emerge as people with these qualities only in the conduct of their jobs, not through paper-based tests.

Importantly, these same qualities also help us to identify the weaknesses of some notorious individuals who have nevertheless excelled in one or more dimensions of leadership. The Roman

Emperor Nero was trained in rhetoric from an early age, but this was insufficient to compensate for his many weaknesses. He was, after all, the man who planned the assassination of his mother, may have been responsible for the great fire of Rome in AD 64, and who brutally martyred Christians. Joseph Stalin was noted for his declamatory speeches, could employ a simple folksy charm, and was a patient listener. Yet he was also responsible for the imprisonment and murder of vast numbers of people. Benito Mussolini was a talented actor, a shrewd propagandist, and a man many felt compelled to obey. Adolf Hitler was a fantastic showman, had immortalistic pretensions, and could be amiable and charming when it suited him. Yet few would describe either Mussolini or Hitler as great leaders given the wars they initiated and the murders they committed.

Leaders such as these may be competent in one or a few dimensions of leadership, but lack something vital, whether it be maturity, wisdom, integrity or courage. To begin with they are all destructive immortalists, megalomaniacs, who believe in their innate right to rule and infallibility. More than this, they tend to suffer from a personality disorder of some sort. Of Nero, the historian David Shotter has written that his was an immature and inadequate personality that showed childlike frustrations and frantic striving for attention.[37] Stalin, five feet four inches tall with a face pitted from smallpox, a partially crippled arm and deformed toes on his left foot, was plagued by an overwhelming inferiority complex. Mussolini was incapable of real affection for anyone, felt inferior to intellectuals and experts, distrusted his subordinates, loved flattery, and would rather be uninformed than hear bad news. Hitler was so disorganized and insecure that he surrounded himself with sycophants loyal to him personally.[38] Such flawed personalities can never be fully multi-dimensional or truly great leaders, as more recent examples ranging from Idi Amin in Uganda to Slobadan Milosevic in Serbia demonstrate.[39]

To Conclude

The commentator on leadership Warren Bennis once wrote: 'To an extent, leadership is like beauty: it's hard to define, but you know it when you see it.'[40] In a sense, my primary goal in writing this book has been to make the essence of leading more easily definable and recognizable. This is increasingly important in our modern world and in our businesses, where we constantly face extraordinary adaptive challenges. To meet these challenges requires a familiarity with the six dimensions of leadership, and a level of comfort with the demands they place upon us. Are you equipped to take up the gauntlet of multi-dimensional leadership?

CHAPTER NOTES

Chapter 1
1. Bennis (1976) p.157.
2. Juckes (1995).
3. Mandela (1994).
4. Farkas & Wetlaufer (1996) p.110.
5. McFarland, Senn & Childress (1993) p.55.

Chapter 2
1. Cleverley (1971) pp.198–199.
2. Deal & Kennedy (1982).
3. Goode (1978) pp.344–345.
4. Duncan (1968) p.237.
5. Kouzes & Posner (1995) p.13.
6. Adair (1988) p.81.
7. Adair (1989) p.203.
8. Adair (1989) p.204.
9. Townsend & Gebhardt (1997) pp.21–22.
10. Bradford & Cohen (1984) pp.26–27.
11. Wilkins et al. (1990).
12. Garfield (1986).
13. Deal & Kennedy (1982).
14. Rowlinson & Hassard (1993).
15. Swasy (1993) p.6.
16. Kotter (1997) p.112.
17. Ramsey (1987) p.17.
18. Kirk (1994) p.21.
19. Baker (1970).
20. Dauphinais & Price (1998) p.190.
21. Burk (1986) p.ix.
22. Sandoz (1997) p.27.
23. Klapp (1964) p.43.

24. Haddad (1986) p.x.
25. O'Boyle (1998) p.374.
26. Deal & Kennedy (1982) p.11.
27. Shell Film & Video Unit (1997).
28. Gardner (1995) p.141.
29. Gross (1996) pp.41–42.
30. Linenthal (1982) p.8.
31. Burk (1986) p.94.
32. Taffinder (1995) p.57.
33. *Printing World* (1998).
34. Bronner (1981) p.45.
35. Bennis & Nanus (1985) p.79.
36. Vaill (1989) p.119.
37. Weinstein (1996).
38. Forbes (1997) p.71.
39. Geneen & Moscow (1985) pp.100–101.
40. *Sunday Telegraph*, 20.10.96.
41. *Financial Times*, London Edition, 5.12.98, p.24.
42. Pagonis (1992) p.123.
43. Farkas, Backer & Sheppard (1995) p.55.
44. Sopel (1995) p.15.
45. http://www.pathfinder.com/fortune/1997/ 971013als.html.
46. http://www.sun.com/corp_emp/working/culture.html.
47. Farkas, Backer & Sheppard (1995) p.70.
48. DeGeorge (1996) p.46.
49. DeGeorge (1996) p.170.
50. Gross (1992) p.109.
51. Brown (1988) p.90.
52. Brown (1988) pp.139–140.
53. Bower (1993) p.7.
54. Haines (1988) pp.18–19.
55. Coward (1991) p.105.
56. Duncan (1968) p.60.
57. Lutz (1998) p.167.
58. O'Boyle (1998) p.15.
59. Balfour (1990) p.61.
60. Lutz (1998) p.184.
61. Schwarzkopf (1988) p.87.
62. Gray (1959) p.51.
63. Boas & Chain (1976) p.15.
64. Boas & Chain (1976) p.20.

65. Alexander (1991).
66. Sharan (1995).
67. Linenthal (1982) p.35.
68. Linenthal (1982) p.37.
69. Linenthal (1982) p.45.
70. Nye (1979) p.55.
71. Lawrence (1933) p.562.
72. De Gaulle, C. (1960) p.57, pp.65–66.
73. Klapp (1964) p.40.
74. Eliot (1993) p.45.
75. Burk (1986) p.x.
76. Klapp (1964) p.18.

Chapter 3

1. Mangham & Overington (1987) p.186.
2. Sculley (1987) pp.180–182.
3. Carlton (1997).
4. Peters (1978) p.10.
5. Getty (1973) p.203.
6. Tichy & Devanna (1986) p.31.
7. Vaill (1989).
8. Bate (1994).
9. Geneen & Moscow (1985) p.3.
10. Quoted in Getty (1973) pp.139–140.
11. Mangham & Overington (1987) p.102.
12. Callow (1984) p.170.
13. Billington (1973) p.187.
14. Callow (1984) p.171.
15. Billington (1973) pp.69–70.
16. Carlzon (1987) p.3.
17. Smircich & Morgan (1982).
18. Conger (1991) p.35.
19. Trading with Communities in Need, Body Shop Corporate video, 1995.
20. Aguilar (1992) p.102.
21. Westley & Mintzberg (1988) p.166.
22. Webber (1992) p.93.
23. Krass (1997) p.116.
24. Collins & Porras (1996) p.74.
25. Conger (1991) p.34.
26. Gardner (1995) p.210.

27. Bhola (1989) p.13.
28. Sculley (1987) pp.111–112.
29. Westley & Mintzberg (1988).
30. Westley & Mintzberg (1988) p.74.
31. Zaleznik (1992) p.129.
32. Geneen & Moscow (1985) p.10.
33. Gross (1992) p.88.
34. Allen (1930) p.x.
35. Tichy & Cohen (1997).
36. Wright (1979) p.37.
37. Martin & Siehl (1983).
38. Bradford (1977) p.140.
39. Gardner (1995) p.156.
40. Carlzon (1987) p.2.
41. Marriott & Brown (1997).
42. Conger (1991).
43. Forbes (1997).
44. Carlzon (1987) p.90.
45. Carlzon (1987) p.93, p.94, p.91.
46. Wallace & Erickson (1992) pp.207–208.
47. Sykes (1994) p.202.
48. Aldridge & Brooks (1998) p.5.
49. Gross (1996) p.86.
50. Much (1998).
51. Emmet & Jeuck (1950) p.84.
52. Alberts (1973) p.x, p.122, p.123.
53. Fendley (1995) p.42.
54. Kouzes & Posner (1995) pp.167–168.
55. Kirk (1994) pp.24–25.
56. Tichy & Devanna (1986) p.75.
57. Greising (1997) p.129, p.130.
58. Bennis & Nanus (1985) pp.36–37.
59. Shennan (1993) p.27.
60. Callow (1984) p.170.
61. Kotter (1997).
62. Chandler & Salsbury (1971).
63. Schuck et al, (1962) pp.6–7.
64. Gardner (1995) p.12.
65. Aguilar (1992) p.645.
66. Gibson & Johnson (1988).
67. Forest, Arnst, Rebello & Burrows (1993).

Chapter 4

1. Quoted in Marriott & Brown (1997) p.165.
2. Sculley (1987).
3. Burk (1986) p.116.
4. Farkas, de Backer & Sheppard (1995) p.80.
5. Bennis & Nanus (1985) p.57.
6. O'Boyle (1998) p.15.
7. Jackson (1997) p.xvi.
8. Morais (1991) p.1.
9. Geneen & Moscow (1985).
10. Kouzes & Posner (1995) p.94.
11. Robinson (1985) p.230.
12. Collins & Porras (1996) p.66.
13. Srivastva (1983) pp.2–3.
14. Sooklal (1991) p.834.
15. Forbes (1997).
16. Gates, Myrvold & Rinearson (1995) p.4.
17. Tait (1995) p.174.
18. Collins & Porras (1996) p.74.
19. Taffinder (1995) p.46.
20. Taffinder (1995) p.46.
21. Ogilvy (1963).
22. Griesing (1997) p.xvii.
23. Fairhurst & Sarr (1996) p.52.
24. Bower (1993) p.7, p.8.
25. Pruitt & Smith (1994) p.2.
26. Kets de Vries (1996) p.37.
27. Ramsey (1987) p.27, p.53.
28. Sculley (1987) p.101, p.7, p.56, p.x.
29. Voltan & Itzkowitz (1984).
30. Macfie (1994) p.1.
31. Morita, Reingold & Shimomura (1987) p.55.
32. Kouzes & Posner (1995) p.99.
33. *General Electric: 1984*, 1985, Harvard Business School Case Number 9-385-315. Cited in Aguilar, 1990: 90.
34. Derived from David Halberstam 1979. *The powers that be.* New York: Dell, by Bennis & Nanus, 1985: 87–88.
35. Brown (1988) pp.181–182.
36. Kets de Vries (1996).
37. Siemens (1993).
38. Royko (1971) p.17.

39. Carlzon (1987) p.5.
40. Darmer (1994).
41. Conger (1990) pp.46–47.
42. Sculley (1987) p.1.
43. Eliot (1993) p.107.
44. Alberts (1973) p.182.
45. Swasy (1993).
46. Dunsing & Matejka (1987) p.63.
65. Sculley (1987) p.157.
47. Sculley (1987) pp.166–167.
48. Carlton (1997) p.11.
49. Haddad (1986) p.8.
50. Haddad (1986).
51. Fendley (1995) p.39.
52. Fendley (1995) p.89.
53. Conger (1990) pp.44–45.
54. Nye (1979) p.27.
55. Forbes (1997) p.7.
56. CEO disease, *Business Week*, 1 April 1991, pp.52–60. Cited in Aguilar, 1992: 165.
57. Conger (1990) p.45.
58. Machiavelli (1981) p.96.
59. Allen (1930) p.253.
60. Geneen & Moscow (1985) pp.130–131.
61. Modic, S. 1989. Cincom bets big on people power: How Tom Niles defines his CEO title. *Industry Week*, Aug. 21 23–26. Used in Fairhurst & Sarr, 1996: 77.
62. Getty (1973) pp.67–68.
63. Jackson (1997) pp.xvi–xix.
64. Gates, Myhrvold & Rinearson (1995) p.37.
65. Ellis (1997) p.6, p.193.
66. Thomas (1977) p.12.
67. Iverson (1998) p.81.
68. Marriott & Brown (1997) p.109.

Chapter 5
1. Sookal (1991) p.838.
2. Brummer & Cowe (1994) p.3.
3. Sharan (1995).
4. Morita, Reingold & Shimomura (1987).
5. McFarland, Senn & Childress (1993) p.66.

6. Haddad (1986) p.xiii.
7. Maurois (1953) p.40, p.51, p.122, p.138.
8. Haines (1988) p.19, 393.
9. Cohen (1994).
10. Kets de Vries (1996) p.59.
11. Swasy (1993) p.44, p.61.
12. *Financial Times* (1998) p.24.
13. Aris (1998) p.101, p.97, p.100.
14. Eliot (1993).
15. Kirk (1994) p.16, p.24.
16. Geneen (1985) p.114. Note: when Geneen took over ITT in 1959 it had sales of $765.6 million and a profit margin of only $29 million. By the time he stepped down in 1977, ITT's annual sales had reached $16.7 billion, with earnings of $562 million. During his tenure he had bought, merged with, or absorbed some 350 different businesses in eighty countries, and fashioned them into 250 different profit centres. Geneen himself described this new creation as 'a unified-management, multi-product company'. At its zenith ITT was the ninth-largest industrial company on the Fortune 500 list.
17. Carroll (1993).
18. Taffinder (1995).
19. Farkas, de Backer & Sheppard (1995) pp.4–6. Note: when Lord Sheppard joined GrandMet it was in a disorderly state, owning a miscellaneous collection of pubs and breweries, some dairies and several bingo and dance halls, and a poorly performing hotel chain. He focused business activities, emphasizing marketing expertise in the food and drink industries. In bringing coherence to GrandMet he sold off the hotel chain, Intercontinental, in 1989 for $2.8 billion. He then proceeded to add Burger King, Pillsbury, and a dozen other food and drink companies.
20. Taylor (1993) p.106.
21. Krass (1997) p.119.
22. Jackson (1997) p.86.
23. Jackson (1997) p.317.
24. *Executive Intelligence Review* (1993) p.4.
25. Bower (1993).
26. Sculley (1987) p.4.
27. DeGeorge (1996) p.131.
28. Ramsey (1987) p.161.
29. Iverson (1998) p.82.
30. Zaleznik (1992).

31. Heifetz & Laurie (1997).
32. Aguilar (1992) p.207.
33. Ellis (1997) p.193.
34. Butcher (1988) pp.140–141.
35. Geneen (1985) p.112.
36. Bradford & Cohen (1984) p.46.
37. Kenyon (1987) p.2.
38. Farkas, de Backer & Sheppard (1995) p.5.
39. Geneen (1985) p.xiii.
40. Greising (1997) p.87.
41. Ellis (1997) p.193.
42. Fordham (1999) p.2.
43. Bradford & Cohen (1984) p.49.
44. Krass (1997) p.138.
45. Farkas, de Backer & Sheppard (1995) p.23.
46. Marriott & Brown (1997) p.52.
47. Tichy & Charan (1995) pp.69–71.
48. Taffinder (1995) p.50.
49. Farkas, de Backer & Sheppard (1995) p.54.
50. Gardner (1995).
51. Kouzes & Posner (1995) p.192.
52. Hatch (1997) p.189.
53. *Financial Times* (12.5.98) p.24.
54. Sir John Harvey-Jones (1989) pp.40–41.
55. Tichy & Devanna (1986) p.203.
56. Carlzon (1987) p.38.
57. McFarland, Senn & Childress (1993) p.70, p.64, p.65, p.74.
58. Peters & Waterman (1982).
59. *Fortune* (1993).
60. Zellner (1993).
61. Edwardes (1983) pp.255–256.
62. Sculley (1987) p.136.
63. Krass (1997) p.131.
64. Dauphinais & Price (1998) p.38.
65. Iverson (1988) p.26.
66. Tichy & Charan (1995) p.77.
67. Krass (1997) p.121.
68. Tait (1995) p.174.
69. Krass (1997) p.132.
70. Geneen (1985) p.113.
71. Tichy & Cohen (1997) p.41.

72. Spears (1998) p.3.
73. Kelly (1988).
74. Iverson (1998) p.viii.
75. Kouzes & Posner (1995) p.185.
76. Kouzes & Posner (1995) p.204.
77. Farkas, de Backer & Sheppard (1995) p.208.
78. Tait (1995) p.15.
79. Machiavelli (1981) p.91.
80. Gross (1992) p.97.
81. Zaleznik (1992) pp.128–129.
82. Haddad (1986) p.xiii.
83. Harlow (1953) p.88.
84. Kennedy (1998).
85. Kotter (1997) p.10.

Chapter 6
1. Charles Handy (1985) p.112.
2. Kirk (1994).
3. Steiner (1983) p.31.
4. Suchman (1995).
5. Steiner (1983) p.32.
6. Steiner (1983) p.32.
7. Farkas, de Backer & Sheppard (1995).
8. Tait (1995) p.22.
9. Steiner (1983) pp.55–56.
10. Shawcross (1992)
11. Handy (1985) pp.111–112.
12. Aris (1998) p.105.
13. Mulford (1992)
14. Iverson (1998).
15. Gardner (1995) p.158.
16. Watson & Petre (1990)
17. Allen (1930) p.253.
18. Steiner (1983) p.29.
19. Greising (1997) p.170.
20. Steiner (1983) p.28, p.23.
21. Brummer & Cowe (1994).
22. Bower (1993).
23. Robinson (1985).
24. Robinson (1985).
25. Haines (1988) p.21.

26. Gross (1992).
27. Shennan (1993) p.28.
28. Baker (1970) p.37.
29. Schreiner (1995).
30. Sykes (1994).
31. Pruitt & Smith (1994).
32. DeGeorge (1996) p.103.
33. O'Boyle (1998) p.7.
34. DeGeorge (1996) p.155.
35. Steiner (1983) p.25.
36. Krass (1997) p.2.
37. Brummer & Cowe (1994) p.5.
38. Gross (1992).
39. Krass (1997) p.121.
40. *Fortune* (October 1962) p.164.
41. Morita, Reingold & Shimomura (1987) p.86, p.92.
42. Morais (1991) p.72.
43. Emmet & Jeuck (1950) p.39.
44. Webber (1992) p.97.
45. Brown (1988) p.154.
46. Jackson (1987) p.186.
47. Kettle (1999) p.2.
48. Fallon & Srodes (1983).
49. Dauphinais & Price (1998) p.38.
50. Carlzon (1988) p.88.
51. Kouzes & Posner (1995) p.169.
52. Steiner (1983) p.42.
53. Marriott & Brown (1997) p.5.
54. Chandler & Salsbury (1971) p.125.
55. Iverson (1998) p.31.
56. Schwarzkopf (1988) p.399.
57. Mangham (1990) p.105.
58. Farkas, de Backer & Sheppard (1995) p.23.
59. Tait (1995) pp.174–175.
60. Hampden-Turner (1990) p.133.
61. Farkas & Wetlaufer (1996) p.48.
62. Edwardes (1983).
63. Tichy & Charan (1995) p.70.
64. Farkas, de Backer & Sheppard (1995) p.63.
65. Gardner (1995) p.158.
66. Chandler & Salsbury (1971) p.28.

67. Harlow (1953) p.96.
68. Deutschman (1992).
69. Hellriegel, Slocum & Woodman (1992) p.416.
70. Marriott & Brown (1997) p.6, p.8.
71. Greising (1997) p.171.
72. Aris (1998) p.49.
73. Hane (1988).
74. Krass (1997) p.121.
75. Much (1998).
76. Boas & Chain (1976).
77. Edwardes (1983) p.260.
78. Robinson (1985) p.222.
79. Gardner (1995) p.212.
80. Marriott & Brown (1997) p.8.
81. Ionescu (1991).
82. Ionescu (1991) p.264, p.308.

Chapter 7
1. Klapp (1964) p.91.
2. White (1998) pp.288–289.
3. Suu Kyi (1995).
4. Shawcross (1992) p.14.
5. Aris (1998) p.213.
6. Jackson (1997) p.xii.
7. Getty (1973) p.189.
8. Carlzon (1987) p.124.
9. Iverson (1998) pp.57–58.
10. Ogilvy (1963) pp.64–65.
11. Sculley (1987) p.333.
12. Peters & Waterman (1982) p.14.
13. Dauphinais & Price (1998) p.276.
14. Marriott & Brown (1997) p.78, p.85, p.86, p.101.
15. Balfour (1990) p.98.
16. Maraniss (1996) p.397.
17. Tait (1995).
18. Tait (1995) p.224.
19. Tichy & Cohen (1997) p.4.
20. Klapp (1964) p.91.
21. Much (1998).
22. Geneen (1985) pp.113–114.
23. Tichy & Devanna (1986) pp.102–103.

24. Tichy & Cohen (1997).
25. Chandler & Salsbury (1971) p.591.
26. Ionescu (1991) p.207.
27. Haigh (1988) p.3.
28. Machiavelli (1981) p.103.
29. Bennis (1976) p.19.
30. Sykes (1994) p.217.
31. Robinson (1985) p.67.
32. Nye (1979) p.13.
33. Allen (1930) pp.295–296, p.309.
34. Winans (1995) p.4, pp.12–13, p.187.
35. Geneen & Moscow (1985).
36. Fendley (1995) p.9.
37. Duncan (1968) p.40.
38. Fallon & Srodes (1983) p.47.
39. DeGeorge (1996).
40. Marriott & Brown (1997) pp.153–154.
41. Thomas (1977) p.78.
42. Alberts (1973).
43. Eliot (1993).
44. Bennis (1976) pp.15–16.
45. Conger (1990) p.48.
46. Gross (1996) p.16.
47. Kirk (1994) p.17.
48. Tichy & Devanna (1986) p.26.
49. Dauphinais & Price (1998) p.42.
50. Jeffcutt (1994).
51. Bennis & Nanus (1985) pp.62–63.
52. Bennis & Nanus (1985) p.72.
53. Machiavelli (1981) pp.94–95.
54. Millin (1952).
55. Kets de Vries (1996) p.31.
56. Levinson (1996).
57. Alberts (1973) pp.23–24.

Chapter 8
1. Heifetz & Laurie (1997: 134).
2. Getty (1973) p.76.
3. Krass (1997) p.142.
4. Geneen & Moscow (1985) p.115.
5. Cleverley (1971).

6. Boje, Fedor & Rowland (1982).
7. Hollander (1978) p.146.
8. Boisot (1987).
9. Laurent (1983).
10. Schermerhorn (1993).
11. Schermerhorn (1996) p.111.
12. Gardner (1988).
13. Tutu (1991) p.59.
14. Schermerhorn (1993).
15. Greenleaf (1970).
16. Spears (1998) p.1, pp.4–6, pp.7–8.
17. Pearson (1995) p.7.
18. Goleman (1996).
19. Chlewinski (1998).
20. Gubrium & Buckholdt (1977).
21. Cunningham (1994) p.93.
22. De Bono (1996) pp.41–42.
23. Cunningham (1994) p.73.
24. Freud (1949).
25. Bigelow (1992).
26. Kohut (1971).
27. Srivastva & Cooperrider (1988) p.xii.
28. Jackson (1985).
29. Srivastva & Cooperrider (1988).
30. Lutz (1998) p.184.
31. Farkas, de Backer & Sheppard (1995) p.63.
32. Gardner (1995) p.157.
33. Krass (1997) p.143.
34. Walton (1986) p.17.
35. Hornstein (1986).
36. Wolfe (1988) p.169.
37. Shotter (1997) pp.56–7.
38. Pauley (1997).
39. Kamau & Cameron (1979).
40. Bennis (1989) p.1.

REFERENCES

Adair, J. 1988. *Developing leaders, the ten key principles.* UK: Talbot Adair Press/McGraw-Hill.

Adair, J. 1989. *Great leaders.* Guildford: Talbot Adair Press.

Aguilar, F.J. 1992. *General managers in action, policies and strategies.* 2nd Ed. Oxford: Oxford University Press.

Alberts, R.C. 1973. *The good provider, H.J. Heinz and his 57 varieties.* London: Arthur Barker Limited.

Aldridge, J. & Brooks, R. 1998. Branson plays the naked goof. The *Observer,* p.5.

Alexander, P.C. 1991. *My Years with Indira Gandhi.* New Delhi: Vision Books.

Allen, W.H. 1930. *Rockefeller, giant, dwarf, symbol.* New York: Institute for Public Service.

Anthony, P. 1994. *Managing culture.* Buckingham: Open University Press.

Aris, S. 1998. *Arnold Weinstock and the making of GEC.* London: Aurum Press.

Baker, W.J. 1970. *A history of the Marconi company.* London: Routledge.

Balfour, S. 1990. *Castro.* London: Longman.

Bate, P. 1994. *Strategies for cultural change.* Oxford: Butterworth-Heinemann.

Bennis, W. 1976. *The unconscious conspiracy.* NY: Amacom.

Bennis, W. 1989. *On becoming a leader.* Kent: Hutchinson Business Books.

Bennis, W. & Nanus, B. 1985. *Leaders, the strategies for taking charge.* New York: Harper & Row.

Bhola, P.L. 1989. *Benazir Bhutto, opportunities and challenges.* New Delhi: Yuvraj Publishers.

Bigelow, J. 1992. Developing managerial wisdom. *Journal of Management Inquiry,* 1, 143–153.

Billington, M. 1973. *The modern actor.* London: Hamish Hamilton.

Boas, M. & Chain, S. 1976. *Big mac, the unauthorized story of McDonald's.* New York: E.P. Dutton & Co.

Boisot, M. 1987. *Information and organizations, the manager as anthropologist.* London: Fontana.

Boje, D.M., Fedor, D.B. & Rowland, K.M. 1982. Myth-making: A qualitative step in OD interventions. *The Journal of Applied Behavioral Science*, 18(1): 17–28.

Bower, T. 1993. *Tiny Rowland, a rebel tycoon.* London: Heinemann.

Bradford, E. 1977. *Nelson, the essential hero.* London: Macmillan.

Bradford, D.L. & Cohen, A.R. 1984. *Managing for excellence, the guide to developing high performance in contemporary organizations.* New York: John Wiley & Sons.

Bronner, S.E. 1981. *A revolutionary for our times: Rosa Luxemburg.* New York: Columbia University Press.

Brown, M. 1988. *Richard Branson, the inside story.* London: Michael Joseph.

Brummer, A. & Cowe, R. 1994. *Hanson, a biography.* London: Fourth Estate.

Burk, R.F. 1986. *Dwight D. Eisenhower, hero and politician.* Boston: Twayne Publishers.

Burns, M. 1978. Cited in Bernard M. Bass 1981. *Stodgill's handbook of leadership.* New York: The Free Press, p.5.

Butcher, L. 1988 *Accidental millionaire.* Paragon House.

Callow, S. 1984. *Being an actor.* London: Methuen.

Carlton, J. 1997. *Apple, the inside story of intrigue, egomania and business blunders.* New York: Random House.

Carlzon J. 1987. *Moments of truth.* Cambridge, MA: Ballinger.

Carroll, P. 1993. *Big Blues: the unmaking of IBM.* London: Orion.

Chandler, A.D. Jr & Salsbury, S. 1971. *Pierre S. du Pont and the making of the modern corporation.* New York: Harper & Row.

Chlewinski, Z. 1998. *Search for maturity, personality, conscience, religion.* New York: Peter Lang.

Cleverley, G. 1971. *Managers and magic.* London: Longman.

Collins, J.C. & Porras, J.I. 1996. Building your company's vision. *Harvard Business Review*, Sep–Oct: 65–77.

Conger, J.A. 1990. The dark side of leadership. *Organizational Dynamics*, 19 (2): 44–55.

Conger, J.A. 1991. 'Inspiring others: the language of leadership'. *Academy of Management Executive*, 5 (1): 31–45.

Coward, B. 1991. *Cromwell.* London: Longman.

Cunningham, I. 1994. *The wisdom of strategic learning, the self-managed learning solution.* London: McGraw-Hill.

Darmer, P. 1994. SAS – Mergers in the air. In: Adam-Smith, D. & Peacock, A. (eds.), *Cases in organizational behaviour.* London: Pitman.

Dauphinais, G.W. & Price, C. 1998. *Straight from the CEO, the world's top business leaders reveal ideas that every manager can use.* London: Nicholas Brealey.

Deal, T.E. & Kennedy, A.A. 1982. *Corporate cultures, the rites and rituals of corporate life.* Reading, Mass.: Addison-Wesley Publishing Company.

De Bono, E. 1996. *Textbook of Wisdom.* London: Penguin.

De Gaulle, C. 1960. *The edge of the sword.* Trans G. Hopkins. New York: Criterion Books.

DeGeorge, G. 1996. *The making of a blockbuster, how Wayne Huizenga built a sports and entertainment empire from trash, grit, and videotape.* New York: John Wiley & Sons.

Deutschman, A. 1992. Bill Gates' next challenge, *Fortune,* 28 December: 30–41.

Duncan, H.D. 1968. *Symbols in society.* New York: Oxford University Press.

Dunsing, R.J. & Matejka, J.K. 1987. Macho management: What HR professionals should watch for. *Personnel,* July: 62–66.

Edwardes, M. 1983. *Back from the brink, an apocalyptic experience.* London: Collins.

Eliot, M. 1993. *Walt Disney, Hollywood's dark prince.* London: Andre Deutsch.

Ellis, G. 1997. *Napoleon.* London: Longman.

Emmet, B. & Jeuck, J.E. 1950. *Catalogues and Counters, A history of Sears, Roebuck and Company.* Chicago: The University of Chicago Press.

Executive Intelligence Review 1993. *Tiny Rowland, the ugly face of neocolonialism in Africa.* Washington: Executive Intelligence Review.

Fairhurst, G.T. & Sarr, R.A. 1996. *The art of framing.* San Francisco: Jossey-Bass.

Fallon, I. & Srodes, J. 1983. *DeLorean, the rise and fall of a dream-maker.* London: Hamish Hamilton.

Farkas, C., de Backer, P. & Sheppard, A. 1995. *Maximum leadership.* London: Orion.

Farkas, C.M. & Wetlaufer, S. 1996. The ways chief executive officers lead. *Harvard Business Review,* May–June: 110–122.

Fayol, H. 1916. *General and industrial management,* Pitman, 1949. Translated by Constance Storrs from the original *Administration Industrielle et Générale.*

Fendley, A. 1995. *Commercial break, the inside story of Saatchi & Saatchi.* London: Hamish Hamilton.

Financial Times, London Edition, 5.12.98, p.24.

Fleishman, E.A. 1953. The measurement of leadership attitudes in industry. *Journal of Applied Psychology,* 37 (3): 153–158.

Forbes 1997. *Forbes great minds of business.* New York: John Wiley & Sons.

Fordham, J. 1999. We love you madly. The *Guardian.* Friday Review, 16 April: 2–3.

Forest, S.A., Arnst, C., Rebello, K., & Burrows, P. 1993. The education of Michael Dell, *Business Week,* 22 March: 82–88.

Fortune, October 1962: 164.

Fortune 1993. A master class in radical change. 13 December: 82–40.

Freud, S. 1949. *Group psychology and the analysis of the ego.* (First published in 1922) London: Hogarth Press.

Gardner, H. 1995. *Leading minds, an anatomy of leadership.* London: HarperCollins.

Gardner, J. 1988. The context and attributes of leadership. *New Management,* 5: 18–22.

Garfield, C. 1986. *Peak performers: The new heroes in business.* London: Hutchinson.

Gates, B., Myhrvold, N. & Rinearson, P. 1995. *The road ahead.* London: Viking.

Geneen, H.S. & Moscow, A. 1985. *Managing.* London: Granada.

General Electric: 1984, 1985, Harvard Business School Case Number 9-385-315. Cited p.90.

Getty, J.P. 1973. *How to be a successful executive.* London: W.H. Allen & Co.

Gibson, R. & Johnson, R. 1988. Why Pillsbury's chief from the '70s is again taking firm's helm, *Wall Street Journal,* 1 March: 1, 21.

Goleman, D. 1996. *Emotional intelligence, why it can matter more than IQ.* London: Bloomsbury.

Goode, W.J. 1978. *The celebration of heroes, prestige as a social control system.* Berkeley: University of California Press.

Gray, J.G. 1959. *The warriors: Reflections on men in battle.* New York: Harper & Row.

Greenleaf, R.K. 1970. *The servant as leader.* Indianapolis: The Robert Greenleaf Center.

Greenleaf, R.K. 1977. *Servant leadership.* New York: Paulist Press.

Greising, D. 1997. *I'd like the world to buy a coke, the life and leadership of Roberto Goizueta.* New York: John Wiley & Sons.

Gross, D. 1996. *Forbes greatest business stories of all time.* New York: John Wiley.

Gross, K. 1992. *Ross Perot, the man behind the myth.* New York: Random House.

Gubrium J.F. & Buckholdt, D.R. 1977. *Toward maturity.* San Francisco: Jossey-Bass.

Haddad, W. 1986. *Hard driving, my years with John DeLorean.* London:

W.H. Allen.

Haigh, C. 1988. *Elizabeth 1*. London: Longman.

Haines, J. 1988. *Maxwell*. London: Macdonald.

Hampden-Turner, C. 1990. *Corporate culture, from vicious to virtuous circles*. London: Economist Books.

Handy, C. 1985. *Understanding organizations*. 3rd Ed. London: Penguin.

Handy, 1993. *Understanding organizations*. Harmondsworth: Penguin.

Hane, P.J. 1988. Allen Paschal discusses plans for the Gale Group (interview). *Information Today, Inc*, 01.10.98.

Harlow, A.H. 1953. *Andrew Carnegie*. London: Blackie.

Hatch, M.J. 1997. Jazzing up the theory of organizational improvisation. *Advances in Strategic Management*, 14: 181–191.

Heifetz, R.A. & Laurie, D.L. 1997. The work of leadership. *Harvard Business Review*, Jan–Feb: 124–134.

Hellriegel, D., Slocum, J.W. & Woodman, R.W. 1992. *Organizational behavior*. 6th Ed. St Paul MN: West.

Hollander, E.P. 1978. *Leadership dynamics, a practical guide to effective relationships*. New York: The Free Press.

http://www.pathfinder.com/fortune/1997/ 971013als.html.

http://www.sun.com/corp_emp/working/culture.html.

Hornstein, H.A. 1986. *Managerial courage, revitalizing your company without sacrificing your job*. New York: John Wiley & Sons.

Ionescu, G. 1991. *Leadership in an interdependent world: the statesmanship of Adenauer, De Gaulle, Thatcher, Reagan and Gorbachev*. Harlow: Longman.

Iverson, K. 1998. *Plain talk, lessons from a business maverick*. New York: John Wiley & Sons.

Jackman, M. 1985. *The Macmillan book of business and economic quotations*. New York: Macmillan.

Jackson, T. 1997. *Inside Intel, how Andy Grove built the world's most successful chip company*. London: HarperCollins.

Jeffcutt, P. 1994. From interpretation to representation in organizational analysis: Postmodernism, ethnography and organizational symbolism. *Organization Studies*, 15 (2) 241–274.

Juckes, T.J. 1995. *Opposition in South Africa, the leadership of Z.K. Mathews, Nelson Mandela, and Stephen Biko*. Westport: Praeger.

Kamau, J. & Cameron, A. 1979. *Lust to kill, the rise and fall of Idi Amin*. London: Corgi.

Kelly, R.E. 1988. In praise of followers. *Harvard Business Review*, Nov–Dec.

Kennedy, C. The roadmap to success: How Gerhard Schulmeyer changed the culture at Siemens Nixdorf. *Long Range Planning*, 31 (2): 262–271.

Kenyon, N. 1987. *Simon Rattle, the making of a conductor.* London: Faber & Faber.

Kets de Vries, M. 1996. *Family business, human dilemmas in the family firm.* London: International Business Thompson Press.

Kettle, M. 1999. Blair's fighting talk wins friends and foes. The *Guardian*, 26.4.99, p.2.

Kirk, D. 1994. *Korean dynasty, Hyundai and Chung Ju Yung.* Hong Kong: Asia 2000.

Klapp, O.E. 1964. *Symbolic leaders, public dramas and public men.* Chicago: Aldine.

Kohut, H. 1971. *The analysis of the self.* NY: International Universities Press.

Kotter, J.P. 1997. *Matsushita leadership, lessons from the 20th century's most remarkable entrepreneur.* New York: The Free Press.

Kouzes, J.M. & Posner, B.Z. 1995. *The leadership challenge.* San Francisco: Jossey-Bass.

Krass, P. 1997. *The book of business wisdom.* New York: John Wiley & Sons.

Laurent, A. 1983. The cultural diversity of western management conceptions. *International Studies of Management and Organization*, XIII, 2:75–96.

Lawrence, T.E. 1933. *Seven Pillars of Wisdom.* NY: Garden City.

Levinson, H. 1996. When executives burn out. *Harvard Business Review*, Jul–Aug: 152–163.

Likert, R. 1961. *New patterns of management.* New York: McGraw-Hill.

Linenthal, E.T. 1982. *Changing images of the warrior hero in America: A history of popular symbolism.* New York: The Edwin Mellen Press.

Lutz, R.A. 1998. *Guts, the seven laws of business that made Chrysler the world's hottest car company.* New York: John Wiley & Sons.

Macfie, A.L. 1994. *Ataturk.* London: Longman.

Machiavelli, N. 1981. *The Prince.* Translated by George Bull. Harmondsworth: Penguin Books

Mandela, N. 1994. *Long walk to freedom, the autobiography of Nelson Mandela.* London: Little, Brown & Company.

Mangham, I.L. 1990. Managing as a performing art. *British Journal of Management*, 1: 105–115.

Mangham, I.L. & Overington, M.A. 1987. *Organizations as theatre: A social psychology of dramatic appearances.* Chichester: John Wiley.

Maraniss, D. 1996. *First in his class, the biography of Bill Clinton.* New York: Touchstone.

Marriott J.W. Jr, & Brown, K.A. 1997. *The spirit to serve.* New York: HarperCollins.

Martin, J. & Siehl, C. 1983. Organizational culture and counter-culture: An uneasy symbiosis. *Organizational Dynamics*, Autumn, 52–64.

Maurois, A. 1953. *Cecil Rhodes*. London: Collins.

McFarland, L.J., Senn, L.E. & Childress, J.R. 1993. *21st century leadership, dialogues with 100 top leaders*. New York: The Leadership Press.

McGregor, D. 1960. *The human side of enterprise*. New York: McGraw-Hill.

Millin, S.G. 1952. *Rhodes*. London: Chatto & Windus.

Mintzberg, H. 1973. *The nature of managerial work*. New York: Harper & Row.

Morais, R. 1991. *Pierre Cardin, the man who became a label*. London: Bantam Press.

Morgan, G. 1986. *Images of organization*. London: Sage.

Morita, A., Reingold, E.M. & Shimomura, M. 1987. *Made in Japan, Akio Morita and Sony*. London: Collins.

Much, M. 1998. Leaders & success – industrialist Robert Wood Johnson. *Investor's Business Daily* 15/10/98.

Mulford, M. 1992. *Elizabeth Dole, public servant*. Hillside, NJ: Enslow Publishers.

Nye, D.E. 1979. *Henry Ford, 'ignorant idealist'*. Port Washington, NY: Kennikat Press.

O'Boyle, T.F. 1998. *At any cost, Jack Welch, General Electric, and the pursuit of profit*. New York: Alfred A. Knopf.

Ogilvy, D. 1963. *Confessions of an advertising man*. London: Longman.

Ott, J.S. 1989. *The organizational culture perspective*. Pacific Grove, CA: Brooks/Cole Publishing Co.

Pagonis, W.G. 1992. The work of the leader. *Harvard Business Review*, Nov–Dec: 118–126.

Pauley, B.F. 1997. *Hitler, Stalin, and Mussolini, totalitarianism in the twentieth century*. Wheeling, Illinois: Harlan Davidson Inc.

Pearson, G. 1995. *Integrity in organizations*. London: McGraw-Hill.

Peters, T.J. 1978. Symbols, patterns and settings: An optimistic case for getting things done. *Organizational Dynamics*, Autumn, 3–23.

Peters, T.J. & Waterman, R. 1982. *In search of excellence*. New York: Harper & Row.

Printing World, 03.08.98.

Pruitt, B.H. & Smith, G.D. 1994. *The making of Harcourt General, a history of growth through diversification 1922-1992*. Boston, MA: Harvard Business School Press.

Ramsey, D.K. 1987. *The corporate warriors*. London: Grafton Books.

Robinson, J. 1985. *The risk takers, portraits of money, ego and power*. London: Unwin.

Rowlinson, M. & Hassard, J. 1993. The invention of corporate culture: A history of the histories of Cadbury. *Human Relations*, 46 (3) 299–326.

Royko, M. 1971. *Boss, Richard J. Daley of Chicago*. Chicago: Signet.

Sandoz, P. 1997. *Canon, global responsibilities and local decisions*. London: Penguin.

Schermerhorn, J.R. 1993. *Management for productivity*. New York: Wiley.

Schermerhorn, J.R. 1996. *Management and organizational behavior essentials*. New York: Wiley.

Schreiner, S.A. Jr. 1995. *Henry Clay Frick, the gospel of greed*. New York: St Martin's Press.

Schuck, H., Sohlman, R., Osterling, A., Liljestrand, G., Westgren, A., Siegbahn, M., Schou, A., Stahle, N.K. 1962. *Nobel, the man and his prizes*. Amsterdam: Elsevier.

Schwarzkopf, H.N. 1988. *It doesn't take a hero*. London: Bantam Press.

Sculley, J. 1987. *Odyssey: Pepsi to Apple*. London: Collins.

Sharan, S. 1995. *Women prime ministers in southeast Asia*. New Delhi: Commonwealth Publications.

Shawcross, W. 1992. *Rupert Murdoch, ringmaster of the information circus*. London: Chatto & Windus.

Shell, 1997. *A family concern* (video). Shell Film & Video Unit.

Shennan, A. 1993. *De Gaulle*. London: Longman.

Shotter, D. 1997. *Nero*. London: Routledge.

Siemens, 1993. *Sir William Siemens – a man of vision*. Siemens plc.

Sloan, A.P. Jr. 1965. *My years with General Motors*. London: Sidgwick & Jackson.

Smircich, L. & Morgan, G. 1982. 'Leadership: The management of meaning'. *The Journal of Applied Behavioral Science*, 18 (3): 257–273.

Smith & Kreuger 1933. Cited in Bernard M. Bass 1981. *Stodgill's handbook of leadership*. New York: The Free Press, p.5.

Sooklal, L. 1991. 'The leader as a broker of dreams'. *Human Relations* 44 (8): 833–856.

Sopel, J. 1995. *Tony Blair: The Moderniser*. London: Bantam.

Sorokin, P.A. 1966. *Sociological theories of today*. New York: Harper & Row.

Spears, L.C. 1998. Tracing the growing impact of servant-leadership. In: *Insights on leadership, service, stewardship, spirit, and servant-leadership*. L.C. Spears (Ed.). New York: John Wiley & Sons, pp.1–12.

Srivastva, S. 1983. Introduction: Common themes in executive thought and action. In Suresh Srivastva 1983. The executive mind: 1–14. San Francisco: Jossey-Bass.

Srivastva, S. & Cooperrider, D.L. The urgency for executive integrity. In Srivastva *et al*, 1988. *Executive integrity, the search for high human values in organizational life*. San Francisco: Jossey Bass, pp.1–28.

Srivastva *et al*, 1988. *Executive integrity, the search for high human values in organizational life.* San Francisco: Jossey Bass, pp.xi–xv.

Steiner, G.A. 1983. *The new CEO.* New York: Macmillan Publishing Company.

Suchman, M.C. 1995. Managing legitimacy: Strategic and institutional approaches. *Academy of Management Review,* 20 (3): 571–610.

Sunday Telegraph, 20.10.96.

Suu Kyi, A.S. 1995. *Freedom from fear, and other writings.* 2nd Ed. London: Penguin.

Swasy, A. 1993. *Soap Opera, the inside story of Proctor & Gamble.* New York: Random House.

Sykes, T. 1994. *The bold riders, behind Australia's corporate collapses.* St Leonards, Australia: Allen & Unwin.

Taffinder, P. 1995. *The new leaders, achieving corporate transformation through dynamic leadership.* London: Kogan Page.

Tait, R. 1995. *Roads to the top, career decisions and development of 18 business leaders.* Basingstoke: Macmillan Press.

Taylor, W. 1993. Message and muscle: An interview with Swatch titan Nicolas Hayek. *Harvard Business Review,* Mar–Apr: 99–120.

Thomas, B. 1977. *The Walt Disney biography.* London: New English Library.

Tichy, N.M. & Charan, R. 1995. The CEO as coach: An interview with AlliedSignal's Lawrence A. Bossidy. *Harvard Business Review,* Mar–Apr: 68–78.

Tichy, N.M. & Cohen, E. 1997. *The leadership engine, how winning companies build leaders at every level.* New York: HarperCollins.

Tichy, N.M. & Devanna, M.A. 1986. *The transformational leader.* New York: John Wiley & Sons.

Townsend, P.L. & Gebhardt, J.E. 1997. *Five-star leadership, the art and strategy of creating leaders at every level.* New York: John Wiley & Sons.

Tutu, D. 1991. Do more than win. *Fortune,* 30 December: 59.

Vaill, P.B. 1989. *Managing as a performing art.* San Francisco: Jossey-Bass.

Voltan, V. & Itzkowitz, N. 1984. *The immortal Ataturk.* Chicago: University of Chicago Press.

Wallace, J. & Erickson, J. 1992. *Hard drive, Bill Gates the making of the Microsoft empire.* New York: John Wiley & Sons.

Walton, D.N. 1986. *Courage, a philosophical investigation.* Berkley: University of California Press.

Watson, T.J. Jr 1963. *A business and its beliefs.* New York: McGraw-Hill.

Watson, T.J. Jr & Petre, P. 1990. *Father Son & Co., my life at IBM and beyond.* London: Bantam Press.

Webber, A.M. 1992. Japanese-style entrepreneurship: An interview with

Softbank's CEO, Masayoshi Son. *Harvard Business Review*, Jan–Feb: 92–103.

Weinstein, M. 1996. *Managing to have fun*. New York: Simon & Schuster.

Westley, F.R. & Mintzberg, H. 1988. Profiles of strategic vision: Levesque and Iacocca. In: Jay A. Conger, Rabindra N. Kanungo and Associates. *Charismatic leadership, the elusive factor in organizational effectiveness*. 161–212. San Francisco: Jossey-Bass.

White, J.A. 1998. Leadership through compassion and understanding. *Journal of Management Inquiry*, 7 (4): 286–293.

Wilkins, A.L., Perry, L.T., & Checketts, A.G. 1990. Please don't make me a hero: A re-examination of corporate heroes. *Human Resource Management*, 29 (3) 327–341.

Winans, C. 1995. *The king of cash, the inside story of Laurence Tisch*. New York: John Wiley & Sons.

Wolfe, D.M. 1988. Is there integrity in the bottom line: managing obstacles to executive integrity. In: Srivastva, *et al*, 1988. *Executive integrity, the search for high human values in organizational life*. San Francisco: Jossey-Bass, pp.140–171.

Wright, J.P. 1979. *On a clear day you can see General Motors*. Grosse Point, Mich.: Wright Enterprises.

Zaleznik, A. 1992. Managers and leaders: Are they different? *Harvard Business Review*, Mar–Apr. 126–135.

Zellner, W. 1993. The fight of his life, *Business Week*, 20 September: 54–64.

INDEX